MW00988580

JOHN FORD SR., MAI[N]
OF MAINE GAME WAR[DEN...]

This book was a great read, one that hopefully will provide many of you with your own pleasant memories from a time long ago. It pleasantly reminded me of summers long ago when I too enjoyed the pleasures of spending a few weeks at a lakeside summer camp. Dale Potter-Clark and Charles Day Jr. have together compiled a thorough record of exactly when (several of) Central Maine's first lodges and camps were established. At the time, they were great retreats built far out in the Maine wilderness. In order to reach them, their clients had to travel by rail. Reading the history of how the development of these camps originated while scanning the many pages of old photo's depicting that era in time was priceless. I highly recommend SUMMER RESORTS AND KIDS' CAMPS to anyone interested in exploring and reading about a special Maine way of life that was second to none. Dale and Charles have superbly recorded these events, both in pictures and print. I think this book should be in every library in Maine!

FROM SCOTT DAVIS, OWNER OF THE FORMER MARANCOOK HOTEL...

I loved the book - the way it was written - the style and the way it flowed. It took me back to the times when I sat and listened to my grandmother talk about the history of this area, from the time when our ancestors settled here in 1789. More than anything, SUMMER RESORTS AND KIDS' CAMPS made me realize that railroad transportation was a major factor in that chapter of history when 'people from away' came to enjoy what our beautiful lakes and forests have to offer. My wife Holly and I are pleased to have played a small part in honoring those who came before us by restoring what was once the Maranacook Hotel. Thank you to Dale, Charlie and all of those who so generously contributed their time and resources to creating what will preserve an important part of our heritage.

First Printing August, 2016
Second Printing May, 2017
ISBN - 978-1-5323-1407-0

More historical publications by the authors

Charles L. Day, Jr:
Maranacook's Southern Lakeside Resorts by Day

Obtain copies from Winthrop Historical Society

Dale Potter-Clark:
To Those Who Led the Way in Readfield, ME 1768-1900
To Those Who Followed the Lead in Readfield, ME 1900-76
The Sanborns of East Readfield, Life in Frog Valley
Joseph Baker of Readfield and Moscow, Maine
Rev. Isaac Case, Baptist Missionary
John Lane and Jere Page homesteads and mills
Elder James Potter, He Preached in Readfield on his way to Paris
Old Houses in Readfield and the People who lived in them – pending

This book and Dale's others can be purchased via:
www.readfieldmaine.blogspot.com

DEDICATION

To my beloved Harvey who has stood by my side for twenty-five
years, through the happiest, proudest, saddest and most worrisome of
times. Thank you Harv for your unwavering support and
encouragement as this book came together.
Without you it would never have come to fruition!
Forever, Dale

———— ∽ ————

ACKNOWLEDGEMENTS

There are more individuals to acknowledge than we can possibly
mention by name. We extend a heartfelt thank you to the dozens of
people from all over the world who returned our phone calls, replied
to our emails and welcomed us into their homes, cottages and kids'
camps in support of our research. Stephanie (Wilson) Hatch was
especially generous and helpful in so many ways. Thank you Milt
Wright for encouraging Dale to continue her research and writing
about Readfield's history. We also give big thumbs up to Charlie
Knight and Bob Harris of Readfield for captaining their pontoon
boats on Torsey and Maranacook Lakes so Dale could see some of
these places from "the other side". The content within these pages is
richer because of the stories and personal photographs that everyone
shared. You know who you are and we hope you feel our gratitude.

We must also recognize Dale's mother, Evelyn Potter, and Charlie
Day's wife, Dot. "Mum" for sharing a lifetime of stories, knowledge
and local adventures that ultimately gave Dale "the bug" and instilled
in her a deep love for Readfield history. Dot, for her years of helping
Charlie find and procure his vast postcard collection. His post cards
were the impetus for *Maranacook's Southern Lakeside Resorts* and for this
book, which was his brainchild.

We extend a special Thank You to Scott Davis. He introduced us to
each other in the summer of 2013 when we were both visiting the old
Maranacook Hotel, which is now the summer home of Scott and his
wife Holly. Unbeknown to us Scott had arranged for us to be there at
the same time knowing that we would hit it off and perhaps enjoy
working on a project together. Little did he know…

ABOUT THE AUTHORS

Dale Potter-Clark is a retired nurse and hospice executive director who currently spends her days (and sometimes nights) doing genealogical and historical research. She writes articles for local newspapers, *Discover Maine Magazine* and has authored several books and monographs pertaining to Readfield's history. Her blogs and websites also include extensive information about early Readfield and its people. She is a founding member of Readfield Historical Society and currently their historical consultant. Dale's family has lived in Readfield for 10 consecutive generations. She is a born 'Maineah' who has loved Maine history for as long as she can remember. The info within is a natural extension of her research which led to her collaboration with Charlie on *Summer Resorts and Kids' Camps.*

Charles L. Day, Jr. is a Connecticut native who summers in Maine and winters in Florida. He worked for the Connecticut State Park Division and retired 1995 as Assistant Director of State Parks after 35 years of service. Charlie is a veteran of the U.S. Army Security Agency and received the Korean Defense Medal for his service. As a young man he became an Eagle Scout and has continued serving in various capacities with Boys Scouts of America (BSA) - most recently on the Gulf Ridge Council BSA and past Chair and current member of the Eagle Scout Recognition and Award Committee for the Sons of the American Revolution, State of Florida. He holds the "Silver Beaver" and the "Robert Burt" Veteran Scouter awards. Charlie joined the Sons of the American Revolution in 2004 and currently is the Color Guard Commander for the Florida Society. He also is the Chaplain of his Mayflower Colony. Since the 1950's Charlie and his wife Dorothy have visited a family cottage on Lake Maranacook. Charlie serves on the board of directors at the Winthrop Maine Historical Society and is a member of the Readfield Historical Society. In 2013 he co-authored *Maranacook's Southern Lakeside Resorts,* and has very much enjoyed working with Dale on *Summer Resorts and Kids' Camps.*

IN REMEMBRANCE

*Five people who granted interviews for this
book have since passed. We wish to remember
them with gratitude and reverence*

Wilbur N. Nelson
June 5, 1925 ~ October 16, 2016

Holly Hock Dumaine
June 2, 1939 ~ October 6, 2016

Geraldine "Midge" (Bryant) Potter
July 12, 1930 ~ July 28, 2016

Robert "Bob" Ifill
January 9, 1924 ~ March 27, 2016

Wendel "Skip" Adell
January 19, 1933 ~ March 18, 2016

FOREWORD by Evelyn Adell Potter, Readfield Historian

Memories which you thought had grown deep will appear as you enjoy this book, "Summer Resorts and Kids' Camps", honoring four of our lakes in Central Maine. The research, taking months going into years, done by its authors Dale-Potter Clark and Charlie Day, have made this reading a treasure of those memories.

Pullman trains hissing into Readfield Depot or Winthrop station; and folks in fine attire being met by chauffeurs in lettered station wagons. Noble people from far away had arrived for the gentlemen to play golf, go boating or fishing. In driving by a fine tourist home, bobbing parasols could be seen as the fashionable ladies strolled the grounds.   Afternoons would see them enjoying the verandas.

The time for the Pullmans to arrive with boys and girls for the "Kids' Camps" was the special time for the town "Kids". It meant the official start of summer when they were allowed to go swimming, (with permission). School was out!!

A week before the campers were to be delivered, the children in town took turns asking the RR station agent for the day and time the Pullman was expected. The time came!! The train was met by the camp vehicles.

The camp kids would be seen from time to time during the summer, at the General Store, riding by in the backs of open trucks, hiking to some unknown spot, canoeing on Echo, Maranacook, Lovejoy or Torsey. They were a part of our summer life.

But, time for departure... too soon, the end of summer, legitimate swimming, the start of school. The camp kids came back to the train stations and the Pullman pulled in to take them back to the city.

I was one of the town kids who had watched their arrival, then their departure. The campers hugged and cried as they boarded the Pullman. I watched as the train went out of sight wondering how I would feel if I were on that train and had to leave Maine...I still wonder.

The Founders and Evolution of

SUMMER RESORTS

AND

KIDS' CAMPS

On four lakes in Central Maine

Dale Potter-Clark

&

Charles L. Day, Jr.

Map indicates approximate locations of the
resorts and camps. See the next page for the key

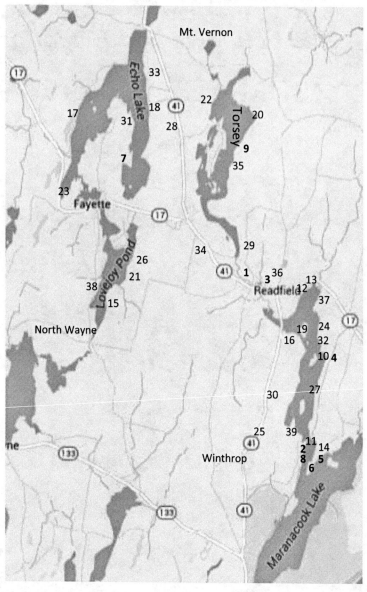

Summer Resorts & Kids Camps on Four Lakes in Central Maine

1.	The Larches -	1870	
2.	Maranacook Grove –	1880	
3.	Maranacook House –	1880	**
4.	Hutchinson House –	1880	
5.	Tallwood Farm –	1888	
6.	Sir Charles Hotel –	1891	**
7.	Bodge Camps -	1891	**
8.	Hotel Maranacook –	1898	**
9.	Cebennek Boys Camp –	1900	**
10.	Coleman's Grove -	1902	**
11.	The Pines –	1903	
12.	The Avalon –	1903	
13.	Tamsonhurst –	1903	**
14.	Townsend Farm –	1903	
15.	Kennebescoggin Camps –	1904	**
16.	Camp Maranacook –	1907	
17.	Echo Lake Lodge -	1910	**
18.	Camp Mowana –	1912	**
19.	Camp Haukeemah –	1914	
20.	Camp Hirundo -	1915	
21.	Camp Abenaki –	1919	**
22.	Armstrong Lodge –	1919	**
23.	Camp Winnebago -	1919	
24.	Newton's Camps -	1920	
25.	Martha Washington Inn –	1924	
26.	Camp Menatoma –	1926	
27.	Kamp Kiwanacook –	1927	**
28.	Interlaken Farm –	1931	
29.	Castle Hill Farm –	1935	
30.	Lanes' Cottages –	1935	
31.	Echo Lake Lodge & Cottages –	1937	
32.	Maces Camps –	1937	
33.	Camp Vega Jr. –	1940	**
34.	Torsey View House –	1940	
35.	Camp Thunderbird –	1945	
36.	Wright House -	1946	
37.	Camp KV –	1949	
38.	Don Bosco Camp –	1952	
39.	Folsom Brothers –	1961	

** Indicates if operated under another name(s) at a later date

Summer Resorts & Kids Camps on Four Lakes in Central Maine

*CHRONOLOGICAL INDEX (Pg. 3 of 4) * Still operating as a business*

INTRODUCTION

In 1880 the Maine Central Railroad opened Maranacook Grove on "North Winthrop Pond" (northern Lake Maranacook) and summer tourism in this area of central Maine officially began.

Twenty years later Maine's first kids' camp, Cebennek, was established on Torsey Pond and more camps followed. The annual July tradition began when year round residents gathered at the train station to watch the camp kids arrive. Come August the locals were back again to watch the same campers board trains bound for Boston, New York City or Philadelphia – all the while wondering what their destinations were and what it was like on the other end. Concurrently many of those campers were looking longingly at the locals for they yearned to stay in the Maine woods they had come to love.

By 1905 several hotels had been built on Lake Maranacook and in the villages of Readfield Corner and Readfield Depot. City dwellers were buying lakeside lots and having private cottages built. Most of these lots were extracted from original farms and homesteads that had been intact for nearly 150 years.

Access to the newly developing lakeshore was oftentimes by boat in the early days. In some cases the farmers who sold the lake lots granted right of ways over their cow paths or logging roads, across their pastures and through the woods to the cottages. The farmers almost always retained the right and privilege to drive their cattle to the lake or pass through to an adjoining pasture. They and summer residents learned to live harmoniously. Locals were wise to realize their part-time neighbors brought with them a major boost to their economy. Many family members of those earliest summer residents have returned for five or more generations, or have moved here year-round.

In 1928 the State of Maine Development Commission printed a booklet that promoted prime areas throughout Maine for vacationing and fishing. Included were dozens of pictures and specific mention of hotels located all over the State but only a small section about the Winthrop Lakes Region. There were no notations of accommodations or photos from this immediate area in either the narrative or advertisements. Easy access by automobile via state roads was mentioned frequently in the publication but there was no reference to railroad transportation.[1]

A year later the stock market crashed and most everyone who'd had the means to vacation here until then "lost their shirts". Although some housekeeping cottages and tourist homes survived into the 1970s or beyond, the Great Depression was the beginning of the end for hotels and the earlier times of grandeur.

After WWII more and more lakeside lots and islands were bought by individuals who wished to own a piece of paradise on the lake. By then summer residents and tourists were coming in their own cars for the most part, although there were still a few who traveled here by train into the 1950s.

Passenger trains no longer come and go from Readfield Depot, Maranacook Station or the Winthrop Station. They were all torn down years ago. Oh we still feel excitement when the huge commercial buses pass through town every summer loaded to the hilt with young campers. But, can that excitement and wonder come even close to when they arrived by train; or when the "sports" traveled in from the city with all their fancified fishing gear; or high society and theater people swept off the Pullman cars, the women wearing bustled dresses and wide-brimmed hats? One can only imagine…

CHANGES ON THE HORIZON ~ 1844

The year was 1844 and the town of Readfield was defined by three villages – Kents Hill, Readfield Corner and East Readfield. "The Depot" had not yet become one of Readfield's four business centers. Instead, that part of town was dotted with a few farms, a store, the town hall, a cattle pound and a tavern run by Mary and J.J. Hutchinson. Theirs was one of several old style taverns on that land route from Hallowell to Farmington and Coos County, NH.

Daniel O. Craig[2] owned a store at what later became the center of Readfield Depot. He also ran a tavern on his 100 acre farm nearby.[3]   Perhaps it was through contacts made at those businesses that Craig learned the railroad would be coming through town. He bought several parcels of ideally located land at auctions between 1844 and 1865 and proceeded to sell strips of it to the Androscoggin & Kennebec Railroad Co. (A&K Railroad). He also sold lots to business men and homeowners in the newly formed Readfield Depot village. There is little doubt that Craig recognized the potential for property development at Readfield Depot but he died in 1867 before that happened on any grand scale. Two decades later his son David W. Craig did become a significant land developer when he bought a 100 acre peninsula on Maranacook Lake.[4]

The A&K Railroad extended their tracks to Readfield and built a train station there in 1849.   Added later were side tracks, a baggage room, coal shed and freight storage shed on the east side of the tracks.   More businesses began to arise such as a granary and elevator, sawmill, livery stable, blacksmith shop and a grocery and dry goods store.   Travelers could switch out horses or wagons at Hutchinson's Exchange House. There was a post office, tenement house, Morrill's Inn and Hutchinson's Tavern. The first town hall and a grammar school had already been built there followed by the Union Chapel. In 1910 the Smith

Memorial Methodist Church was erected. By that time Readfield Depot had become a busy, self-sustaining village.

From the first, railroad passengers could not help but notice the beautiful countryside as their trains rumbled along the lakeside tracks and through the little hamlets of Readfield Depot and Winthrop. Word spread that salmon and trout fishing was good in Lake Maranacook and men began to come here via the train to enjoy the sport. Their wives and children wanted to come too, but most were from the city and unaccustomed to outdoor camping and rustic accommodations. The questions were asked... Where could families from the city stay? What would they do all day while the men fished? Railroad executives wondered that too.

Daniel O. Craig homestead as it looked in 1910. Owned by J.J. and Mary Hutchinson after their first tavern burned. The original house was recently replaced by the Payson family.

ANDROSCOGGIN & KENNEBEC RAILROAD ~ 1849

The Androscoggin and Kennebec Railroad Company (A&KRR) was chartered in 1845 and soon began building a route of about sixty-miles, called "the back road" which linked Portland to Bangor across an inland route. Dozens of Kennebec County deeds, dated 1848, reflect the flurry that occurred that year when local farmers on both sides of Lake Maranacook sold strips of land to the A&KRR for their right of way and rail beds. The tracks would cross the Lake at its narrowest point – what adjacent landowners called "the narrows of the North Winthrop Pond".[5] The thought of that alone would have created great excitement, but the entire year of 1849 surely brought ever increasing anticipation as the tracks edged closer to Winthrop and Readfield.

On December 4, 1848 the back road from Danville Junction to Lewiston opened; from there the expansion through Greene and Monmouth to Winthrop was completed on July 4, 1849; the next leg to Readfield was finalized on October 15th; and on December 3rd the section through Belgrade and Oakland to Waterville was opened for public travel and freight.[6] Prior to that day, on Tuesday November 27th, an introductory trip of eighty miles from Portland to Waterville took place. It had been exactly three years since the A&KRR first presented their work plan for a back road, and twenty-eight months since they'd begun laying tracks. According to one reporter the railroad bed above Readfield was still "course and run on the sub-grade but with entire safety and good speed." [7] In those days trains were powered by wood-fired steam engines. What a sight it must have been when that first one rolled into the stations with the whistle blowing and smoke streaming from its stack.

The K&ARR borrowed seven passenger cars from the Atlantic Railroad for that trip, and began the excursion in Portland loaded with two-hundred stockholders and railroad executives from other lines. It was an "uncommonly mild and brilliant day for that late in the season." [8] At each station as well as along the tracks in the countryside there was great fanfare. People of all ages came afoot and by wagons and carriages from miles around to celebrate the first arrival of a train. All dressed in their finery and with smiling faces they cheered and waved a grand welcome to the engineer, crewmen, passengers and dignitaries aboard. At Lewiston more stockholders and passengers boarded, as did others at subsequent stops along the way. Below are excerpts from a *Kennebec Journal* report of the event.[9]

> ...The crowds at several stations and the additions to the company at every stopping place, manifested hearty satisfaction... At Winthrop there was, of course, a large and hearty throng, to unite in the festivities of the day, and a well-filled platform...At the Readfield station, which for some weeks has been the terminus of the company's trains, a still greater crowd was awaiting the arrival of the cars and many hearty cheers were exchanged between the different portions of the train and the surrounding crowds. An engine with two passenger cars had come (to Readfield) from Waterville the same morning, to meet and join the advancing train, bringing several Waterville gentlemen with salutations to their friends from below. These two cars were added to the seven, and two other platform cars were filled with increasing swarms and added to the lengthened line. This imposing cortege of twelve cars, with the powerful steam horse – the Ticonic – in front, set out from Readfield to penetrate the valleys and lake margins, which had never before seen a sight so strange and imposing...

The train continued on to Belgrade and West Waterville (Oakland) stations where still more passengers came aboard. Up to four-thousand children and adults greeted the entourage of one-thousand or more passengers at the terminus in Waterville. Cannons were fired and church bells rang throughout the city. Invited guests proceeded to the newly built 250-foot long railroad freight shed where tables had been set up for the entire length. Over the course of one-hour ten speeches were heard – including one from Readfield resident Anson P. Morrill.[10] Proficient hostesses had prepared ample food – including twelve-hundred pounds of meat - for an elegant dinner that served two-thousand diners. Some guests were disappointed they could not stay longer for an evening party which organizers promised would be magnificently illuminated. Instead, they watched in awe as the direction of the massive steam engine was changed on the newly constructed turn-table and reconnected to the passenger cars. Passengers filled the cars again and the lively procession departed at 2:45 p.m. making its way southward and leaving people off at their respective stations along the way. At the Readfield station the engineer steered onto the side tracks to allow passage of an up train from Portland – no doubt transporting more guests to the evening party in Waterville. The celebratory procession arrived in Portland at 8:00 p.m. that same evening. As passengers disembarked they surely were bursting with enthusiastic tales about the day!

Thirteen years later the Maine Central Railroad Company (MCRR) was created when the directors of the A&KRR and the Penobscot & Kennebec Railroad Companies agreed to re-organize as such. In 1873 MCRR grew yet again when they consolidated with four smaller railroad companies. A little hamlet had evolved around the Readfield train station and residents were grateful for the convenience of the railroad – especially local farmers and businessmen who could send and receive freight and produce by rail. Sportsmen started coming from the city by train in the summertime to fish the area lakes, ponds and streams. Little else had changed since the first train, especially the outlying landscape.

All that said there were risks and tragedies that also came with the railroad. Train wrecks were not unusual and accidental deaths were all too common. But that did not deter men from flocking to town in search of employment. Hopefuls who were not hired by the railroad often found other jobs that offered supplemental services such as stagecoach drivers, wheelwrights, delivery wagons, livery stables, blacksmiths, innkeepers, storekeepers, mail carriers, handymen and freight handlers. Likewise, women found work as seamstresses or as cooks and housekeepers at local inns.

The passenger's ride was rough and tumble on those early trains, but the convenience and speed with which they reached their destinations outweighed the risks and discomfort.

Despite all the obstacles and risks, rail travel and the number of passengers flourished. By the 1870s the MCRR was gradually replacing wooden tracks and bridges with iron. In 1880 MCRR built a lakeside excursion center between Readfield Depot and Winthrop called Maranacook Grove, complete with its own station and turn-table. The wooden trestle over Lake Maranacook was replaced with iron in 1887. MCRR added a 30x15 ft. baggage room and a new coal shed at Readfield Depot in 1881. Between 1891 and 1893 twenty-three passenger cars, ten baggage cars and two mail cars were added to MCRR's overall rolling stock.[11]

By 1900 the MCRR was running six passenger cars and twelve mail stops a day through Readfield and Winthrop. A grain elevator and warehouse were built by Morrill & Gordon adjacent to the tracks at Readfield Depot and received several grain deliveries a day.[12] The Kennebec, Kathadin, Penobscot, Skipper and The Pine Tree were engines commonly seen on the route through Winthrop and Readfield. In the mid 1930s another engine named the Flying Yankee made its debut. That train witnessed a lot of fanfare because of its futuristic design and the public was absolutely amazed by its sleek look and incredibly fast speed. The Yankee operated for more than 20 years.[13]

Readfield Depot became a buzzing village that, along with Winthrop, soon transitioned into final destination points that burst forth with a new kind of summer activity.

1856 map of Readfield Depot.
Courtesy of Readfield Historical Society

Carriages waiting at the train crossing in Readfield Depot

The Readfield Depot train station as it looked in its heyday.
Freight shed is on the right. Baggage shed is behind the station.

From the trestle over "North Winthrop Pond" appeared in
an 1880 MCRR publication promoting Maine tourism by rail

Bar Harbor Express, Readfield, Me.

The *Bar Harbor Express* provided through-service during
the summer season from New York into northern
New England. It was one of the region's few
all-Pullman operations and considered one of the
most important trains in "Vacationland".

Left: John C. Adell of
Readfield Depot worked for
the MCRR as the Assistant
Station Agent at the
Readfield Depot station and
later as the Telegraph
Operator at Winthrop
station.

Courtesy of Townsend family

Mary (Gordon) Adell with Ruth and Marion Townsend, two of her grandchildren, sitting on the porch at the tenement house near Readfield Depot station. *Courtesy of Townsend family*

Approaching the trestle crossing over
Lake Maranacook via the railroad

"Maranacook Lake is at the head of a line of lakes, all now well filled with black bass, pickerel and the favorite white perch..." ~ Forest and Stream, October 1889

COMETH THE "SPORTS" ~ 1860

When travel by rail was soundly established the Maine Central Railroad (MCRR) began to expand into related endeavors. Their marketing was initially geared towards businesses and later towards luring would-be adventurers and fishermen into the State of Maine.

Henry David Thoreau's excursions upcountry, and the publication of his book "The Maine Woods" in 1864, sparked immediate interest in what the Maine wilderness had to offer sportsmen. To further prompt interest, in 1867 Henry O. Stanley of Dixfield, with his cousin George Shepard Page,[14] a Readfield native, caught a record breaking 12 lb. brook trout in the Rangeley Lakes Region. The next year Page transported a live 10 lb. male trout and an 8 lb. female to his home in Stanley, New Jersey in an attempt to propagate them and restore that state's brook trout fishery.[15] Newspaper stories about his catches appeared all over New York and New Jersey which caused a sensation and further excited sportsmen about fishing in Maine's northwoods.

In 1868 Page helped create, and was the first president, of the "Oquossoc Anglers Association" and soon after he and the group built the rustic Camp Kennebago for fishermen.[16] Camp Kennebago was one of many such camps that appeared throughout Maine.

Interestingly, Page introduced black bass into Maine when in 1869 he brought thirty-one live fish from Newburgh, NY to Winthrop and released them into Lake Maranacook.[17] This was done to counteract the presence of pickerel which had been released into Maranacook without authorization. The trout fishery was devastated as a result.[18] Thereafter any publicity distributed by the MCRR and the Maine Publicity Bureau, about fishing Lake Maranacook, was dominated by the promise of great catches of black bass.

By 1870 "sports" began flocking north by rail from New York, New Jersey and southern New England making their way "upcountry" for canoeing, fishing and "rusticating" in Maine's northwoods.

Over the next decade the MCRR's focus turned to their next expansion - capitalizing on an untapped market, the everyday Maine resident.

George Shepard Page was a Readfield native who eventually lived in Stanley, New Jersey. On the right is his cousin Henry O. Stanley. Stanley's father Isaac was a Winthrop native who moved his family to Dixfield. H.O. Stanley became Maine's Fisheries Commissioner in 1872 and held the post for many years. These two men were both cousins of the Stanley twins of Kingfield who invented the Stanley Steamer.

Sports are showing off their catch from Lake Maranacook.

Fishing at the outlet of Dead Stream into Lake Maranacook

IS IT MARANACOOK OR MARANOCOOK?
Kennebec Journal Daily, August 30, 1880

Dr. William B. Lapham, agricultural editor of the *Maine Farmer,* has made a careful investigation of the derivation and orthography of that lake in Winthrop over which there has been so much controversy. The following is the result of his lucubrations.

There does not seem to be any good authority for the present orthography of "Maranacook" as applied to the North Winthrop Pond. Colonel Lithgow and Jabez Bradbury, both old residents on the Kennebec (River), testified before a court in Boston, the former in 1762 and the later in 1765 that the Indian name of this pond was "Maroonscook", and Capt. Joseph Bane of York[19], who was eight years captive among the Indians, gives the same orthography.

The late William Willis of Portland who has given much attention to the language of the Abenaqui Indians, in his list of Indian words spells it "Maranocook".

Now we cannot state which one of these two spellings is correct, but we feel quite sure that "Maranacook" is wrong. As this is to become a famous resort (Maranacook Grove), we suggest that the true name should be applied, or if this cannot be ascertained beyond a reasonable doubt, then the orthography sustained by the preponderance of testimony should be used. In our judgment the evidence of such men as Col. Lithgow, Jabez Bradbury and Capt. Bane, all of whom were acquainted with the Indians and more or less familiar with their language, is entitled to great weight.

"The largest number of (53) excursion tickets on record were sold Sunday at Readfield Station." Readfield Depot news, Kennebec Journal, August 1906

MARANACOOK GROVE ~ 1880

By the 1870s the MCRR began making arrangements for pleasure parties. They planned to create a place where guests could enjoy quiet attractive day excursions away from their business cares and the hot dusty city streets. The "back road" route had already captured the notice of passengers. It meandered through pristine valleys and followed the edges of several bodies of water in the Winthrop and Belgrade Lakes Regions. The trestle over Lake Maranacook in Readfield also provided views up and down the Lake which enthralled passengers.

James Sedgley's 200 acre farm was located at the trestle's end on the western shore of Lake Maranacook – partly in Winthrop and partly in Readfield. He sold a strip of land to the A&KRR in 1848[20] and in 1880 he leased ten lakeside acres to the MCRR on both sides of the tracks. The five year lease included the option to extend another twenty years at the MCRR's discretion. Sedgley stipulated that the MCRR could clear only enough trees for ornamental purposes and to make way for the construction of an excursion center.[21] In August of 1880 the MCRR opened Maranacook Grove. [22]

The MCRR put up several structures including a 30x100ft pavilion and a dining hall of the same proportions. They added a 67x30ft boathouse, a 16x16ft baggage room, a 13x13ft store house and a wharf. The following year they added an ice house and coat room. The grounds included seating, gravel paths, arbors and lovely Chinese like lanterns along the pathway. The crème de la crème, for efficient railroad operations, were side tracks and Maranacook Grove's own engine turn-table. Both were vital to the safe delivery of thousands of guests on opening day. Thereafter the same set-up helped secure the arrival of northbound and southbound trains whenever the Maranacook Grove hosted large events.[23] .

Come July of 1880 the MCRR started running promotional ads about a Regatta that would take place on opening day on August 4th. The MCRR ran their train schedule on the front page of the Kennebec Journal (KJ) every day that summer. On August 3rd an article stated "a large force of boating men are in town tonight… everything is arranged on a grand scale and the grounds are considered one of the most delightful spots in Maine. Area hotels are full, the streets lively, and the stage is set for tomorrow." [24] But it wasn't meant to be. The following morning telegrams were sent to local hotels announcing postponement due to rain.[25] Attendance would have been far higher on August 4th than it was on the rain date of August 5th.

The happenings described by the Kennebec Journal on August 6th are hard to fathom. One hundred and fourteen railroad passenger cars came from Portland, Lewiston, Brunswick, Farmington, Bangor, Waterville and Augusta. The MCRR borrowed cars from Ogdensburg, Rochester, Grand Trunk and Moosehead Lake Railroads to meet their needs. Estimates said eight to nine thousand people arrived by rail, two or three thousand more came afoot, by boat or teams. "At Mr. James Sedgley's place near the Grove some one-hundred horses were taken care of in first-class style". Some overzealous enthusiasts claimed there were 60,000 attendees.[26]

The Regatta was a highlight of the day which included professional and amateur levels of scullers and four-oared races. There was a bateau race, and four teams from the Penobscot Nation entered the Indian canoe race. Two men per vessel "paddled the birch bark canoes with all the grace and ease of their ancestors... and elicited much cheering and applause…" Significant purses were awarded to those who won first, second, third and fourth place which added to the excitement of the day.

Two bands entertained guests. The Bangor Band, dressed in splendid uniforms, consisted of nineteen pieces and Johnson's Band of Lewiston boasted twenty-two musicians. The large pavilion dance floor provided ample space for those who wished to trip the light fantastic.

The only hitch of the day, other than a few young men becoming inebriated and a bit unruly, was a shortage of food. The Portland caterers in charge of refreshments telegraphed their home base in Portland for more food, but even then they could not come close to feeding everyone.

At the end of the day, as the last train pulled out towards Readfield Depot at 15 mph, a young man lost his balance and fell off a platform car. Fortunately he was not badly hurt but he lost his pride and his ride home. All was well that ended well, except for that one unhappy excursionist who got left behind.

This MCRR trip became more and more popular as time went on. There was opposition by some groups and individuals when the MCRR began offering Sunday trips. Naysayers believed that Sunday excursions infringed on the peace, prayerful reflection and physical rest of the Sabbath. They were also against MCRR's requirement that railroad employees work on Sundays. In 1904 The New England Sabbath Protection League wrote in their monthly publication:[27]

> "…This (MCRR) road has done more to debauch public sentiment in Maine… It has gone into the Sunday excursion business in wholesale way. It has by its business spoiled such wholesome resorts as Old Orchard and made a scandal and a reproach to the State. Is it not time for the residents of the Pine Tree State to rise in might and disprove the oft statement that the Maine Central Railroad owns the legislature and the State of Maine, by demanding that unnecessary Sunday travel shall be abolished by its principal railroad?…"

In spite of any opposition to the MCRR and their Sunday excursions it all remained intact. Additionally, sporting camps and hotels – some privately owned and some built by the MCRR - sprung up in this immediate area and elsewhere along the MCRR back road rail. Included were establishments in Poland Spring, Lewiston, Lake Auburn, Oakland, Belgrade, Waterville, Winthrop and Readfield.[28]. The excursion centers and hotels were here to stay – at least until competition, a bad economy and / or tragedy struck.

In 1902 the local electric railway company extended street car service from Augusta to Winthrop and built a popular excursion center on Cobbosseeconte Lake, called Island Park that remained active well into the 20th century. (see pg.90)

Maranacook Grove ceased operations in 1915 and the buildings were absorbed by the Maranacook Camps, Cottages and Hotel Company.

Water sports and boat races were popular activities for the excursionists who visited Maranacook Grove.

The first Maranacook Station and beyond that is the trestle.
Train passengers left the siding by walking under the sign.
They descended a flight of stairs and entered directly into
Maranacook Grove pictured below. Note the barrels of
drinking water lined up in the center of the Grove.
In 1915 a new Maranacook Station was built
closer to the hotel. This archway and the stairs were
moved to that location.

"Maranacook has become a great resort for taking black bass, and with its elegant accommodations, row, sail and steamboats I fear the fish are getting the worst of it." Forest and Stream, October 1889

STEAMBOATS COME TO LAKE MARANACOOK ~ 1880

History tells us that steamboats appeared on Maine's inland waters as early as 1836. During the "golden age" of steamboating (1830-1930) more than 60 steamboats plied the waters of Moosehead Lake alone. The first such boat, the *Moosehead*, was 96 feet long.[29] Early operation was unregulated and boats were sometimes overcrowded and poorly maintained. There were some regulations by 1850 but in the years that followed the number of boats increased dramatically as did the demand for power and speed.[30]

In 1874 the Maine State Legislature mandated the annual inspection of all steamboats as well as a licensing process for the engineers and captains who operated them. Two state inspectors were required – one with a practical knowledge of ship building and the other with expertise in the construction and use of boilers and engines.[31]

Steamboats were powered by coal and wood so fire was the biggest threat to steamboat passengers. Woodwork around the boilers, chimneys, fire boxes and steam pipes had to be shielded by non-combustible materials leaving adequate space for heat ventilation. In order to pass inspection all steamboats had to include a life boat, axes, water buckets, enough life preservers for every passenger, unobstructed egress and stairways, and crew training in the use and maintenance of this safety equipment. Inspectors also determined the amount of pressure and speed that each steam engine could safely attain; as well as the number of passengers a vessel could carry. Failure of steamboat owners or operators to comply would result in fines or, in the event of a death due to lack of compliance, imprisonment for manslaughter.[32] No doubt these laws and the principles of navigation were taken very seriously by the men plying the waters of Lake Maranacook because there has not been any record found of an accident or mishap resulting in fatalities or collisions.

Another legislative action occurred in 1885 when the Maine Central Railroad (MCRR) was given State authorization to form steamboat connections. With that approval the MCRR could purchase, hold, maintain and operate, either by itself or jointly with others, steamboats for the transportation of passengers and freight beyond the line of its railroad tracks.[33] Although the MCRR owned and operated their own steamers and hotels in other parts of the State, such as those on Moosehead Lake and the Kineo Hotel, no record has been found of their actually owning either a steamboat or a hotel on Lake Maranacook. Certainly summer passengers disembarked directly to and from steamboats to MCRR's Winthrop and Maranacook Stations, but from all we can gather those steamboats were owned by either Margaret Butler at the Sir Charles Hotel, Mark S. Collins of Maranacook Hotel or the pioneer of steamboats on Lake Maranacook, Simeon Davis.

Lake Maranacook never floated a steamer as large as the *Moosehead*, and there are no fantabulous stories to tell about the steam powered vessels there. But the captains and engineers who operated them were an important part of the early days of tourism on Lake Maranacook and thus worthy of mention.

SOME STEAMBOAT MEN ON LAKE MARANACOOK

Simeon Davis launched his first vessel on Lake Maranacook in 1880 – the same year the MCRR premiered Maranacook Grove. Two years later he put a larger one into service.[34] No doubt transporting passengers to and from that popular destination was the impetus for launching the steamboats *Annie* and *Amarascoggin*. Davis had spent a lifetime building skills apropos to such an enterprise. He was born in Mount Vernon in 1834, the son of Benjamin Davis, an affluent farmer. The family homestead was "Interlaken Farm" on Echo Lake (see pg 269) in West Mount Vernon. Simeon attended Maine Wesleyan Seminary (Kents Hill School) two miles from his home and then he taught in local schools for several years. Teaching did not fulfill his bent for entrepreneurism so at age twenty-five he moved to Winthrop, worked as a blacksmith's apprentice, and soon opened his own business. Davis was also a staunch abolitionist so one cannot help but wonder if moving to the antislavery hotbed of Winthrop was also an incentive. At any rate, from blacksmithing he expanded into retail sales of iron, steel, wood and coal until 1880 when Maranacook Grove opened. By that time Davis had the skills and interest for running passengers on the Lake, he had established business contacts and accumulated significant resources which all made the steamboat business a natural and lucrative move. In subsequent years he also ran the *Davis* on Lake Annabesasook and *We Two* on Lake Maranacook. He became widely known for his business acumen.[35]

Mark S. Collins was another steamboat captain on Lake Maranacook. Born in 1868 Collins was an Anson native who came from a long line of saw mill operators but he and his older brother Charles took another direction. Both worked as station agents for the MCRR as young men – Charles in Yarmouth and Mark in Readfield. The exact year Collins arrived in the Readfield and Winthrop area is not known, but we do know he came before 1889 when he made his first land acquisition. Steamboats were but one of his lifetime business ventures. As you will see elsewhere in this book, Collins was an entrepreneur and investor extraordinaire. He married Nellie Townsend in 1893, and their daughter was born three years later. Nellie's father owned Townsend Farm (see pg. 99) on Tallwood Peninsula at that time. By 1895 Collins owned 100 acres of land along the west shore of Lake Maranacook in Winthrop and soon after he acquired the steamboat *Lorna*, which he named in honor of his baby daughter. In 1902, when the trolley came through

Winthrop (see pg. 90), he immediately leased a 20 foot right of way on the southern tip of Lake Maranacook adjacent to the trolley station. There he built a rather elaborate wharf that was commonly called "Collins" Landing. He retained that right of way for 15 years.[36]

Mark Collins was also fiercely competitive. His steamer *Maranacook* was the largest and perhaps the best known steam powered vessel of them all in this area. In 1901 Mrs. Margaret Butler, the owner of the Sir Charles Hotel, launched her own vessel, the 40 foot *Anita*. She had apparently been low key about telling of its size which was larger than the *Maranacook*! When Collins saw that he had been outdone he brought the *Maranacook* into dry dock, cut it in two and added ten feet in the middle. The townspeople and summer folks were entertained by hearing tales about that particular Collins undertaking and the story has endured for generations.

Capt. Charles W. "C.W." Howard, who built the *Anita* for Mrs. Butler,[37] is also worth mention. Charles was a Readfield native, born on the northern part of Tallwood Peninsula in 1847, on what later became the Townsend Farm (see pg. 99). His grandfather, Joel Howard, was the last person to own Tallwood Peninsula in its 200 acre entirety (1840s). He divided it between his sons – one being Charles' father Anderson, who moved his family nearer to Readfield Depot in 1850 (Fickett 2016) and died soon afterwards.

After his father's death Charles attended Maine Wesleyan Seminary (Kents Hill School) then worked as a machinist in Readfield for a time before moving to Rangeley Lakes. There he captained the *Molly Chunkamunk* between Indian Rock and Haines Landing in Oquossoc and became known as Capt. C.W. Howard.[38] By 1884 he had moved to Peak's Island in Casco Bay where he worked towards becoming a Master Mariner and steamboat builder.[39] He became known as "the steamboat man" for those reasons. In 1905 he bought Bay View House and Bay

View Landing on Peaks Island[40] and converted the landing into a free public wharf for yachtsmen and motor boat owners.[41] Charles died on Peaks Island sixteen years later.[42]

Others who captained steamboats on Lake Maranacook in the early 1900s included:

Raymond Brewer, a young carpenter born in Freeport in 1888. Brewer later went into the grocery business in Freeport.[43]

William Toomey, who emigrated from Prince Edward Island in 1907. Two years later he became licensed as a captain and engineer and worked alongside Mark S. Collins on the *Maranacook*. Toomey went on to become an apprentice steam fitter and eventually became an engineer in Manchester, NH.[44]

Harry C. Soule was from Somerset County. We know little about him except that he was likely related to "old Uncle George Soule", a renowned Rangeley guide and owner of Camp Henry, Mountain View House and a steamboat on Mooselucmaguntic Lake in the late 19th century.

Clement Willard "Clem" Knight was born in Newburg, Penobscot County in 1868. Through his father he acquired a taste for the Maine wilderness of northern Maine. His mother, who was born in Winterport, and an older brother who settled on Matinicus Island, inspired Clem's interest in coastal Maine and boating. His other older brother, Edward (Ed), was perhaps the biggest influence on the course of Clem's life. Sometime before 1898 Ed acquired an old lumber camp on Molunkus Lake in Macwahoc, a remote part of southern Aroostook County. Knight's Sporting Camps (Lake Molunkus Sporting Camps, 2016) drew sports in from throughout New England and New York. Clem worked with his brother as a guide on fishing and hunting excursions and both men were crack shots and adept fishermen.[45]

It is not known what brought Clem, also known as C.W., to Winthrop. In 1900 he was living with Mark Collins' family at the

Maranacook Hotel and working as an (steamboat) engineer.[46] He later became licensed as a steamboat captain.[47] This story has been passed down over the years and tells us that Clem became very confident as a steamboat operator. It had been a dry summer and Maranacook Lake was low when Clem piloted summer guests on an evening excursion. One of the passengers asked Clem if he worried about hitting one of the boulders that lay near the surface. Clem replied "not to worry, I know every ledge in this lake". At that moment the *Maranacook* hit one and without missing a beat Clem said "and there's one right now!"[48]

Clem Knight was also among the guides on Lake Maranacook. Angling is what drew most summer guests to this area so local hotels offered guided fishing excursions on a daily basis. The guides tied row boats or canoes to the steamboats and ferried them to a good fishing spot. They anchored the steamboat, transferred the fishermen to the smaller boats and paddled them about while the guests cast their lines. The day's catch became dinner.

The guides had campgrounds set-up at various strategic points where they cooked shore dinners. Some were in wooded settings and others were located on sandy beaches. In some cases the hotels created elaborate areas complete with fireplaces and picnic tables. At least one campground was set-up to appeal to men, women and children alike in an effort to make the experience enjoyable for all. [49]

Tall tales about fishing and hunting were told by Clem Knight and his contemporaries. Perhaps Clem told of his brother Ed, who once took down three deer with one bullet; or the day he shot three raging black bears on the attack, in one encounter?[50] No doubt the guides and steamboat captains on Lake Maranacook were proficient storytellers and shared a wide range of exciting tales about fishing and hunting in "the Maine northwoods".

The *Amarascoggin* near Maranacook Landing. This was one of three steamboats that Simeon Davis' ran on Lake Maranacook.

Capt. C.W. "Clem" Knight.
Behind him is the *Maranacook* in dry dock.
Photo courtesy of Andrew Knight, Jr.

The 40 ft. *Anita* near her home base, the Sir Charles Hotel. She was built by Readfield native Capt. C. W. Howard of Peaks Island, and commissioned in 1901 by Mrs. Margaret Butler.

The Maranacook at the Hotel Maranacook landing. Standing front and center is Capt. Mark Collins.

Ignacio and Carrie Martinetti of New York City (center) aboard a steamer on Maranacook. They owned a cottage called "The Pines" near the Sir Charles Hotel from 1916 until 1924 (see pg 62)

Tamsonhurst guests about to go on a steamboat excursion. Owners of the Tamsonhurst in Readfield were Ed & Tamson Nelson. (see pg. 109)
Photo courtesy of the Nelson - Johnson family

MARANACOOK HOUSE ~ 1880

This establishment went by several names during its existence. For six years there were two structures at this location with different names, which explains the overlap: Elmwood House 1869 – 1880; Asa Gile Hotel 1874 – 1880; Maranacook House 1880 – 1900; Elmwood Hotel 1900 - 1930

The Elmwood Hotel is probably the most recognized name of any of the old hotels in Readfield. But few people know anything about its early history or that it went by other names prior to 1900.[51]

The Elmwood sat on land owned by John O. Craig[52] and before him by his father Thomas and his grandfather James.[53] The Craigs were an industrious lot. This is evidenced in our chapters about J.O.'s cousin Daniel and his son David W. Craig of Readfield Depot.[54] J.O.'s enterprises included woodlots, a logging operation, a saw mill, land development and he owned the Elmwood House (before it became Elmwood Hotel). Yet, on every U.S. Census he simply gave his occupation as farmer.[55]

By 1842 J. O. and his wife, Sally, had eleven children and had outgrown their little Cape Cod on Church Street that he had inherited from his father.[56] J.O. borrowed $3,500 that year, using the 30 acres of land that remained of his grandfather's estate as collateral.[57] The loan was to build a new and larger house on the main road at Readfield Corner. A much more advantageous location for someone with their sights set on building a new business. Their eldest daughter Rozilla, who was newly married, got the Cape Cod house with a half acre. (Guimont 2016)

About that same time J.O.'s cousin Daniel was busy accumulating land near Readfield Depot, in proximity to where the railroad would be passing through town in 1849. Imagine the discussions J.O. and Daniel must have had about the coming of the railroad and the impact that would have on the town's growth and new business opportunities.

From his new home at Readfield Corner J.O. could observe the ever increasing traffic as people passed back and forth from Readfield Depot and points beyond. Business at Readfield Corner was bustling in those years with dry good and grocery stores, tailors, shoe, coat and dress shops and several manufactories at Factory Square. Colonial era taverns like J.J Hutchinson's at Readfield Depot, Samuel Fogg's and Peter Kittredge's at Readfield Corner and Dudley Moody's at Kents Hill no longer satisfied travelers' expectations like they once had. With the advent of trains more people were making pleasure excursions rather than trips of necessity. Railroad travel was rough by today's standards but for those times it was luxurious and efficient. People wanted to come and stay awhile in the privacy of their own rooms and with a higher level of decorum than the old taverns had to offer. They wanted to be fed three meals a day, have easy access to transportation, be closer to churches, shopping and have the option of recreational activities. Hotels that offered amenities and conveniences such as those, in a small village like Readfield Corner, were beyond anyone's comprehension. J.O. Craig and Asa Gile changed all that.

Remarkably, J.O. was seventy-four years old in 1869 when he added an east wing on his home and the Elmwood House was born.[58] It is a mystery why he sold it only one year later. Perhaps J.O. had hoped that one of his children would take over the Elmwood and that did not work out? He may have given it up due to his or his wife's ill health? Perhaps he was made an offer he could not refuse? Whatever the reason, he sold the Elmwood House to Asa Gile, who lived next door. The Craigs moved back to Church Street to live with Rozilla and her family. Sally died there in 1874 and J.O. died seven years after her.

Asa Gile was a Mt. Vernon native who married Ursula Smith of Readfield in 1844. She was a daughter of Capt. John Smith and granddaughter of Mathias Smith who, in 1768, was one of the first men to settle in town. Like the Craigs, the Smith family was well known and held in high esteem in Readfield's circles. Capt. John owned a profitable store at Readfield Corner and he was also a successful attorney. His participation in various organizations included the Universalist Church, and his significant land holdings added to his prominent standing in the community. Asa married well when he wed Ursula Smith.

Asa Gile was also involved in several business ventures. He owned a woodworking shop at Factory Square where fly rods and coffins were made. He also ran a sashes and blinds factory on the Square.[59] Gile studied law under Lot. M. Morrill, Esq. of Readfield and built-up an active law practice as well.[60] As an opportunistic lawyer he became involved in many land deals and investments. He was also a philanthropist, as evidenced by his contribution to the Town of Readfield in 1860. With his money a second floor was added to the fifth district schoolhouse, complete with stage and assembly hall.[61] Townspeople were encouraged to use the space and they hailed Gile for his generosity. Plays, meetings and various gatherings were cheerfully held there, including temperance meetings that Gile himself attended and fully endorsed.[62]

In spite of his philanthropic nature and business savvy Gile did have a downfall.

The story goes that Asa Gile became competitive with his law tutor's brother, Anson P. Morrill. Like Gile, Morrill's business ventures centered in Readfield but his tentacles reached far beyond town. The Readfield Woolen Factory was floundering when Anson P. Morrill bought it in the 1850s but he turned it around and received acclaim for doing so.[63] Hundreds of people received income from that factory's success, both directly and indirectly, and the townspeople were grateful. When Readfield's sons marched off to fight in the Civil War the future looked mighty grim for their wives and children. How would they ever survive without the muscle power or earned income from their men folk? About that time the woolen factory was awarded a contract to make material for the Union soldiers' uniforms. Additional workers were hired in order to meet orders, and many of those new hires were those women and their teenage daughters and sons. This was a blessed relief that kept the families afloat on the home front. Morrill was a hero yet again. In 1855 Morrill was elected Governor of Maine and his journey towards even wider notoriety began. When he received the Republican nomination for U.S. House of Representatives in 1861 Asa Gile reared-up and ran against him on the Democratic ticket. Not only did Morrill soundly win that election,[64] but he went on to serve in various other political posts and boards of directors over the years, including president of the Maine Central Railroad.[65] By all indications Morrill flew right past Gile in his business and political pursuits, but when he began construction on a new mansion house on Sturtevant Hill Road,[66] Gile was not to be outdone.

Asa and Ursula Gile bought her father's homestead on Main Street in 1854 but Capt. Smith continued to live there.[67] Within a few years after he died in 1860 the Giles began making plans for the construction of their own grand manor. In 1868 they donated Capt. Smith's mansion to the Union Meeting House (UMH) on Church Street and arranged for it to be moved onto a lot adjacent to the UMH. The Giles had a magnificent home built where the more modest Smith mansion formerly stood. Their new home dominates the Readfield Corner landscape to this day. According to oral tradition every time Morrill added an ostentatious feature to his estate, Gile did the same at his. His Italianate style mansion boasted features such as seven Italian marble fireplaces, hand carved woodwork, six bedrooms, a modern kitchen, tennis court, and an ornate fountain. Elaborate staircases led to the second and third floors. From the "captain's nest" atop the third floor one could see for miles around.

Framing the impressive grounds was a decorative wrought iron fence set in a granite foundation.[68] (Doorebos 2016)

When Asa Gile bought J.O. Craig's property in 1870 it included Craig's residence and The Elmwood House. In typical Gile style he set his standards high and proceeded to build a hotel like no one had ever seen in this area. By the spring of 1874 construction was complete. A local newspaper reported *"The Elmwood House has recently been remodeled, and with extensive additions made, is one of the most commodious hotels to be found outside of city limits; and much credit is due the proprietor Asa Gile, Esq. for his liberal expenditure for the public convenience."* [69] This new building was remarkably well-built and could accommodate fifty guests.[70] It boasted more than twenty large guest rooms, a spacious dining room and a ballroom with a raised platform for musicians. An expansive stable was available for boarding the clientele's horses. [71] The hotel also provided transportation with its own carriage, horses and hostler. In 1879 the new structure was called Asa Gile Hotel and The Elmwood House was separate, but still there.[72] By 1882 the entire property had become "Maranacook House".[73] Why did Gile give it this name when his hotel was not located on or even near Lake Maranacook?

From the 1760s until after 1880 Lake Maranacook was called Chandler's Pond and Winthrop Pond. After Maranacook Grove opened in 1880 people began calling the pond Lake Maranacook on occasion, but that name was not commonly used for several more years. The name Maranacook was not associated with the lake at all in 1880, but with Maranacook Grove.[74] It is apparent that Gile changed the name of his hotel to "Maranacook House" to attract excursionists and to capitalize on the success of Maranacook Grove. There were no other large hotels of this nature anywhere in town at that point. The Sir Charles was the second to open its doors, but that did not happen until 1894. Gile had Readfield's hotel market cornered for nearly fifteen years. Had it not been for his extravagant spending the Maranacook House would have been a splendid money maker.

Ursula died in 1878 and Asa's health and earning power began declining soon after. Excessive expenditures on the mansion and the hotel spun Asa deeply into debt and he never recovered from that or his health issues. The bank foreclosed on his house and the hotel in 1887, followed by an auction which fetched far less than the properties were worth. A Lewiston Journal news report described the situation in some detail and then concluded "...the estates in question were too large for Readfield and that is all there is to it..." [75] William Harvey, a prominent Readfield entrepreneur, [76] placed the winning bid of $1,550 on the house. That was less than eight percent of what Gile had spent on its construction twenty years earlier. [77] Four men placed the winning bid of $1,650 [78] on the Maranacook House.

Sadly, Asa Gile died one year after the auction – broken hearted no doubt. The inventory of his remaining real estate included a machine shop and machinery; a field, orchard, corn and orchard barns; store house; wood lot; Gile hall and its scenery. The total value was $2,095. [79]

The new hotel owners were Benjamin Harriman, Judge Emery O. Beane [80] and George Twitchell of Readfield and Reuel Soule of Augusta. They hired a manager and continued to operate the hotel until 1895 when, in the midst of a two year long major recession, they sold it for $2,025. [81]

"The Panic of 1893" resulted in declining stock prices, 500 bank closings, 15,000 businesses failures, and foreclosure on numerous farms across the country. The unemployment rate hit double digits and long soup lines formed in the big cities. [82] Conditions such as those negatively impacted summer sojourns to Maine as they have during every recession since then. Perhaps Harriman et al saw this as a good time to "get out" while they could still recoup their investment? The Sir Charles Hotel had opened the year before, giving the Maranacook House owners competition for the first time. Most likely both situations weighed into their decision to sell when they did.

Charles E. Stevens became the new owner of Maranacook House in 1895. He was a native son of Waterbury, Connecticut where his father owned Blake & Johnson, a brass wire and fixtures manufacturory.[83] His father died in 1894 but Charles declined the opportunity to carry on in his father's footsteps at Blake & Johnson. Instead, he struck out for Maine to become his own man. Charles was single and had worked in the hotel industry in Poland, Maine before he bought Maranacook House. Twenty days later he married Sadie Gordon of Readfield. It is not known where or how the couple met, but it is known that Sadie was working as a housekeeper at the time of their marriage – perhaps at Maranacook House or at Poland Spring House?[84] It was Charles' second marriage, he was forty-one. Sadie was a maiden lady, age forty-four.[85] They never had children.

Charles had an advantage that boosted his new business - familial connections to other hotel owners and managers on Lake Maranacook.[86] His success was remarkable and he soon earned a fine reputation and was highly regarded as a Readfield resident and hotel proprietor.[87]

In 1900 Mark Collins opened the Maranacook Hotel adjacent to Maranacook Grove. (see pg. 15) That same year Charles Stevens changed the name of his establishment from Maranacook House to Elmwood Hotel. This change was, no doubt, to avoid confusion between the two establishments. It is also an example of how those, and other fellow proprietors, collaborated and agreed to the benefit of all. They also referred guests to each other when their rooms were filled to capacity, and helped each other out when there was a shortage of workers or hardships of other types.

Perhaps the Elmwood received more publicity in August of 1905, than at any other time in its history. Mattie Hackett was an employee at the Elmwood that summer, when she was murdered near her home on Kents Hill. The woman accused was Mrs. Raymond, whose husband worked with Mattie at the Elmwood.

The investigators theorized the murder was an act of jealous rage. News stories appeared nationwide for months afterwards, and the Elmwood was mentioned in nearly every one. Surely Charles Stevens did not appreciate that kind of publicity. The murder was never solved. (see pg. 125)

After fifteen years of operating the Elmwood Hotel, Charles and Sadie sold it back to the same investors they had bought it from. The couple moved to Waterbury, CT where Charles became a partner in Blake & Johnson until 1923 when he sold his shares of that business. The Stevens returned to Maine to live in Cape Elizabeth for the rest of their days.

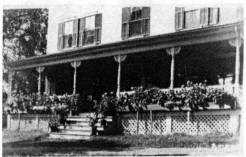

The front piazza at the Elmwood Hotel

In later years the Elmwood was run as an old soldiers' home for Civil War veterans. The front porch, graced with rocking chairs, was a perfect setting for the old patriots to sit 'n rock as they puffed on their corn cob pipes and swapped war stories. That was a common sight in the 1930s.[88]

Supervision of the building eventually fell to Benjamin Harriman's son Merle. It had deteriorated significantly by then and he razed the main part of the building before he died in 1949.[89] His widow, Helen, spent most of the next ten years clearing the title so she could sell the property.[90] She rented apartments there in the interim.

In 1958 Lawrence Cushing, Sr. bought what was left of the old Elmwood Hotel[91] and from that day forward it has been a private residence. The rear el and a stable are all that remain. (Hickmann 2016)

The Elmwood in 1910. All that remains is
the rear el today. Note the large stable.

The Asa Gile mansion as it looked in 1892.

"Mr. J.J. Hutchinson whose hotel was burned at Readfield Depot, Wednesday, estimates his loss at about $4,000. Four or five hundred dollars worth of hay is a total loss. The Maine Central Railroad freight house at Readfield Depot caught fire from the sparks, Wednesday, but the fire was extinguished without damage. Mr. Hutchinson's insurance of $2,300, is wholly in the "Home" (Insurance Company), New York. ~ Lewiston Evening Journal, October 8, 1881

HUTCHINSON TAVERN and HUTCHINSON HOUSE

Hutchinson was a familiar name in Readfield Depot in the nineteenth century thanks to J.J. and Mary Hutchinson. They began operating an old fashioned tavern there years before the railroad passed through, and it existed for nearly sixty years.[92] The Hutchinsons offered the only hotel type accommodations available in the village of Readfield Depot until William O'Neal changed that.

"Willie" was the son of an Irishman from Boston named Patrick O'Neal. The O'Neal family had been living in the outreaches of East Readfield for some years when Patrick seized the chance to buy a property closer to town on South Road. He, his wife and five children moved into their new home in 1862. Among their brood were "Willie", the oldest, and "Katie" who was six years younger than her brother.

With this South Road acquisition the O'Neals became the proud owners of a sixty acre farm that included more than a quarter-mile of frontage on Lake Maranacook. Their residence was located around the corner from Readfield Depot where a curious boy like Willie O'Neal could easily watch the ever increasing activity of train passengers coming and going. Sports and their fishing guides were among them which surely fed his adventuresome imagination. Oh the conversations that must have taken place around the O'Neal's supper table about all the happenings in town. Conversations like how many fish Mr. So and So from Boston caught that day and of the fancy fishing gear used; the impressive sales and deliveries at the train station and local mercantiles; or perhaps the rising number of patrons staying at Hutchinson's Tavern.

Willie's young friend was a cousin of the tavern keeper J.J. Hutchinson. His name was Edwin Hutchinson and he lived next door to the O'Neals. Willie and Edwin must have talked to each other about those changes too as they became more inquisitive about opportunities that the outside world might offer. When Edwin was fifteen he moved to Malden, Massachusetts to live with his uncle and attend high school. Willie soon followed to Fall River where he worked for the railroad. There he met a girl and was married in 1878. Willie was still a resident of Fall River when he bought eight acres of land near his father's farm on South Road in 1880.

J.J. and Mary Hutchinson's tavern was destroyed by fire in 1881[93] one year after Maranacook Grove had opened. The property was a total loss and they were only insured for about half its value.[94] At the same time Willie O'Neal was constructing a new eight room hotel on his South Road lot. When the old tavern burned he took advantage of the situation and called his new hotel "Hutchinson House".[95] No doubt he chose that name because Hutchinson's tavern had just burned flat and he did not expect it to be rebuilt. His aim was to capture the clientele that would have otherwise stayed at the tavern.

The number of people coming through Readfield Depot on day excursions to Maranacook Grove (see pg. 14) was increasing dramatically and many of them were seeking overnight accommodations. J.J. and Mary could not sit back and miss out on this kind of gainful opportunity. They bought another large house near their original location[96] within days of the fire and started preparations to resume their lodging business. They were both sexagenarians by then and it must have been very challenging to keep up the pace as they once had. At the same time they would have lamented about mounting competition from Willie O'Neal's new establishment as well as from Asa Gile's "Maranacook House". [97]

J.J. died in 1884 leaving Mary to run their new tavern on her own. It is reassuring to imagine that Willie O'Neal's hotel reduced some of Mary Hutchinson's burden thus making her final years easier; and let's suppose that Mary supported Willie's new endeavor by sending him referrals or giving valuable advice. Whatever the case, the two institutions overlapped for a decade and Mary began to list her establishment as "Depot - Hutchinson House" to delineate the two. [98]

The tavern became outdated and did not meet the expectations and higher standards set by some of the "modern" travelers. With the railroad came more jobs for local people - both directly and indirectly. Mary had no sons to give her a hand and it became more and more difficult for her to secure the male help she needed in order to run her tavern efficiently. As she continued to age and falter so did her business. [99] When Mary actually stopped running the tavern is not known for sure. She died of "general debility" in 1895 at age seventy-five. [100]

In 1893 Willie sold Hutchinson House to his sister Katie and her husband Orrin Stanley. [101] Willie had owned it during the first big growth spurt in Lake Maranacook's history. He remained a resident of Fall River throughout that time so it is likely that Katie managed Hutchinson House until she could afford to buy it from her brother. By that time Katie had also inherited her father's farm that he had bought nearly thirty years earlier. The two structures sat almost opposite each other on South Road.

Meanwhile, Edwin Hutchinson had done very well in the shoe industry. He made a fortune as a shoe and boot salesman, first in Boston then later in Chicago and throughout the Midwest. In 1896 he returned, with his wife and two young sons, to live near his mother and sister at Readfield Depot. He must have made Katie and Orrin an awfully good offer because they sold both the O'Neal farm and the Hutchinson House to Edwin on the same day.[102]

Katie's husband, Orrin began making carriages with his father but Katie continued in the hotel business. From Readfield she went to Winthrop and helped her mother-in-law run the "Stanley House" on Bowdoin Street.

The Hutchinson House ceased to operate as a hotel when it was purchased by Edwin. He hired carpenters to create a grand residence there for his family.[103] After three years he sold the O'Neal farm with a quarter-mile of shoreline on Lake Maranacook. [104] He reserved several hundred feet of waterfront and use of the pasture lane that led to it for himself. No doubt Edwin did this so his own children could experience the joys of fishing and exploring Lake Maranacook as he and Willie O'Neal had during their own childhoods.

Edwin moved his family into their new home in 1899 and from that day forward the family called it "the big house on the hill".[105] Over the next six years Edwin and his wife Ida had four more children as they lived in the grandeur of their new home. Sadly, soon after their sixth child was born, Edwin's wife fell into despair and was committed to the Maine State Insane Asylum. Edwin made sure she was provided with a comfortable private room. He visited her regularly, often with their children and later their grandchildren in tow, but Ida never came to live at home again except for short visits.[106]

In Edwin's later years, after the children were grown and on their own, he spent more and more time in Portland where he had established a large shoe store called the Hutchison Shoe Company. The big house on the hill in Readfield became his "summer house" but he never let it go.[107] After Edwin's death in 1931 his heirs sold his summer house, but they retained that long beloved lakeside property.[108] Ida outlived Edwin by twenty-four years. [109]

Edwin M. Hutchinson and Ida Pullen Hutchinson

Photos Courtesy of Hutchinson grandchildren Elizabeth Giles Bailey and Bill Tyner.

This home on South Road replaced an eight room hotel
that had been built here about 1880. In 1896
Edwin M. Hutchinson bought the property and razed or
expanded it and had this grand family home built at
the same location. This house burned in 1948 when it
was a convalescent home called "Sunset Home".

Left: Edwin M. Hutchinson, Jr. and a friend after a day of fishing. Behind them is the Hutchinson's log cabin on Lake Maranacook, near Coleman's Grove.

Photos courtesy of Elizabeth Giles Bailey

Below: A group from Brann's Camps (formerly Colemans) and some members of the Hutchinson family in 1929.

"My location is as quiet and secluded as if it were miles away in the woods, yet a walk of less than fifteen minutes will bring you to the railroad station, near which is the post office, grocery stores and the express office."
~ *George E. Coleman, 1904*

COLEMAN GROVE ~ 1902
BRANN'S CAMPS ~ 1924
PINEREST ~ 1944

Like most hotels, resorts and camps that are covered in this book, Coleman's Grove was built on an old farm property that encompassed some lakeside frontage. In this part of our story George and Hattie Coleman bought the original Levi Prescott homestead on South Road, which was settled by Prescott in 1821.[110]

Several owners followed Prescott, including an Irishman from Boston named Patrick O'Neal.[111] His daughter Katie inherited the farm and, in 1896, sold it to Edwin Hutchinson, a childhood friend of the O'Neal kids. Edwin's mother was a Readfield native but his father was an Irish immigrant so Edwin had something in common with O'Neal's sons besides being rambunctious boys. They spent many happy days of their boyhood together romping and fishing along this section of undeveloped lakeshore. When Edwin Hutchinson sold this farm to George Coleman in 1899 he retained several hundred feet along the shore and a right of way across the pasture lane to reach it. Edwin was keeping more than just a patch of land and a right of way. He was keeping a piece of his heart.[112]

George Coleman was an Augusta native who, like many other men during that era, came to town as a Maine Central Railroad employee. He worked as an insurance agent for some years, as well as a train station master and telegraph operator. The Colemans and their four children lived in the farmhouse,[113] cultivated the land, maintained an orchard, raised berries and kept animals.[114] Then in 1902 George borrowed $500 and began constructing rental cottages on his lake frontage. He named what Edwin Hutchinson and Willie O'Neal had formerly known as their playground - "Coleman Grove".

Given George's job as a station master for the Maine Central Railroad he made a lot of contacts so it is not surprising that his new enterprise was successful. While he was working his wife Hattie stayed close to home and oversaw the camps.

"A tennis court has been laid out in a clearing in the midst of the grove." ~ *George E. Coleman, 1904*

"A new steamer has been purchased by Mr. Coleman for stops at Maranacook and Coleman's Grove. ~ *Kennebec Journal, July 4, 1905*

"Cottages at Coleman's Grove have been in good demand during the season. When vacated they are immediately occupied by other families." ~ *Kennebec Journal, Sept. 28, 1907*

The Colemans had run Coleman Grove for twenty-two years when they sold the entire property to Bob and Eleanor Brann of Readfield in 1924. Bob Brann owned a livery stable at Readfield Depot but with the advent of automobiles his services were becoming less and less in demand. They changed the name of the business to Brann's Camps and remained the proprietors for twenty years. After Eleanor died in 1941 Bob was unable to carry on alone and sold the business three years later. Four more proprietors followed the Branns.

Albert and Mae Golsner of Queens, NY were next in line. They had already been summer residents on Lake Maranacook for ten years when they bought Brann's Camps. The Golsners' private cottage was located further south on the east shore. (see pg.121) They are credited with naming this enterprise "Pinerest", a name that stuck until the operation ceased three decades later.

Earle and Pauline Higgins owned Pinerest for four years after the Golsners; in 1953 Wallace and Madeline Beardsell of Littleton, MA bought it; and finally Fred and Catherine Bliss of Plymouth, MA took over the helm in 1956.

Fred, Catherine and their children moved to Readfield and eventually bought a house in town in addition to Pinerest. Fred was a plumber and ran his own company while Catherine was largely responsible for the day to day operations of Pinerest. Catherine tells the story of how she and Fred borrowed money from their parents and used it to buy the cottages a full five years before they bought their home on Old Kents Hill Road (Knox 2016). In retrospect she shakes her head. "We were young and green and knew nothing about running summer cottages" she said, "and I was pregnant besides." They had little time to pull everything together because, when they signed the sales agreement, they were only one month away from opening day. Fortunately Catherine was referred to someone in town who'd worked at Pinerest and was willing to help them get settled.[115]

During the Beardsell and Bliss eras there were thirteen[116] cottages that had two, three and four bedrooms. Each of them had a large screen porch, flush toilet, gas stove, an electric refrigerator and were completely furnished. Among the amenities was a laundry, a small store, table tennis, Badminton, basketball, a children's playground and a horseshoe pit.[117]

The Bliss' brochure described Pinerest in detail:
> "Located in a grove of huge pine trees and hemlocks on fifty acres…running along a quarter mile of privately owned lakefront… Facing west on one of the finest all around vacationing and sporting lakes in Maine. Here and there along the shore are roomy housekeeping cottages – not too gilded to make them beyond your reach or to hamper informality that should go with your vacation – yet carefully planned and equipped for easy living. Pinerest Cottages are particularly suited for the entire family's

> *vacation — safe and secure without isolation…Our safe, sandy beach offers a fine spot for swimming and all other water activities…Boats and outboard motors are available…The fireplace and cook-out facilities are also located at the beach and it is the center for camp entertainments and parties…Hiking groups and camera fans will enjoy many hours traversing through the forest…"*

Unlike other housekeeping cottages in the area, that closed down at the end of the summer, Pinerest cottages were heated and remained open through the autumn season. Their brochure stressed that point:

> *"In these woods abound all kinds of wild game, offering excellent hunting in season and we do offer accommodations for autumn hunting parties…Our own supervised rifle and archery ranges are safely located well away from the cottages, in these woods…"*

Last but not least, of course, the Blisses brochure spoke to fishing, which had long since become one of Lake Maranacook's greatest draws:

> *"Beginners and experienced anglers alike will find that Lake Maranacook offers some of the finest small mouth bass and white perch fishing in Maine, and excellent trout and pickerel fishing as well…"*

Fred and Catherine ran Pinerest successfully for sixteen years and developed a tried and true following of clientele. But, when the day came to pass the torch this time, Pinerest was not sold intact. Instead, Fred and Catherine sold each cottage individually with its own patch of land. Most went to families who had been coming to Pinerest for generations. After 1971 families named Desjardins, Trearchis, Czekonski, Cronin and Reeves from Attleboro, MA; Innocenti from Somerville, MA; Nyberg from Chagrin, OH; and Rebane from Havertown, PA[118] owned and played on the same shores where those rambunctious Irish kids had romped so many years before. Today that pasture lane leading to the lakeshore is aptly named Pine Rest Cottage Road. What a fine tribute.

Looking southeast from Coleman's Point

Civil War veteran H.A. Johnson of Waterville fishing from Coleman's Camps dock circa 1920. His son was married to Bertha Nelson whose parents ran Tamsonhurst. (see pg. 109) After Tamsonhurst closed the family vacationed at Coleman's.
Photo Courtesy Steve Johnson

SEVEN ROOM COTTAGE AT COLEMAN'S POINT, LAKE MARANACOOK, ME.

Seven Room Cottage at Coleman's Point, Lake Maranacook

**Ruth Brann, Bob's daughter, and "Ma Richie"
at Brann's Camps**

Rev. Heath and Family - Lake Maranacook

— Our Sail Is Set. —

START NO HOME AGAIN

Rev. George Heath and his family vacationed at Coleman's Grove between 1918 and 1928. Each time he sent typewritten post cards to his church flock in West Somerville, MA. The bottom photo, dated 9/3/1918, shows the family with their baggage packed in a wagon and ready to head home. The card said in part "...Our boys 'over there' are meeting the challenge of God and humankind magnificently..."

GLIMPSES INTO OLD READFIELD DEPOT VILLAGE

Main St, Readfield Depot looking eastward across
the tracks. On the right is the grain elevator and grist mill and
behind that a saw mill. On the left is the tenement house,
formerly Craig's Store, and the school.

Gordon & Henry grist mill before the elevator was installed
(See picture above). Before that an oilcloth carpet factory was
operated at this location (1856 map).

Readfield Depot School in 1918. Union Chapel was upstairs until the Smith Memorial Methodist Church (below) was built in 1910. After that school classes were held on both floors. Readfield's original town house sat at this location 1824-1873, where all town meetings were held. It fell into ruin, was torn down, and the school was built here. Readfield Historical Society has owned this building since 1986.

Smith Memorial Methodist Church was built in 1910 on the east corner of Main Street and South Road. It was purchased by Eric Elvin and torn down in the 1960s.

Brann's Livery sat on the knoll slightly west of the tracks. The residence there today was originally that of Arian & Fan (Adell) Jones then Ruth and Marion Townsend. Arian Jones was an old railroad man and upon retirement he had a house built here, next to the tracks, so to watch the trains.

Gordon's Store became the hub of Readfield Depot by the early 20th century. Gordon sold groceries, hardware and kerosene. The Readfield Depot post office was in the store, a saw mill was located in the rear, and the adjacent grain elevator and storage warehouse were owned and operated by Gordon. Pictured here L to R: Ruel Adams, Nelson Gordon, Sr. and Frank Ramsey

Built by Samuel and Sarah (Hutchinson) Morrill about 1824.
It came to be known as "the Depot House" after the railroad
came through in 1849. From the late 19th into the early 20th
centuries rooms were let-out here. (Kingsbury 2015)

George Childs ran this store in the 1920s and 30s. It was located
on the north side of the road, west of the tracks, just beyond the
Depot House. In 1910 Roy Curtis was renting and running this
store and living in the apartment overhead. That same year he
joined in with brothers Mark and Charles Collins as partners in
the Maranacook Hotel on Maranacook Lake. Curtis bought out
the Collins brothers in 1918 and, with his own brother Oliver,
remained owner of the hotel until his death in 1938.

Gordon's store, the Sherburne house and beyond that Chesley's blacksmith shop on south side of main road at Readfield Depot.

"The tenement house" sat west of Depot School. Originally William Luce's store was here. Then it went to his step-son Daniel O. Craig and from there to his son David W. Craig who operated it until 1882. (see pg 58) Mark Collins (see pg 74) owned this store 1891 – 1897. He sold it to Nelson "Nels" Gordon who converted it to a tenement house. There Gordon provided housing and groceries to the poor for which the town reimbursed him. This type of public assistance was preferred by most indigents who wished to remain in their own residences rather than live on the town poor farm. (see pg 59)
Pictured is George K. Adell with one of his grandchildren.

At Hutchinson's Exchange House highway travelers could switch out horses or railroad passengers could rent a wagon or carriage. George Luce was a trucker (wagoneer) who once owned this property. (Gay 2015)

Hutchinson's Tavern was built at this location in 1835 and burned in 1881. Several families who have lived here played a part in developing the summer tourist industry in one way or another. J.J and Mary Hutchinson ran their landmark tavern until it burned in 1881. Then they bought the Daniel O. Craig homestead (see pg. 2) and continued business there. In 1896 Granville Sanborn, carpenter, bought the vacant lot and built the house pictured above. He moved on and bought Depot House (see pg. 54) in 1900, selling this house to Mark S. Collins, the proprietor of Maranacook Hotel.
Readfield Depot businessman Nelson Gordon and his wife Emma also lived here for many years. (Winter 2015)

Mark and Nellie Collins sold the house (previous page) in 1906 and bought the one pictured above (Bourque 2015). The Collins lived here until 1914 when they moved to California. During most of those years Mark Collins owned Maranacook Cottages, Camps and Hotel on Lake Maranacook. (see pg.75)

Collins also became heavily involved in other ventures during those years. In March of 1905 he began buying large woodlots in Readfield, Wayne, Belgrade, Mt. Vernon and elsewhere. He leased a saw mill on Belgrade Stream and he also became heavily invested in buying and selling real estate. Additionally he developed an apple orchard of 1,000+ trees on the old county road (Ledgewood Drive 2015). Before Collins moved to California in 1914 he sold that to Sturtevant's Orchard of Winthrop. The house pictured above was in proximity to much of his woodlands and the apple orchard as well as the train station. On the 1910 US Census he gave his occupation as mill owner, dealing in lumber.

When Maranacook Hotel burned in August, 1905 Collins had already sold it, but he soon bought it back. (see pg. 75)

DAVID WHITE CRAIG, ENTREPRENEUR

David White Craig was the youngest child of Daniel and Mary (White) Craig but responsibility fell on him when his father died. Of David's four brothers two predeceased their father, one had moved to Bangor where he was involved in his own business, and the other brother was on the road as a commercial cattle broker. David continued to live at the family homestead with his mother while he ran his father's store. She died in 1868 and one year later David married a Massachusetts girl named Flora Elisabeth Van Campen. Her father owned the Van Campen Insurance Agency in New Bedford, MA. The Craigs lived at Readfield Depot where David ran his father's store until 1882. That year he sold his own home and his father's store and homestead. He and Flora moved to Malden, MA where David turned his eye towards new endeavors.

In Massachusetts his new occupation as a safe salesman soon turned to developer. No doubt his father-in-law was helpful in pointing him towards business contacts and investors. In 1888 David Craig fell into a land deal that cemented a solid financial base for the rest of his life – back in his own home town.

David W. Craig and his wife Flora lived here 1871-1882
(Plante 2016)

TALLWOOD FARM ~ 1768 - 1888

There is a 200 acre peninsula on Lake Maranacook – partly in Readfield and partly in Winthrop – that was first settled 250 years ago. The name and its purpose have changed several times since.

Robert Waugh settled at this location in 1768, with his wife Elisabeth (White) from New Ipswich., N.H. Waugh's property also included a 12 acre island he called Pine Island.[119] He built his farm here and also established a landing for waterway travelers called "Waugh's landing".

James Craig (g-grandfather of David W. Craig) came the same year and settled on Maranacook's western shore. He operated a ferry in proximity to where Martha Washington Inn was built years later. (see pg 153) Together, Waugh and James Craig became vital links for early travelers as they paddled up the Cobbosseeconte waterway through Winthrop and Readfield.[120]

The Waugh homestead remained in the family for three generations, until 1834, and then changed hands five times over the next 27 years. One of those owners was Joel Howard who split the property between his three sons in the 1840s. The northern 100 acres was conveyed to Thomas Townsend in 1858 and three years later the Inhabitants of Readfield purchased the southern half. The town poor-farm was moved there from Hawes (Walker) Road and the old homestead was dubbed Tallwood Farm. Twenty seven years later it was sold it to David W. Craig for $1,000, the same amount the town had paid for it.[121]

Readfield's decision to sell can be traced to the effects of a severe depression that occurred from 1873 to 1876. As factories and workshops shut down in the cities, tens of thousands of workers - many Civil War veterans - became homeless transients. The terms "tramp" and "bum" became common during those years and was used for many decades thereafter. Relief rolls exploded in major cities, and 100,000 were unemployed in New York City alone.[122] Some of those tramps came as stowaways via the trains through Readfield where the railroad tracks were in proximity to Tallwood Farm. That made for easy foot access from Readfield Depot or across the trestle from Maranacook Station, to get a free meal and a good night's sleep.. The influx created significant demands on the poor-farm manager and added financial strain on taxpayers.

By 1888 the town fathers decided to relocate the Poor Farm again. This time to the western reaches of town near North Wayne – today known as the Readfield Town Forest. Their thinking was that tramps would not walk that far from the Depot just to capture a free meal and one overnight. The town fathers also put a plan into place that tramps and other inmates, as they were then called, would be required to work for their board, but that did not work out as hoped. Most of the permanent inmates were insane, elderly or too sick to work. Most of the tramps chose to eat a hot meal then sleep in the barn rather than take a room. By early the next morning, when the poor-farm manager awoke, the transients were long gone.[123]

David W. Craig was already living in Malden, MA when he caught wind of the sale. Hearing about the successes at Maranacook Grove probably added to Craig's attraction towards this investment. Tallwood Peninsula was fully visible from Maranacook Grove and from the railroad trestle. A hotel would surely appeal to Maranacook Grove excursionists and others who yearned to stay on the lake for extended periods of time and immerse themselves in the beauty of the area. He paid $1,000 for Tallwood Farm and 90 acres in 1888. The acreage was half of Waugh's original lot, but still included a significant amount of shoreline.

Craig built a hotel on Tallwood Point, in addition to several cottages, which became an instant success. For several years the peninsula was called "Craig's Point" in his honor.[124]

From the hillside overlooking Tallwood Farm
Lake Maranacook is in the distance
Notice Tallwood Drive winding along the shore

Pictures on this page from Jean (Wills) Macomber collection

Tallwood Farm was the Readfield Poor Farm 1861 – 1888
This was originally the Robert Waugh homestead

"The horses in this locality are getting quite accustomed to automobiles, as added to others on the road are two at Craig's Point in daily use, one owned by Mr. Hall, the other by Mr. Raymond, both gentlemen from Boston."
Readfield Depot news, Kennebec Journal, July 1906

SIR CHARLES HOTEL, CRAIG'S POINT ~ 1894
MOHICAN INN ~ 1907
TALLWOOD INN ~ 1917

David Craig, now 39 years old, moved quickly with help from local carpenters and workers. Within three years he began selling cottages and camp lots, and also built some as rentals. The first to own a summer residence was Margaret Butler of Boston, whose cottage sat at the end of the point. Others followed until there were seventeen in all. From 1891 to 1893 Craig sold five of them – all to Boston residents - and he had a cottage built for himself as well.

Construction began on the Sir Charles Hotel in October 1893, about 250 yards from the western shore of Craig's Point.[125] Craig hired Henry Whittier to do the job - a local house carpenter and Readfield Depot native.[126] In addition to other staff Craig hired George K. Adell of Readfield Depot as the first hotel manager when it opened to guests.[127]

During this time opportunities arose for Craig to augment his land holdings for little to nothing by today's standards. In June, 1892 he paid $200 for 12 ½ acre Cochran Island,[128] and two years later he and two Boston investors picked up the 8 acre Center Island for $55.[129]

Within five years from the time Craig bought Tallwood Farm he developed the peninsula into an impressive and popular summer resort. Bostonians, for the most part, flocked to the Sir Charles Hotel by train for summer vacations. The hotel could accommodate seventy-five guests. Those who rented private cottages enjoyed taking their meals in the hotel dining room.

The peninsula became known as "Craig's Point".

When the Sir Charles opened in 1894 guests included John McNally of the Boston Herald, along with his family and several other prominent Boston newspaper men. That fall the Forest and Stream magazine wrote of McNally's experience with fly fishing off Craig's Point. In five hours, the article said, McNally and his colleagues hooked thirty-two 2 to 3 lb. black bass and his catch was equally as satisfying in the days that followed. "Hundreds of bass rods are being used this season on the Maine lakes and ponds", reported the magazine, "and a really good deal of sport is obtained from black bass fishing."[130] Apparently, at that time, fishermen were appreciative that George Shepard Page had introduced the species into Lake Maranacook twenty-five years earlier.

David Craig must have liked the taste of entrepreneurism because by 1899 he again looked towards new horizons. In June 1899 he and Flora sold the Sir Charles Hotel to Margaret Butler and they moved to Port Angeles, WA. He operated Craig's Fish Products Co. there and died on the west coast in 1912 at age 62.

Margaret Butler was an interesting woman and by all indications she was not afraid to reach for what she wanted. She was born in Sebago, Maine in 1844 to John and Mary McDonald. Margaret stood at 5 foot 8 inches – tall for a woman in her time. She made her way to Boston as young lady and there she married twice. The first time was at age 21 in the midst of the Civil War to a Union soldier named George Folsom. They parted ways. In 1884 she married a second time, to a Boston merchant named William Butler. He must have been a man of means because one year after he died Margaret bought the Sir Charles Hotel, 90 acres and the cottages. That was a big undertaking for a 55 year old widow.

Butler was owner operator 1899 – 1913 and the business flourished. Guests could enjoy the usual fishing, swimming and boating. In 1901 she commissioned Capt. C.W. Howard of Peak's Island to build a 40 foot steam boat she christened

Anita.[131] In 1905 Butler began making plans to enhance the facilities.[132] She enlarged and remodeled her cottage in 1910 which subsequent owners named "Gran Liden Lodge." The resort grew to include a dance pavilion and theater where live shows were performed. There was shuffle board, horse shoes and badminton. Local farmers offered hay rides and corn roasts. Guests could wander carriage paths throughout the tall pines. When electricity became available wire was strung from tree to tree and lamps added to light the trails at night.[133]

Some say that both Butler and Craig were involved in the Boston theater but documentation to confirm that has not been found. Butler gave her occupation as physician and clairvoyant on the 1910 census.

Stories have been passed down about Margaret Butler's séances. She held them at her cottage with help from Henry Whittier - the same man who built the Sir Charles Hotel. Butler's séances were the talk of the town, and perhaps beyond. One story was kept alive by Helen Cushman of Mt. Vernon. Cushman was famous in these parts during the 1950s as a ghost storyteller. Among her stories were two unsolved murders that took place in Readfield - Mattie Hackett in 1905 (see pg 124) and this one.

> *Around the year 1782 a cattle drover disappeared on one of his regular rounds and a search ensued to no avail. It seems the man had delivered a herd of cattle to Hallowell, sold them and headed home with a bag of gold. He stopped at a spring near Beaver Brook on the way home to water his horse, he was murdered and his body was stuffed in a beaver dam. The bag of gold he had with him was buried in road not far from Beaver Dam Bridge. The murder was revealed by Margaret Butler at a Spiritualist convention at Tallwood Inn. She went into a trance and added the fact that the gold was buried in the road.*[134]

By 1913 Butler was almost 70 years old and ready to retire. Sam Patterson, a flamboyant and good natured man from New York City, had vacationed on Lake Maranacook with his wife Mary since 1907 at their own cottage on the west shore near the Hotel Maranacook.[135] They had come to love the area so when the Sir Charles Hotel went up for sale Patterson grabbed it. Butler and Patterson entered into a 10 year lease agreement whereby he would pay Butler $9,500 over the course of ten years. The lease outlined additional demands. Patterson was to enlarge the hotel dining room to 200 seats; add a bowling alley, billiard and pool hall; a soda fountain; and a hotel laundry – all at his own expense. A bowling alley, café and a night club were added later. Included in the agreement were all kinds of boats and the steam boat *Anita*.

The WWI years presented many challenges for those in the vacation and resort business. Many young family men who had once graced our lakeshores were in the military, and civilians were committed year round to supporting the Country in their own ways. The armed services accepted women on a very limited basis during WWI so they helped by raising money or gathering food and clothing for the soldiers. Women also had to keep their homesteads operating while soldiers were gone. Some even took the place of men in the workplace. Added to that was the devastating influenza epidemic of 1918 which struck hard everywhere and took many lives both in and out of the military. Daily survival was foremost on the minds of most everyone. There was little inclination and no extra money or time for leisurely summer vacations. In 1919 Charles A. Collins of Readfield, a former proprietor of Maranacook Hotel, wrote his son Parkman saying "…We hear that Sam Patterson wants to sell out his hotel business. He and Mrs. P. are south this winter…"[136] But Patterson hung on well beyond WWI and the Great Depression.

During the economic upswing of the "Roaring twenties" big city consumers had extra money to spend on mass-produced electrical appliances such as radios, washing machines and vacuum cleaners. More importantly the average family could now afford an automobile as well as those with significant means. Cars became a preferred mode of travel and by 1929 there was one car on the road for every five Americans. With the flood of automobiles came road trips and motels, in competition with stationary vacations at the Maine resorts.

Sam Patterson and the Sir Charles Hotel adapted to the changing times. They continued to cater to the older guests who came to fish, converse and relax. He also found ways to appeal to a new generation who wanted to recreate like never before. Live theater productions gave way to a movie theater. Films were secured and delivered by entertainment magnate Lou Walters, who brought his young daughter Barbara Walters along for vacations.[137] Some of the features that Patterson began offering the younger set included music and dancing; baseball, basketball and tennis tournaments; swim meets; ping-pong; horse-back riding; and transportation to the Augusta Country Club. All this for $35 a week!

Patterson's brochure subtly appealed to the new age in another way. The young people were, in the opinion of the older generation, running amok with their new style of dancing, short dresses, loose morals and drinking alcohol on the sly. With that in mind one cannot help but notice photos that emphasize moonlight "canoe rides and inspiration" as well as one of Bearce Road captioned "Lover's Lane".

The "Great Depression" of the 1930s had a negative impact everywhere – most of all on vacationers. Many of the wealthy clientele, who had come here for years, lost their fortunes in the crash. Between 1924 and 1939 Patterson borrowed more than $30,000 in order to keep the business going, but tumultuous times finally caught up with him. In the late 1930s Readfield and Winthrop (Tallwood falls within both towns) started placing liens on the property. In 1938 Patterson sold his private cottage on the west shore of Lake Maranacook, which the family had owned for more than twenty years.[138] By the end of the summer of 1940 the bank foreclosed and the Sir Charles ceased operating.

The buildings began to deteriorate and the peninsula became a shadow of its former glory. Enter Benjamin Bloomfield.

Bloomfield was a steamboat manufacturer from Houston, Texas who bought Tallwood Inn from the bank in 1941. He was able to save some of the buildings but the hotel and several cottages had to be torn down. Members of the Bloomfield family and friends vacationed there in the remaining cottages. Patterson was included and returned every summer well into his twilight years. The colossal flurry of summer activity that once existed on Craig's Point was no more.

Many changes have occurred since then. Tallwood Farm burned long ago. Over the years the hotel was known as Sir Charles Hotel 1894-1907, Mohican Inn 1907-1916, and Tallwood Inn 1917-1941.[139] The peninsula has been called "Craig's Point", "Among the Pines" and finally "Tallwood Point". In July, 1952 a twister set down there and destroyed many of the stately pines (see pg 195). In August, 1988 a plan named "Tallwood on Lake Maranacook" was approved by the Winthrop Planning Board and part of the peninsula was subdivided.

Owners subsequent to Bloomfield have included Mary Glowacki of Nanticoke, PA, 1953; Granville Piper, a Readfield native, 1986; and Michael Fiori and Dora Anne Mills since 1996.[140]

Fiori and Mills own Margaret Butler's Gran Liden Lodge and four of the remaining cottages which have been restored and are currently available to rent. Fiori and Mills built another farm, which they call Tallwood, on the same spot as the original. Tallwood Inn has been gone for many years but Tallwood Peninsula Cottages are now open for business once again.[141]

Margaret Butler standing on the porch of her cottage

**Sir Charles Hotel was built on Craig's Point in 1893-1894.
In some of the older deeds this point of land is referred to as
"Among the Pines".**

Local boys and men came to play baseball with summer guests at Tallwood Inn. This photo was taken in 1915. Notice even the steam boat captain is included, sitting near top right.

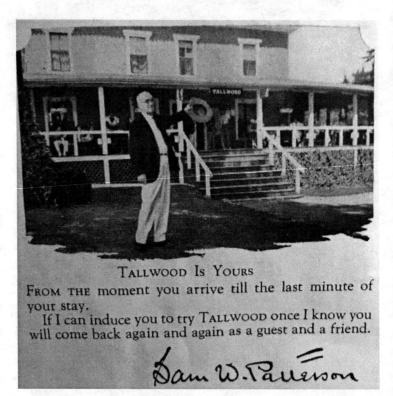

TALLWOOD IS YOURS

FROM THE moment you arrive till the last minute of your stay.

If I can induce you to try TALLWOOD once I know you will come back again and again as a guest and a friend.

Sam W. Patterson

MAINE'S CHANGING SCENE ~ 1890's

By 1890 the Maine Central Railroad (MCRR) had become keenly aware that young people were leaving their farms to work in city factories and that Maine's population was declining. Adding to that was an unstable international financial system and fear of an economical crisis like the one of 1873 (see pg 59). Coinciding with those issues the MCRR's freight business had begun to falter. The security of the Gilded Age of the 1870s and 1880s had passed.[142]

The MCRR shifted their focus in 1891 towards how and where they could attract more tourists into Maine. That same year the Sandy River & Rangeley Lakes Railroad completed a 28 mile narrow gauge road connecting Rangeley to the MCRR terminus at Farmington. The timing was advantageous and the MCRR began to aggressively market the Rangeley Lakes Region.[143]

Cornelia Crosby was a native of Phillips who was a recognized expert at promoting Maine's outdoor sporting industry. Dubbed as "Fly Rod Crosby" she had learned to fly fish in 1886 and quickly became an adept angler, catching as many as 200 trout a day. She took notes and began penning a local newspaper column called Rod's Notebook. Her lively writings included stories about her fishing adventures and mishaps, places to board in the Rangeley Lakes Region and intriguing accounts of what the sporting camps were like. Her column went syndicated in New York, Boston, Philadelphia and Chicago newspapers. Adding to Crosby's public image was a 6 ft. stature and her bent for wearing unusual attire for women of the day. She seemed like the perfect choice to promote tourism on MCRR's behalf.[144]

Crosby organized Maine's exhibit at the First Annual Sportsmen's Show at Madison Square Garden in 1895. The following year she caused a sensation by wearing a Paris-inspired green leather hunting outfit with a skirt that stopped short at mid-calf, matching tall green lace-up boots, a tailored jacket with a red sweater and a peaked red and green hat. Record crowds came to watch her demonstrate fly fishing as she praised the virtues of Maine's forests, lakes and streams. The pièce de résistance was the backdrop she had shipped from Maine - a spruce log cabin that held mounted deer heads and fish tanks with live Maine salmon and trout.[145]

Forest and Stream, the premiere national sportsmen magazine of the times, included an extensive article about the exhibit saying it "...brought a breath of the pine forest... and many a man touched the spruce logs... and sat on the fragrant balsam bed and wished they were in the woods of Maine..." Fly Rod was accompanied by men from Dead River, Rangeley, Moosehead and Aroostook. "All the guides were courteous and obliging and had many a bout of spinning yarns with former or future customers..." [146]

In the same issue of *Forest and Stream* the lakes of Readfield and Winthrop were specifically mentioned, but not in a way that was advantageous to the hotel and sporting camp industry there. The report pertained to the unfortunate introduction of pickerel into the Winthrop and Belgrade Lakes. Because of it the Maine Fisheries Commissioner, Henry O. Stanley, and another interviewee, shared comments about those fisheries saying they were "... especially concerned about the ponds in Winthrop and Readfield..." They also said those fisheries were doomed unless local residents dropped back on their extent of ice fishing. Bass were stocked in those lakes to drive out the voracious pickerel. The hope was that ponds in Belgrade, Winthrop and Readfield would return to their former prestige of excellent trout ponds. They were at one time, said the Commissioner, "fully equal to the Rangeley Lakes".[147]

In 1897 Fly Rod Crosby lobbied the Maine Legislature for a state-run system to register Maine hunting and fishing guides. The Legislature passed a bill requiring that guides buy an annual license and 1,316 were distributed that year. Fly Rod was issued

Maine's first ever Registered Maine Guide license which caused yet another sensation. Besides her adept fishing, writing and guiding, Fly Rod was a crack shot with a rifle and bagged the last caribou in Maine in 1897. At the height of her career, in the 1890s, she served as a guide for "sports" from all over the U.S. including Teddy Roosevelt.[148] Interestingly, it has been said that Roosevelt fished at Lake Maranacook with his famous guide Bill Sewell of Island Falls,[149] but conclusive documentation of that has not been found.

Fly Rod coined the first-ever Maine tourism motto, "Maine, the Playground of the Nation," [150] and the proof was in the punch. Sportsmen were buzzing everywhere about her fabulous successes. Thus the Rangeley and nearby Moosehead Lakes regions were becoming wildly popular and drawing more and more out-of-state "sports" further north into the deeper woods. As more privately owned hotels and sporting camps sprung up in central Maine their owners entered the competition and began offering their own guided fishing excursions and advertised in the big city newspapers and tourist publications.

It has been said that Teddy Roosevelt (far right) once fished Lake Maranacook with his guide Bill Sewell.

Maranacook Hotel and Camper's Point letterhead, 1900

Spend Your Vacation in the . . **Maine Woods**

Cottages Furnished for Housekeeping,
$25.00 to $50.00

Janitor service and ice free ; also free steam launch ride day and evening. First-class hotel accommodations if desired. **The home of theatrical people.** Send for illustrated circulars and references.

Address,

CAPTAIN COLLINS, Maranacook, Maine.

← Maranacook Cottages, Camps and Hotel Company placed this ad in a New York newspaper in 1904. The focus on this ad is the cottages rather than the Hotel even though the ad was placed by the same establishment and proprietor.

← John Chase of Kents Hill started Camp Cebennek on Torsey Pond in 1900. This ad appeared in a national publication.

CAMP CEBENNEK *Famous Allagash Canoe Trip*

ONE month at fully equipped main camp on Torsey Lake. All land and water sports. One month on Allagash Canoe Trip through the big woods of Maine. Best fishing and photography of big game. Information given concerning Cebennek's twenty wonderful summers. Junior Camp for boys nine to twelve.

JOHN A. CHASE, Kents Hill, Me.

"F. W. Brown had the seating capacity of a hayrack well tested the other evening by a merry crowd, who were improving the moonlight night by riding around the lake." ~ Kennebec Journal, August 1906

MARANACOOK COTTAGES, CAMPS AND HOTEL
WHERE TO START?

In reviewing the existing information about the Maranacook Hotel, we find that some of it is contradictory in nature. These questions always come up: EXACTLY WHAT YEAR WAS THE MARANACOOK HOTEL BUILT AND WHO BUILT IT? [151] These questions were foremost on your authors' minds as we researched the materials relevant to this chapter. We were determined to do our utmost to find the answers. After more than two years of searching and organizing primary and secondary sources; touring the Hotel and grounds as they exist today; and conducting a number of personal interviews, we did not find the substantiating documentation we hoped to unearth. So, we poured through every source within our grasp to determine the most likely answers through a process of elimination. The stories of the evolution of Maranacook Cottages, Camps and Hotel shared in this chapter are based on that research. All towns mentioned are located in the State of Maine unless noted otherwise.

1889 ~ 1897

The Maranacook Grove excursion center (see pg.15) had been in full swing for nine years when a young man named Mark S. Collins appeared on the scene. Mark was born in Anson in 1868, the younger son of a miller and descended from a long line of saw mill men. His family moved from Anson to Clinton when he was 9 years old, where his father operated mills in the middle of the town's industrial center. [152] By then, Mark was at an age when parents generally gave boys more freedom to explore. His home was near enough to the town's business district so he experienced the hustle and bustle of community life. They also lived in proximity to Twelve Mile Stream, Beaver Brook and the Sebasticook River.[153] Mark lived a Tom Sawyer type existence during those years, and gained a passion for the water, fishing and hunting which remained a part of his soul throughout his life.[154] The trunk line of the Maine Central Railroad (MCRR) from Portland to Bangor passed near the Collins' house and the train station was also nearby, so Mark could easily watch the comings and goings. He became enamored with the railroad and thought about what adventures and destinations the trains might hold for a young man with ambitious goals. About 1889 Mark accepted a position with the MCRR as station agent and moved to the Winthrop Lakes Region. His older brother Charles had already accepted the same position, but in Yarmouth.[155]

From the first, Collins was a wise investor and businessman. In 1889 he bought a 96 acre farm in Winthrop, with house and barn, for twenty-one cents an acre.[156] A strategic move because this farm held a land route to Maranacook Grove. It appears he was already planning for how he might capitalize on the growing tourist industry.

It did not take long for Collins to recognize another opportunity. The MCRR needed more capacity for transporting passengers to and from the Maranacook and Winthrop train stations via steamers on Lake Maranacook. Without delay, Collins earned a Maine steamboat captain license and bought his own steamer, the *Lorna*. He also built a team road through his farm towards Maranacook Grove and kept a team of horses and hay in his barn.[157] Local farmers commonly took summer excursionists and hotel guests for hayrides so, no doubt, that offering was part of Collins plan as well.

In 1891 Collins bought Craig's Store (see pg.58) adjacent to the Readfield Depot train station.[158] The mercantile had a booming business from train passengers and highway travelers, and was also the closest store to Maranacook Grove. Business was good and, better yet, the store is likely where he met his wife Nellie

Townsend. Her family traded at Readfield Depot which was the closest business center to their farm. Mark and Nellie married in 1893.[159]

Collins' plan for further developing and profiting from the tourist industry on Lake Maranacook moved forward in April, 1895. At that time he and neighbor George Sedgley essentially switched some of their property - Collins' 96 acre farm for 100 acres of Sedgley's land. With that exchange Collins became the owner of significant frontage on Lake Maranacook and, more importantly, Maranacook Grove sat on ten of those acres.[160] Like Sedgley had before him, Collins leased the land where Maranacook Grove sat to the MCRR, but he charged four times more than Sedgley had.[161]

Collins' father-in-law, Thomas Townsend, died in 1896 which may have delayed Mark's progress on his business plans. The Townsend farm encompassed 100 acres on Tallwood Peninsula, adjacent to the up and coming Sir Charles Hotel. (see pg. 62) Collins bought the farm from his mother-in-law in 1897.[162] By that time Mark's brother Charles had married Lottie Townsend (Nellie's sister) and he helped Mark finance this transaction.[163] Most likely Mark had thoughts about converting the farm into his own summer hotel but considered the location first. Land travel to the Townsend farm was via primitive secondary roads. The property included waterfront on Lake Maranacook but the frontage was on a back cove.[164] The buildings were not visible from the main body of the Lake or from the railroad trestle like the Sir Charles Hotel and Maranacook Grove were. A wise investor and business promoter like Mark Collins would have recognized those things as a hindrance to attaining his goals. He sold the Townsend farm months later, to an investor from Wisconsin[165] for $1,400, and he also sold the store for $900.[166] With money in hand Mark refocused on his original plan.

1898 ~ 1907

With an eye towards attracting rusticators[167] and sports to his Maine northwoods Mark Collins built two clusters of camps and cottages near Maranacook Grove. One was "Camper's Point" which held a group of primitive camps and tent platforms on four wooded acres. Those were separated from Maranacook Grove by the railroad tracks. Another group of cottages were set up for housekeeping and located south of Maranacook Grove, along the lakeshore and closer to the mainstream. They were all completed by June 1899 and two months later Collins took out two mortgages totaling $1,400.[168] As collateral he put up those camps and cottages along with these assets: furniture, furnishings, bedding, linen, dishes, three flat bottomed boats, one fantail boat, one pair of oars for each boat, the steamboat *Lorna*, her barge boat carriage and all the lumber stored on Camper's Point.[169] Not only had Maranacook Cottages and Camps been born but they also served as equity for Collins' further expansion – the Maranacook Hotel.

By July 1, 1900 Mark Collins was living at the Maranacook Hotel and his occupation was "hotel proprietor".[170] Living under the same roof were his wife, daughter, and five boarders including a station agent, steamboat engineer[171], two lady "hotel servants",[172] and a day tender (desk clerk). [173] It is plausible, and may be what has created past confusion about the age of the Hotel, that Collins actually added on to the MCRR's existing dining hall. That building was erected in 1880 as a one story 30x100 ft. building.[174] The Maranacook Hotel was a two and a half story building with dimensions of 35x110 feet.[175] Incorporating the Hotel into the existing dining hall rather than creating a new building at the same location, would have been the logical move.

The next six years were volatile. Collins tried selling the establishment twice, but it fell back to him each time. In April 1905 he sold it to the Maranacook Hotel, Cottages and Camp Co., a corporation that had formed in Massachusetts earlier that year. He then returned to his roots – the logging and lumbering industry.[176] Four months later the Hotel burned and four lives were lost but the cottages and Camper's Point were spared. The Hotel was rebuilt by the new owners in time for the 1906 summer season.[177]

In reading a Kennebec Journal article dated August, 1906 one gets the impression that the new management was lacking in efficiency. The Waterville Elks Club hosted a day outing at Maranacook Grove and invited clubs from every large city in Maine and Boston, MA. Four-hundred fifty people showed up and all were enjoying a grand event until it was time for dinner in the Hotel dining hall. According to the news report there was neither enough food nor space to accommodate everyone. The group had been pleased with their day of playing baseball, boating and competitive games, but in spite of all that, the hungry guests were left with a bad impression. Word spread far and wide about the shortcomings they had experienced at the Maranacook Hotel that day. By October, 1906 the business reverted back to Mark Collins again.[178]

1908 ~ 1918

Through the next ten years the Collins brothers were the driving force behind the successes at Maranacook Hotel. In 1908 Mark brought his brother Charles on as full partner. Charles moved, with his wife Lottie, their daughter Edith and son Parkman, from Yarmouth to Winthrop. Two years later the Collins brothers brought Roy Curtis on as a third partner and the three men incorporated as the Maranacook Hotel Co.

Their promotional advertisements were plentiful during those years, appearing in national magazines and city newspapers in New York and Boston. In 1910 they hired James Magness, a 40 year old Irish immigrant and artist cartoonist.[179] Undoubtedly Magness created the postcards that were "published by Collins Brothers, Maranacook, Maine".[180]

Although Mark Collins continued as a full partner at the Hotel his energies soon turned towards new real estate investments. He bought and sold many properties in towns throughout Kennebec County.[181] He also bought several hundred acres of woodlots[182] and became a saw mill owner and lumber dealer.[183]

Collins' life took yet a different turn when he developed asthma and his doctor advised him to relocate to a warmer climate.[184] Mark, Nellie and their two children moved to southern California in 1914 and he immediately began looking for land to develop out there. He gave Nellie power of attorney so she could conduct business on his behalf in either Maine or California and every summer he returned to Readfield, sometimes for extended stays, to manage his real estate investments in Maine.[185]

Meanwhile, in 1915, a boon came for the Maranacook Hotel partners when the MCRR discharged their lease ten years sooner than expected and Maranacook Grove became theirs.[186] That same year the original Maranacook Station burned and the MCRR built a new one much closer to the Hotel.[187] This was an advantage as well, because passengers who did not disembark at Maranacook Station could get a good look at the hotel and grounds while the train stood still.[188] Perhaps some returned to vacation there as a result?

In 1918 the Collins brothers sold their shares of the partnership to Roy Curtis who ran the Hotel, with his own brother Oliver as secretary of the corporation.[189] Roy was a favorite of the local people who found work at the Hotel – especially during the Great Depression. Jobs such as guides, cooks, housekeeping, waitressing, maintenance, re-setting bowling pins and even cutting ice for the ice house come winter were available.[190] Like the Collins brothers the Curtises were masters at promoting the business and drew repeat clientele back year after year. Some Maranacook Hotel "alumni" became so fond of friendships made at the hotel during the summer that they held winter reunions in Boston for years after.[191]

During the Curtis era the compound included the lakeside cottages and camps on Campers Point, the Hotel, tennis courts, a bowling alley, ice house, oil house, wood shed, passenger station and platform, post office, fountain house, lakefront wharf, soda shop, swing house, band stand, baseball field, package room, tank house, store house, dancing pavilion and a lakeside sleeping apartment.[192] The Curtis brothers continued to run the steamer *Maranacook*, during their tenure. One of the steamboat operators was Charles Collins' son, Parkman, who came there every summer throughout his high school and college years to captain the *Maranacook* in his "Uncle Mark's" footsteps.[193] During this time a three story wing with twenty guest rooms was added. [194] It still stands to this day.

Unlike Sam Patterson at the Sir Charles Hotel, the Curtis brothers managed to keep their business going during the difficult years of the Great Depression and beyond.

Arthur Lahaye bought the property from the Curtis family in 1942 and it remained intact until 1958 when Lahaye created a subdivision called "Maranacook Development".[195] All that remained was the hotel, tennis court, the bowling alley and eleven small cabins along the shoreline, including those on Campers' Point.[196] The Maranacook Hotel never saw its days of grandeur again. Subsequent owners went through bankruptcies, including one who ran a boys camp there for a short time.[197] The section of the hotel that was built immediately after the fire fell to ruin and was torn down. The cottages south of the Hotel were split off and are now individually owned. Scott and Holly Davis currently own what remains of the hotel, which they have beautifully restored and enjoy as a private family compound.

There are several cottages on Camper's Point these days but all are second generation except one. Emil and Alverta Petrovick of Peterborough, NH bought one of the originals in 1977 but it was destroyed by a falling tree during Hurricane Bob in 1991. "The old camp was very small and rustic" said Emil "with low ceilings and a kitchen that was only about 5x5 feet." Across the way from the Petrovicks stands a two story white cottage, the last surviving original on Campers' Point. It is owned today by Allan and Betty Cobb. Betty's parents, Stanley and Marian Perkins of Augusta, began vacationing at this camp in 1945 and they bought it in 1958. There were two bedrooms upstairs, a main room downstairs and a porch. The Cobbs have since added an el that includes a kitchen and dining area. On a recent sunny July afternoon I found Betty outside husking corn while Allan was in the kitchen preparing a meal for a houseful of guests. Betty hustled me inside to show some cherished photos of her father sitting on the porch steps nearly sixty years ago. Like so many other seasonal residents I have had the privilege of meeting lately, the Cobbs have returned to their sacred place on the lake every summer for several generations.

WHERE DID ALL THE COLLINS GO?

Charles and Lottie Collins followed Mark and Nellie to California in 1920, where Charles continued to work with his brother in real estate development. Before leaving Readfield Charles bought Center Island on Lake Maranacook which remained in the family for three generations. Charles died in La Crescenta in 1942 and Lottie in 1951. Their son "Park" (Parkman) married Violet French of Winthrop and they lived in Quincy, Massachusetts until their three children were grown. They moved to Wayne, Maine after retirement where Parkman died in 1967 and Violet in 1990.[198]

Mark Collins became a successful land investor and developer in southern California, but continued to travel to Readfield every summer for decades. He drove east in "his big black car" and stopped in Detroit enroute to buy a new automobile on every trip. Mark's love for fishing endured so he always brought his fly rods and a "unique rubberized fold-out canvas canoe" along too, for his Maine fishing adventures. His businesses in California included a popular restaurant called "Hilltop Inn" and his home was adjacent to it. Collins also developed Highway Highlands in La Crescenta, and a settlement of thirty rental houses called Collins Village in Montrose.

Joseph "Joe" Maloney of Auburn related this story. His great-aunt was Mrs. George (Mary Fogg) Carson. She and her husband followed the Collins to southern CA where George engaged in the real estate business (see pgs.117-118). Some years later Joe visited his aunt and uncle out west where he also visited Mark Collins, at his home on the Hilltop. Collins eagerly showed Joe his study which, he explained, was the old Maranacook (train) Station. It seems that Collins had the train station disassembled and shipped to CA where he repurposed the lumber to panel his study. Surely, that was an indication of the affection that Collins continued to hold for his home state of Maine and the Hotel Maranacook.[199]

Mark and Nellie's two children moved west with them. Their daughter, Lorna, died of appendicitis in 1918. Mark's wife Nellie died in California in 1929. Her remains were brought back to Mark's town of origin in Anson, ME for interment. Their son "Stuart" (Mark II) went into business with his father; his son Mark III continues to live in southern California to this day.

When Mark Collins died in La Crescenta in 1960 he owned 179 rental houses and storefronts. Collins Lane and Collins Hill in La Crescenta are named in his honor. He is buried in Forest Lawn Memorial Park in Glendale, California "among the Stars".[200]

Above:
Mark and Nellie Collins at
Maranacook Hotel
Note the keys hanging from
her waistband
*Courtesy of Katherine and
Mark Collins III*

Left:
Charles and Lottie Collins
later in life, after they moved
to California.
Courtesy of Judy Collins

The Hotel Maranacook staff when the Collins brothers became partners. Standing far left Charles A. Collins; far right Mark S. Collins; sitting far left is steamer captain C.W. "Clem" Knight; sitting on the ground is Charles' son Parkman who later operated the steamer Maranacook while on summer vacations from (Kents Hill) high school and college.

Long House, Maranacook, Maine
These camps on Campers Point provided more rustic accommodations than the Hotel and housekeeping cottages.

Dining Room, Maranacook Hotel
Mark Collins added one-and-a-half stories onto the MCRR's
dining room to create the Maranacook Hotel, in 1900. Five
years later it burned and all was loss.

Part of the lobby in the new Hotel that was built after the fire

The dance pavilion at Maranacook Grove later became part of
the Maranacook Cottages, Camps and Hotel complex.
From the collection of Jean (Wills) Macomber

The back side of Maranacook Hotel with the Curtis wing
added. That is the only part of the Hotel that remains today.
In the foreground is the post office. Maranacook Lake
is on the opposite side of the Hotel building.

Stanley Perkins sitting on the steps of "Camp Lookout" on Campers Point. Stanley and his wife Marian started vacationing there in 1945 and they bought this cottage from Arthur Lahaye in 1958. Their daughter Betty and husband own it today.
Courtesy of Betty (Perkins) Cobb

Florence Dorman of Brighton, MA standing on the bow of the steamboat Maranacook. She and her husband Raymond spent their honeymoon at the Maranacook Hotel in June 1946.
Photo courtesy of Jim Dorman

The building on the right depicts the "Regulation Bowling Alley" that was located at the Maranacook Hotel. Many local people were hired to set pins there and in later years locals were allowed to come bowl there.

Post Office, Maranacook, Maine. Some believe the old gazebo from Maranacook Grove was converted to the post office.

The "Fountain House" at the Maranacook Hotel. This building was a popular spot on a hot day because the spring inside created a lower temperature. *Courtesy of Steve Johnson*

On close inspection of this photo "Maranacook Lodge" can be seen written on the side of the steamer Maranacook. Hotel Maranacook was called Maranacook Lodge later in its history. Also pictured here is the boathouse, the bunkhouse and note the vintage 1930s automobiles.

"Along the line of this proposed railroad are some of the most charming lakes in Maine…" State of Maine Board of Railroad Commissioners, 1900

CLANG, CLANG, CLANG WENT THE TROLLEY ~ 1902

In the 1880s electric streetcars, also known as trams, were invented. Like cable cars they ran on steel rails, but they had no slot between the tracks or underground cable. Instead, they were propelled by onboard electric motors and required a trolley pole to draw power from an overhead wire.[201] In 1886, only seven years after electricity came into common use in urban areas, the first electric streetcar line opened in the U.S. In the early part of 1888 the U.S. held 86 miles of electric railroad with about 172 cars operating. Four years later there were 22,589 miles of electric railroads using 67,199 cars. The total number of passengers carried nationwide in 1902 was nearly six **billion**. The enormous development was principally from picking up and dropping off passengers along highways. In 1904 projections were that large cities, such as Chicago and New York, would be connected by tramlines.[202]

Electric trolley lines first appeared in Maine in April 1889 when Bangor opened a line. Three months later the Augusta, Hallowell and Gardiner Street Railway (AH&G) built seven miles of rail along the Kennebec River from the Maine Central Railroad (MCRR) station in Gardiner, through Farmingdale to Hallowell, and into Augusta as far as Water Street. The line had nine passenger cars when operations began and a year later there were eighteen cars in service. About that time the Augusta and Togus Electric Railway added a line, from Augusta to Togus, which AH&G later acquired.

In view of those successes it is not surprising that AH&G looked towards expanding further. In 1900 they applied to the

State of Maine Board of Railroad Commissioners for an extension from Augusta to Sabattus. Since the stretch from Monmouth to Sabattus was sparsely populated that part was rejected, but the Commissioners did approve the section from Augusta to Monmouth.[203] The Commissioners knew that a trolley line from Augusta to the Winthrop Lakes region would be patronized by both local residents and summer tourists and that it would be an invaluable convenience to local businesses. They also knew that the State of Maine was making significant efforts to promote tourism and the proposed trolley line would expose travelers to some of "…the most charming lakes in Maine…" They observed that development had already taken place on Lake Maranacook, where thousands of people visited every season, and the addition of this line would help transform other lakes in the area into tourist attractions as well. The Commissioners concurred that, "for public convenience", they had no hesitation about approving a street railway from Augusta to Winthrop and Monmouth.[204]

The AH&G were pioneers in this effort because no electric railways yet existed in any of Maine's rural areas. For that reason the AH&G found it challenging to make accurate cost projections. Thus the company ran out of money before the line was completed and the tracks stopped in Winthrop.[205] The newly constructed line went live in July, 1902 and became an instant success.

By 1902 the Maine Central Railroad (MCRR) had been delivering freight, mail and passengers to this area for half a century. The Railroad's managers were initially concerned that trolley service would siphon that business away. As it turned out the trolley worked well for moving light weight high-grade freight and express packages, while the steam trains were still needed for lower-grade and heavier freight. The trolley carried express mail, from Augusta to Winthrop, but mail sent or delivered from greater distances was still carried via the MCRR. Passengers coming and going out of Maine continued to travel by train, so transportation by both railroad and trolley were in demand. Fortunately the two companies did not enter into a rate competition because their administrators knew it could be ruinous to both. In the end the companies worked hand in hand for the benefit of all their customers.[206]

Capt. Mark S. Collins was the owner of Maranacook (Lake) Hotel, Cottages & Camps when the trolley came to town. He also owned the steamboats *Lorna* and *Maranacook* as well as a barge boat carriage and several other types of boats. Within days of the trolley line's opening Collins signed a 15 year lease for a 20ft wide "right of passageway for himself and passengers and travelers on his steamers and other boats." The right of way was located at the Winthrop end of Lake Maranacook near the trolley terminus[207] and Collins' wharf became a popular transfer point for tourists at the height of the summer season. Some were bound for Collins' establishment and others were bound for hotels and camps at the northern end of Lake Maranacook and connections to points beyond.

The Augusta to Winthrop trolley route began near the Augusta Hotel, where Memorial Circle is today. Passenger cars pulled express cars carrying mail, freight and baggage. The tracks ran up Western Avenue and through Manchester towards Winthrop. There were many stops along the way enroute to Lake Maranacook and several fell within the boundaries of Winthrop (see pg 98). Bearce Crossing, also known as "Tallwood Landing", was the first stop on Lake Maranacook. The Crossing was located on the east shore of "Townsend Cove"[208] directly opposite Tallwood Peninsula. Many of the guests who stayed at Townsend Farm (see pg 99) and the Sir Charles Hotel (see pg 62) were picked up there by wagon or boat. The Sir Charles Hotel had launched its own 40 foot steamboat *Anita* in 1901. No doubt she caused quite a sensation when the summer guests arrived.[209] From Tallwood / Bearce Crossing the trams followed the eastern shore of Lake Maranacook to a siding at Big Pine Point, then on to Collins Landing, and finally to the terminus at the Maine Central Railroad train station in Winthrop village. From that connection passengers could easily transfer to trains or horse drawn carriages and continue on to their destinations.

Historically, the State of Maine and the MCRR had geared tourism publicity towards wealthy Americans in Boston and New York. The electric tramways and their new trolley parks opened tourism to local people and to those with less financial means, thus resulting in new and exciting opportunities! In addition to the scheduled stops, residents who lived further out of town could simply stand by an accessible spot on the line and flag down one of "the electrics". Men who lived close enough to the line could take higher paying factory jobs in the city, a commute that was impossible before. Students used electric cars for transportation to school and families rode to church together. For twenty-five cents residents could ride into the city to shop, visit with friends and family for the day, or take in a show. The thrill of boarding a trolley bound for Island Park on Cobbosseeconte Lake was extra special.

Island Park, which opened July 4, 1903, was one of many "trolley parks" built by the electric streetcar companies in Maine. The parks ranged from simple outdoor dance platforms to full-fledged hotels, complete with eateries and theater. They offered musical entertainment, boating, swimming and other recreational activities. Trolley fare typically included admission to the park and often to its theater or a movie as well. For less than $1.00 a young man could escort his best girl on the trolley to Island Park, enjoy a picnic on the beach followed by a boat ride; take her dancing and to a show in the evening; enjoy a moonlit walk along the shore, and return home afterwards.[210] For an additional $2.00 married couples could enjoy a weekend excursion that included all of the above plus a night's stay at Island Park's "Hotel in the Pines"

Speaking of walks by moonlight, the popular song "On Moonlight Bay" was written near Island Park. The story goes that as songwriter Edward Madden paddled his canoe nearby, on a warm moonlit evening, he heard singing and laughter wafting over the lake from other boats and Island Park. In that moment he became inspired to write "On Moonlight Bay". He knew that was just the type of song that any lakeside resort would play as the last dance of the evening and that local patrons would forever associate it with the Island Park dance pavilion.[211] Not only did the song become popular at Island Park but nationwide. It was recorded by Bill Murray and The American Quartet in 1912 and became a favorite of barbershop quartets for all time. A movie musical was released by the same name in 1951, starring Doris Day and Gordon McRae, and two years later they starred in the sequel "By the Light of the Silvery Moon". Since its release the song has appeared in dozens of feature and animated films and television shows.[212]

Island Park had it all, and the trolley provided convenient, affordable transportation and access to entertainment like rural folks around here had never known. Great crowds were drawn there – sometimes hundreds or even thousands in a day when special musical or theatrical events were held. Island Park remained one of the local's favorite entertainment spots well into the mid 20th century.

On another note, it was not easy for "country kids" to attend high school in the early 1900s. It was common for rural Maine towns to not have public high schools and this was true for Readfield. Families who wanted their children to get a secondary education had to make choices, which could include their moving to another town that had a high school. Automobiles were rare for the average family until the 1920s so Readfield students could walk to Maine Wesleyan Seminary at Kents Hill or the high school in Winthrop; they could take their chances on hitching a ride with someone; take the train from Readfield

Depot to Winthrop or the stage to Kents Hill; or find room and board close to a high school and live away from home during school terms. Most families could not afford the last choice and money was scarce for daily train or stage fares. Some teenagers simply chose not to go to high school at all. Bill Brown was a Readfield farm boy who was born in 1899 and lived all his life on South Road. In his oral history taken some years ago, he talked about the trolley and its impact on his ability to get a high school education. Unlike many boys his age Bill wanted to go past the eighth grade. He was fortunate to live not far from Tallwood / Bearce Crossing so he walked that far and rode a streetcar from there to Winthrop High School every day for four years. Seventy years later Bill and the Townsend sisters, who grew up on nearby Townsend Farm, were still delighted at the chance to talk about that trolley. So you see, for some local people the opportunities provided by the electric rail changed the course of their lives in profound ways![213]

The Augusta Winthrop line became an instant success and, as hard as it is to believe now, the entire AH&G line sold two million fares in 1906 alone.[214] In 1907 the AH&G was absorbed by the Lewiston Augusta & Waterville Railway (LA&W) [215] which eventually joined with the line from Lewiston to Brunswick and Bath. Eventually the line ran from Waterville all the way to Portland, Portsmouth and on to Boston making it one of the longest in New England.[216]

By 1919 the local trolley company was financially weakened from the impact of WWI. In addition, Maine experienced the worst winter that trolley line employees ever had to endure in 1920. In February of that year severe snowstorms and freezing temperatures slowed a trip from central Maine to Boston from the normal three hours to thirteen, making for many distraught customers. Soon after that automobiles became the preferred mode of travel. As a result the number of trolley passengers dropped by more than half between 1920 and 1927. Running at a deficit, as were some area resorts at that time, the trolley company discontinued the Augusta to Winthrop line in August of 1928.[217]

When the trolley ceased operation the town of Winthrop immediately took over the old trolley line and in May, 1929 issued a plan for a "road around the lake"[218] that would be built right over the tracks in some places. Early on that road was called "Whoopee Lane" but some residents did not care for the connotation so it was officially changed to "Memorial Road".[219]

Today some trolley rails that run through the woods are still visible to the knowing eye but the memories of riding "the electrics" have been lost with time. From Tallwood / Bearce Crossing eastward part of the old route is now open to hiking and snowmobile traffic.[220] The section from Gardiner to Augusta was converted to a walking path in 1996, called the "Kennebec River Rail Trail".[221]

STATE ST. AND AUGUSTA HOUSE, AUGUSTA, ME.

The Winthrop trolley line began on State Street near the Augusta House and proceeded up Western Avenue towards Island Park and Winthrop.

A trolley approaching Winthrop, near Lake Maranacook

Bearce's Crossing (Tallwood Landing) was located at the north end of Memorial Drive and was often used by summer people bound for Readfield Depot and the resorts and cottages on the northern end Lake Maranacook.

The AH&G trolley line to Winthrop began in Augusta, where Memorial Circle is today, and proceeded up Western Ave. Stops included Granite Hill and Hammond's Grove in Manchester. This 1909 map shows the flow through Winthrop, the first stop being Island Park on Cobbosseeconte Lake. In East Winthrop the direction went southward towards Winthrop Center, east of and parallel to South Road; then west towards Bailey's Oilcloth Factory. From there it proceeded northwest through the woods, parallel and east of route 135. Protected by a "block guard signal" it crossed route 202 and continued to run parallel to route 135 (Stanley Road) until about halfway to the Readfield town line. At that point the rail turned due west through the woods towards "Bearce's Crossing", also called "Tallwood Landing", on Lake Maranacook. It then followed the east shore to stops at Big Pine Point and Jenkins Cove, and then on to the Maranacook siding at the south end of the Lake. The terminus was at the MCRR train station in Winthrop village. In 1906 a short extension was added from MCRR up Main Street through the village. Some stops were simple wooden sidings and others had waiting rooms i.e. Island Park, East Winthrop, Winthrop Center, the MCRR train station and the electric streetcar power station at East Winthrop. (Day & Beattie)

TOWNSEND FARM ~ 1913

In 1858 Thomas Townsend moved his family, from Limerick in southern Maine to Readfield, and bought a 100 acre farm on the northern part of Tallwood Peninsula. About the same time his brother Eben left Limerick and settled in Dyer Brook, Aroostook County. Thomas died in 1896 and Eben in 1898. Soon afterwards Eben's son Linwood moved from Dyer Brook to Readfield, with his mother and brother in tow. Linwood settled on an early Whittier[222] homestead in Readfield with 90 acres of land.[223] The house was Cape Cod style and a barn sat across the road.[224] Adjacent to it was his uncle Thomas' old homestead which Linwood eventually purchased too.[225]

At the same time Linwood was settling into his new home Myrtle Adell was working for Mark Collins as a housekeeper at the Maranacook Hotel.[226] Both Linwood and Myrtle had strong familial connections to the summer hotel industry. Linwood's first cousin, Nellie, was Mrs. Mark Collins.[227] His aunt Mary (Townsend) Brainard ran an inn at East Readfield (see pg 184). Myrtle's father, George Adell, was the first manager of the Sir Charles Hotel (see pg 62). Linwood and Myrtle were destined to meet. They were wed on Christmas Eve of 1900.[228]

The Sir Charles Hotel was in full swing by the time Linwood and Myrtle were married. When the Hotel received requests beyond their capacity the Townsends were asked to board the "overload" and they accepted the opportunity. Linwood and Myrtle made a good team. His easy going persona and love for gardening, farming, visiting and fishing complemented Myrtle's bent towards housekeeping and cooking. Both had a strong work ethic, and Myrtle was good at managing the business end, which further helped their success.[229] They soon gained a reputation that brought guests back year after year.

The setting was pristine and provided the taste of farm and country life that many city dwellers yearned for. On first approach visitors saw Jersey cows in the pasture with Lake

Maranacook as the backdrop. The grounds were graced with vegetable gardens, a barn, and a large, but cozy, farmhouse complete with piazza. Beaver Brook entered "Townsend Cove" on the east side of the property where a natural meadow graced the edge of the Brook. In the spring of the year, during high water season, that section of the Peninsula became a four acre island known to this day as "Townsend Island." During the warmer months the high water receded giving way to marshland that abounded with birds and wildlife. A pathway across the south pasture led to a sandy beach overlooking "Townsend Cove." All of these features offered summer guests many opportunities for nature activities such as picking wildflowers and berries, swimming, fishing, birding, boating and exploring.[230]

Sometime around 1908 the Townsend's barn burned and they built a new one adjacent to the house. Linwood and Myrtle's family was growing as were opportunities for summer guests, so they made the decision to add a larger dwelling too. Between 1908 and 1912 they borrowed $6,600[231] and built a new farmhouse large enough to serve as a summer hotel but, unlike the other hotels, they wanted to create a farm atmosphere rather than a resort. Upon completion of the new construction, in 1913, they hung a sign over their barn door that officially named it "Townsend Farm". The old house was torn down a short time later.[232]

The new farmhouse consisted of twenty rooms on three stories. There were eleven guest rooms plus the family's living quarters on the second floor. A large dining room, which ran from the front to the back of the house, held enough tables so each "party" could eat at their own. In the middle of the dining room an archway with pocket doors made it possible to divide the room in two when necessary.[233] A parlor of equal size was across the center hallway. On the rear of the farmhouse was a rustic two story annex. The interior walls were made of nice wood but unfinished which radiated a "camp-like" atmosphere. Clientele were assigned beds in the annex when the regular guest rooms were full. The first and second floors had half baths and there were full baths with tub and shower on the second and third floors. The third floor also had a large gathering area between the guest rooms. Cooking and drinking water came from a dug well on the property. A gas-powered pump fed water from Lake Maranacook, through an above ground pipe into a "huge cistern" in the cellar. That water was used for laundry and the indoor bathrooms.[234]

The kitchen was set-up with a wood cook stove and a cast iron sink with a hand pump and in later years a water spigot. There was very little counter space in the kitchen so food was prepared in the pantry. An old-fashioned ice box sat in the summer kitchen where it was cooler and the blocks of ice would last longer. Laundry was done in the summer kitchen as well. A small opening between the kitchen and dining room was used to pass plates through to a waitress. Myrtle was the main cook and is especially remembered for her cookies, pies, donuts and brown bread. Every Sunday guests were treated to homemade vanilla ice cream flavored with berries in season. Myrtle prepared three meals a day, from a menu that remained consistent from week to week, using good old-fashioned Maine food and recipes. Each morning she arose at 3:00 a.m. to bake pastries enough to last the day. Breakfast oftentimes consisted of oatmeal and stewed prunes. A big meal of meat, potato and vegetables was served at noon but supper was a lighter fare. The Townsends raised all their own vegetables, poultry, berries and apples; and had farm animals that produced milk, cream and eggs. After dinner every day Myrtle took an afternoon nap and left clean-up to her helpers.[235]

Linwood and Myrtle had five children: Eben "Lee", born 1907; Alice (Couture), born 1910; Ruth, born 1913; Marion, born 1914; and Mary (Hock), born 1916. Ruth and Marion loved to tell stories about their youthful days and growing up on "the Farm". When Marion was asked how many guests Townsend Farm could accommodate she replied "at one time (we) had fifty-four guests tucked in everywhere, but that was exceptional."[236] When the Townsend children became old enough they were given chores and helped out on the farm. Marion helped her mother with cooking pastries and other indoor chores. From an early age Ruth took an interest in carpentry, mechanics and other duties considered men's work at the time. She loved athletics and aspired to be a physical education teacher but when it came down to it she chose to stay home and help her father on the farm instead.[237] She and her brother Lee worked with their father and sometimes a young man was hired temporarily to help harvest crops.

Don Whittier, who lived next door, did some carpentry work for the Townsends. "The Whittiers were good neighbors" said Townsend's grandaughter Holly Hock Dumaine.[238] They could always count on the Whittiers to help in most any situation.

Linwood was a sociable sort who interacted and shared stories with the guests during the evening hours, which they enjoyed very much. Myrtle or "Mrs. Townsend" as the clientele always called her often played cards with the guests after supper. Alice was somewhat of a social butterfly and helped keep them entertained.[239] Local women were hired to work inside as waitresses and housekeepers. Myrtle was in charge of the house staff and she could "run that place like a drill sergeant", a former employee once said.

Myrtle was not in favor of having alcoholic beverages around, and one time Linwood brought home a barrel of hard cider. Myrtle informed him she was moving to Readfield Depot and would stay there until the cider was gone, which it was by the following day. Myrtle immediately moved back home and business returned to normal. In later years, though, the basement did hold a designated space that male guests called "the Bar Fly Club". The men gathered there to tip a few, swap stories, and sing in barber shop harmony. Ever the sentry, Myrtle informed the men that when impressionable young children were within hearing distance the room should be called "the milk room".[240]

Linwood drove his carriage to meet guests whether they arrived by trolley at Tallwood Landing[241] or by train at Readfield Depot. When guests came with an abundance of trunks and luggage a wagon went to pick up and deliver those to the farm separately. Neighbor Fred Brown, followed by his son Bill, were sometimes hired for that task. In later years Ruth often met the train with the Townsend's car and transported them and their baggage to the farm.[242]

An added treat for guests was Linwood's hayride excursions around the lake or to Island Park in East Winthrop.[243] Spirited games of croquet, baseball, Bridge or board games were also enjoyed. As guests returned year after year they became more like family. One was Billy Barker, a vaudevillian from Boston, and his wife Reggie. He often brought a troop of fellow entertainers along with him, which made for an extra lively time for everyone. Most of the guests were married, retired couples although two young families with children did visit routinely. There were a few single men who sojourned to Townsend Farm every summer also. Louie Daniels was a regular. He is remembered for his big cigars and kindness to the Townsend grandchildren. A stay of two weeks was common for many guests.[244]

The day came when Townsend Farm also reached capacity. They referred their overload to nearby "Beaver Brook Farm", run by Mrs. E. M. Flanders.[245] When Flanders went out of business in 1916 Linwood Townsend bought Beaver Brook Farm and kept it going for a year until he could find another buyer.[246] The next owner of Beaver Brook Farm, Fred Leavitt, continued to take guests until the mid 1940s, as did Mrs. Iva Rourke after him, into the 1950s.[247]

The Townsend Farm brochure described the business this way:

"...For 'restricted clientele' [248] *Townsend's has two principal attractions. It combines the modern summer resort...with its facilities for boating, bathing (swimming) and fishing... with the good old fashioned farm life and all which that implies. This means fresh milk, eggs, berries and poultry. All vegetables are picked and served on the table the same day; real New England home-cooked food...The home-like atmosphere and the friendly class of guests attract many of the same people year after year. Townsend Farm has been in the same family for forty years..."* [249]

By 1947 Linwood and Myrtle were ready to retire so their son Lee and his wife Helen took over the business. The elders went to live with their daughter Alice, whose home was within sight of the farm. Lee and Helen lived in Winthrop during the school year but every June they moved back to Townsend Farm and prepared for the arrival of their summer guests. "One winter we did stay at the farm" shared their son Lin, "but it was so cold! My father worked evenings at Bonafide Mill at the south end of the Lake in Winthrop. One cold night after work his car wouldn't start so he walked all the way up the lake from Winthrop to the farm in a snow storm" said Lee shaking his head. "My father and mother worked so hard!"

Lin was born in 1941 and his brother Richard in 1943. "We loved living there" said Lin. They swam, fished, explored and spent quality time with their grandparents as well as aunts Alice, Ruth and Marion. "We didn't know Mary as well because she didn't live close" says Lin. Mary and her daughter Holly lived in Readfield Depot two miles away.

By the time Lee and Helen took over on the heels of WWII this kind of tourist industry was waning. They carried on the established traditions but by then the number of guests averaged only twelve[250] rather than two or three dozen as in the earlier days. Linwood and Myrtle were living nearby during that era, so they continued to socialize and play cards with "Townsend Farm alumni". Linwood died in 1950, but Myrtle continued to stay in touch with some of the former clientele for years afterwards. She lived to be ninety-seven.[251]

While Lee worked the evening shift in Winthrop Helen managed Townsend Farm and their two young sons. Added to Helen's load her mother died in December 1951 so she and Lee brought her elderly father, Colfax Hinds, to live with them at Townsend Farm the following summer. He died there suddenly, from a heart attack, early that August.[252] Helen carried on with grace. She was a wonderful cook but there was much more to do, so they hired one or two young women to help.[253] While Helen cooked, and attended to managerial and other duties, her helpers did the chamber work and waitressing.[254]

Most guests were arriving by automobile by the 1940s and their cars were lined up all along the expansive driveway. Summer activities of old endured but a new one was added when a television was set-up in the guests' parlor. Lin and Richard were allowed to watch on occasion, but they had to sit quietly and could only watch what the guests wanted to watch. Romps through the countryside were more fun anyways for the two young brothers. The boys enjoyed life on the farm throughout their childhood, until they went off to college in the late 1950s.[255]

Lee died unexpectedly at age 54 and Helen was unable to manage everything single handedly. She sold Townsend Farm a few months after Lee's death. She died five years later. The property changed hands three times between then and 1973 when it was purchased by Dr. Alex McPhedran and his wife Winnie.[256]

On the day the McPhedrans were moving in a car full of women pulled into the driveway. One of the passengers was the elderly Myrtle Townsend and Marion was behind the wheel. These seven words came from Marion's mouth as she popped out of the car - "You are not taking down the sign?" She said this in the form of a question but with an implied expectation. To this

Winnie replied "Well we really have not had a chance to think about that yet." Marion said "There are a lot of people around here that sign means a great deal to." The McPhedrans perceptively understood. The large sign that reads "Townsend Farm 1913" remains over the barn door to this day.[257]

Townsend's Farm, Readfield Depot, Maine

Townsend farmhouse and barn
A sign saying "Townsend Farm 1913" was hung
over the barn door the year the farmhouse and barn were
built. It can be seen in this photo and is still there to this day.

R to L: Myrtle Townsend (pregnant with Ruth), Julia Wadleigh Butler, Myrtle's sister Fan Adell (with the dinner bell), hired man Arthur Lovejoy, Myrtle's mother Mary Adell and sister Maude Adell. Sitting are Alice and Lee Townsend.

Lake Maranacook, Beaver Dam Bridge, Townsend Cove
This was a favorite fishing spot for
summer guests and the Townsend family

Lee, Marion, Linwood, Myrtle and Alice Townsend
at the Townsend Farm.
Photo courtesy of Linwood Townsend

"Beaver Brook Farm" on South Road started taking
Townsend's overflow and evolved into a tourist home also.
William and Iva Rourke moved here in 1945 and continued to
take in summer guests calling it "Rourke's Tourist Home".

Lee, Helen and their younger son Linwood "Lin"
Photo courtesy of Linwood Townsend

**Ruth and Alice Townsend waiting to pick up
guests at Readfield Depot train station.**
Photo courtesy of Linwood Townsend

TAMSONHURST ~ 1903
ARROWHEAD ~ 1914
MILLETT MANOR ~ 1948

Edwin J. "Ed" and Tamson Nelson of Oakland, ME were in their forties when, in 1888, they purchased the Joel & Philura (Bean) homestead[258] on the northern shore of Lake Maranacook. In 1903 they took out a $500 mortgage; presumably to enlarge their home into a summer hotel they called "Tamsonhurst."[259] They also built a rental cabin at the edge of the lake. Whether the Nelsons took in summer guests prior to 1903 is not known, but it seems likely they did and needed more room for a growing business.

In 1907 the Boston and Maine Railroad published a directory of New England vacation resorts. Tamsonhurst was one of the hotels listed, naming Mrs. E. J. Nelson as proprietor. The establishment accommodated 30 guests for $2.00/night or $9.00/week. Most guests came by train to Readfield Depot less than a mile away, where Ed Nelson waited to pick them up in his carriage.

Ed's trade was scythe plate welder[260] but he also helped operate Tamsonhurst.[261] Ed and Tamson complemented each other well and the business flourished. In addition to relaxation and Tamson's good cooking the guests enjoyed fishing. No one liked angling more than Ed himself so he made a great guide. For their guests' convenience the Nelsons set up a dock on their property, called "Nelson's Landing" which was large enough for steamboats to berth. From there guests could board for excursions on the lake, connect with the trolley or the Winthrop train station.

The couple's reign at Tamsonhurst ended too soon. In December, 1910 Ed was working in the field adjacent to Tamsonhurst when he lifted a large rock and developed a strangulated hernia. He died of complications at age 64.

Tamson carried on the business until the summer of 1914 when she sold it to Lillian E. F. Ann of Brooklyn, NY. Tamson moved to Mill Valley, CA and lived there for two years, until she returned to Maine and died in Waterville of liver cancer in September 1916.[262] She was remembered as "a tireless worker of the Congregational Church… for her keen intellect, practical sense and humorous acceptance of the realities of life…" [263]

Details included in the deed at the time of the Tamsonhurst sale give insight into the extent of the Nelson's operation.

> *"…included in this sale… all boats, a canoe, all personal property in the barn and other outbuildings, all furniture, fixtures and furnishings in the house that have been used by said grantor while operating said house as a summer boarding house excepting and reserving ten oil paintings, all family pictures, all books, wearing apparel, Lady's desk, work basket, twenty pieces of fancy china dishes and a case of mounted birds and animals including everything within said case, meaning and intending to convey to said grantee the summer boarding house called "Tamsonhurst"…which was (last) used by said grantor in conducting said house during the season of 1914…"*

Lillian Ann renamed the business "Arrow Head" which she operated until 1920. At that time she forfeited on her mortgage agreement and Tamson's heirs foreclosed. The property was sold next to Edwin C. and Mary Frost of New Jersey, when again there was a detailed list of furnishings and personal belongings included in the sale. The stuffed birds were still there as was a soda fountain, which all went to Tamson Nelson's heirs.

Edwin C. Frost was, as some might say, a "wheeler – dealer". He bought rental properties in Readfield as well as the original Joshua Bean homestead directly across the road. In fact, the land where Tamsonhurst sat had once been a part of that property. Frost named the Bean homestead "Kennecook Farm" [264] and hired a manager to oversee his large lumbering, and farming operation.[265] At that time he separated his holdings by signing

Tamsonhurst over to his wife Mary. By then assets also included "…speed boats, canoes, motor boats and other boats…and one Packard, eight cylinder, seven passenger sedan…" The Frosts lived at Tamsonhurst but they never ran it as a hotel.[266]

Subsequent owners were James & Margaret Woolcott who built an ice cream stand called "Woolcott's" which was later enlarged and became the Weathervane restaurant. They also built a rental cottage adjacent to the Weathervane. Woolcotts retained the ground where the Weathervane and the Readfield Beach are now located when they sold to Lewis and Ann Millett in 1948. The Millets renamed Tamsonhurst "Millett Manor" and operated a summer guest house there for many years. The current owners, Russell and Tracey Cahn, call it "Maranacook Inn".[267]

Tamsonhurst photos courtesy of the Nelson – Johnson family

Tamson and Ed Nelson. He is demonstrating one of his scythe blades. Both photos were taken at Tamsonhurst.

Above and below: Tamsonhurst before it was remodeled, in 1903. Note the stone wall bordering the pasture on the north side of Main St. and the beautiful old barn.
Left: Ed Nelson with a day's catch

Nelson's rental cabin and to the right can be seen
part of the main house, Tamsonhurst.

Lake Maranacook from Tamsonhurst, Readfield, Maine

Nelson's Landing. The barn of Tamsonhurst is the closest
building. On the shore in the distance is part of the Wyman
Corn Shop, which sat on land previously owned by the Nelsons.

Tamson Nelson captioned this photo "The Elms at
Tamsonhurst". Looking east on Main St., see a corner of
the lake on the right, which is about where the town beach is now.
When "Dutch Elm Disease" struck Readfield in the 1950s there
were 800 Elms counted along Main St, between the tracks at
Readfield Depot and Kents Hill. *(per 1957 Readfield Town Report)*

From Tingley Brook looking west towards Lake Maranacook and Tamsonhurst. Some of the Elms in the previous picture can be seen in the distance in this photo.

When Jim Woolcott owned Tamsonhurst he built an ice cream stand named "Woolcotts". It was later expanded into the Weathervane restaurant and became a favorite eatery for summer residents. Small parts of the Weathervane rental cottage and the barn at Tamsonhurst can be seen beyond (1950s).

"Two women who were out driving Friday evening, encountered an automobile near W. F. Whittier's, at which the horse became frightened and upset the wagon...the ladies were fortunate enough to escape with a few slight bruises and severe fright." ~ Readfield news, Kennebec Journal, August 1906

THE AVALON ~ 1903

George & Mary Carson
Courtesy Joanne Fogg Fournier

On May 5, 1903 the Kennebec Journal reported "Mr. Carson's summer hotel is nearly completed and looks very inviting for summer guests." A report three weeks later said "Mr. C. C. Hunt from Augusta was here last week to install the engine and water pipes for George Carson to draw water from the lake to the beautiful summer resort The Avalon." An interesting side note is that same news column mentioned there was a severe drought that summer. Finally, on June 11th a report read that "Mr. Carson is completing the work on his summer hotel, having one of the most attractive houses in this vicinity." No doubt the Avalon was open for business during peak season, the summer of 1903.

There was, by that time, competition from two other hotels in Readfield. Tamsonhurst was only steps away, and the Elmwood was located near the intersection at Readfield Corner. Traveling salesmen, people visiting townsfolk, workers from Wyman's Corn Shop and the mills at Factory Square tended to be the clientele during the week at the Avalon and Elmwood. Tamsonhurst guests were most often long term summer vacationers.[268]

In 1907 the Boston and Maine Railroad published a directory of New England vacation resorts. The Avalon was listed naming George W. Carson as the proprietor, accommodations for thirty-five guests and rates of $2.00/night or $10.00-$12.00/week. Sadly, that was the last season of operation for The Avalon. It burned and was never rebuilt. Many years later the ground where it once sat was subdivided into house lots and a road named Hunt's Lane was built where the Avalon once stood.

THE CARSONS

George W. Carson was a boot and shoe dealer from Mt. Vernon when he married Mary Fogg in 1901. She was born on the Fogg homestead in Readfield, a grandaughter of the Fogg family pioneer, Dudley Fogg. As a single woman Mary taught primary school in Readfield for six years and served on the school supervisory committee. She married George one month shy of her 30th birthday and the couple soon after bought what was then known as the Fillebrown house (Henderson 2016).

The Carsons lived across the street from Charles Collins (Drake 2016) and George eventually became involved in the real estate field with him. This was the same Charles Collins, who formerly co-owned the Maranacook Hotel with his brother Mark.

In 1907 the Carsons sold their house and the land where the Avalon had once been, to the parents of William Morgan who founded Camp Maranacook. The Carsons lived on Church Road until they moved to California.[269] (Foster 2016)

George and Mary Carson eventually joined the Collins brothers in Los Angeles County, California, sometime between 1915 and 1920; George continued working as a real estate broker. The Carsons never had children and they both died in California.[270]

Avalon Hotel, Readfield, Me.

The Avalon and in the distance, on the left, can be seen the rooftops of Wyman's Corn Shop.

Avalon Boat Landing, Lake Maranacook, Me.

Avalon Boat Landing, Lake Maranacook, Maine.
The Hotel burned in 1907, before the Carsons could build a significant landing. They never rebuilt the Hotel.

Carsons sold a 50x50ft piece, adjacent to the Corn Shop land, to Edson D. Scofield in 1907. Scofield built this boathouse on that land. In 1915 Bill Morgan bought the land and boathouse from Scofield, to use as a landing to and from his boys camp on Birch Island. NOTE: E.D. Scofield was an attorney who lived on Old Kents Hill Rd. (Knight 2016)

While summer visitors were recreating nearby, the employees at Wyman's Corn Shop were working their days away.
Photo courtesy of Nelson-Johnson family

THE PINES ~ 1903

We have uncovered many firsthand accounts and alluring echoes from the past at all the locations described within these pages, but this story is quite extraordinary. It came to me (Dale) as I researched for a Readfield History Walk in the fall of 2014.

I learned that one of the oldest private cottages on Lake Maranacook was "The Pines", built on the east shore in 1903. I asked my mother, Evelyn Potter the Readfield Historian, if she knew anything about it. To my amazement she did and we were soon off on one of our many local adventures.

It all started in 1998, she told me, when a Mr. Ferris, who was a Maine summer resident on Flying Pond in Vienna, reached out to her. He was trying to find the old cottage on Lake Maranacook that his grandparents, Ignacio "Nash" and Caroline "Carrie" Martinetti, had owned from 1913 until the 1930s.[271] They were theater people from New York City as many of the summer visitors were in those days. After some deed searching and inquiries Evelyn identified a cottage on Big Pines Lane as the one that Ferris was looking for. I asked her to show me the cottage.

As we made our way to Big Pines Lane on a beautiful September afternoon, she told me some of her discoveries about the Martinetti cottage. It was built in 1903 by local carpenters for a Pennsylvania man. Fred Brown, a nearby farmer, had moved the first furniture to the cottage with his team of horses and wagon the following June.

The camp road was barely visible from the town road, tucked in between two houses near Tallwood Peninsula. After we passed through the entrance I felt as if I'd been transported back in time. A beautiful pasture and an apple orchard embraced either side of the road. From there we entered a majestic pine woods which was reminiscent of my visits to the primeval forests on the west coast. The narrow camp road was challenging in places as I carefully maneuvered my minivan. I could not help but think of the days when this lane would have comfortably accommodated farm wagons drawn by teams of horses. Oftentimes they were coming from the train station at Readfield Depot, or the trolley stop at Tallwood Landing, toting tired but happy city dwellers who had finally reached their destinations; in the back of the wagons there were steamer trunks packed with enough clothing and necessities to fit them through the entire summer.

Evelyn's search had also led her to Ann Corbitt, the current owner of The Pines. After our "field trip" I contacted Ann to gain more information about the cottage and she pointed me towards William Godfrey. He would, Ann assured me, have a story to tell. I called Godfrey in New Jersey and indeed, his story was remarkable.

William is a New York native and the son of an Episcopal priest. When he was a kid his parents were friends of Rev. Harold Lemoine who was, at that time, the Dean of the Episcopal Cathedral in Garden City, Long Island, New York. "Uncle Harold", as William called him, was raised in Kennebunk, Maine and attended Colby College, class of 1932. Years later he yearned to come back to Maine so he bought the Martinetti cottage in 1958.[272]

Rev. Lemoine was unmarried but he generously shared his Lake Maranacook retreat with good friends and their children. The five bedroom cottage was not large enough to accommodate everyone so he built a bunkhouse. Every summer he brought a group of boys up from New York City to stay at The Pines for the better part of the summer. William was one of those boys.

He recalled that mornings they would paint, work on the road, or do other chores and afternoons they would play on the lake. On Sunday mornings Uncle Harold conducted services on the front porch. "Some of my happiest childhood memories took place there" said William. "We were all sad when the cottage got sold in 1970."

There was more to his story...

William Godfrey was working at the World Trade Center in New York City when it was attacked on September 11, 2001. That tragic event made him and his wife realize they wanted to find a retreat where they could escape the city for part of the summer and "live life to the fullest". Since William had spent some of his happiest summers "somewhere" in central Maine as a child, the couple decided to focus their real estate search in that area. William did not remember what lake he had visited in his childhood, but he and his wife were happy with a seasonal home they found on Lake Maranacook. William had followed his heart and it felt right.

As they settled in, the Godfreys were unaware of how close they were to where William had actually spent his summers many years before. They were in for a surprise. It was not long before he recognized a bordering cottage as the very one he had visited as a boy. The bunkhouse, ice house and boat house he remembered were all still there as well. It was The Pines!

Recently, Ann Corbitt made William an offer. She would continue to spend her summers at The Pines for as long as she wished to, but the century old cottage would be his. What a remarkable twist of fate that this beloved cottage, where William found immeasurable joy as a boy, has now fallen into his care.

The Martinetti cottage known as "The Pines"

Left: Nash and Carrie Martinetti. See another photo of the
Martinettis on page 28. Right: Harold Lemoine in 1932, at the
time of his graduation from Colby College. He owned
"The Pines" for 12 years and brought several sons
of friends there from New York in the summer.

TRAGEDIES STRIKE ~ 1905

August, 1905 was not a particularly eventful month in most parts of the country. Nothing in particular made titillating headline news on the national level except for two tragic events, and one near miss, which occurred in Readfield and Winthrop, Maine.

The stage was set when a young Readfield woman named Mattie Hackett was murdered on August 17th. She had been a student at Maine Wesleyan Seminary and Female College (Kents Hill School) and was working at the Elmwood Hotel in Readfield Corner. After supper that evening Mattie's father found her near their farmhouse on P Ridge - lying in the road and gasping for air. He carried Mattie to their farmhouse where he found a cord wrapped around her neck but it was too late - she died minutes later.

A novice reporter was sent from the *Kennebec Journal* to cover the story but his editor soon realized he had fodder for headline news and assigned an investigative reporter. Articles began to appear across the country with headlines like "ALL SHROUDED IN MYSTERY. NO CLUES IN MATTIE HACKETT MURDER". In the days that followed all eyes were focused on the small town Readfield, Maine and details of every movement on or near the Hackett farm on Kents Hill gave rise to another news report.

By August 24th a suspect had been identified – Mrs. Elsie Raymond of Readfield Corner. Mattie worked with Raymond's husband at the Elmwood and investigators theorized it may have been a crime of jealousy. A guard was stationed outside Raymond's home and Maine's Attorney General Hannibal Hamlin took personal interest in the inquiry. Townspeople were all abuzz and emotions of fear and insecurity were running high.

Meanwhile, only two miles away as the crow flies, Maranacook Hotel was in full swing for the season. Guests had arrived by train and filled the hotel to capacity. It was exceptionally hot that summer. Starting in June temperatures hit 100 degrees in New York and New England and stayed above 90 from then on. The lakeside resort gave blessed relief to the weary city dwellers. A Malden, MA resident - 17 year old Robert D. Boutwell - was among the employees at Maranacook Hotel that year. He was a well-fit student athlete, who had worked there as a hotel clerk in 1904, when his strong swimming skills were discovered by the hotelkeepers. So, upon his return in 1905, in addition to his duties as clerk, Boutwell was asked to ride on excursions when the 75 passenger steamboat *Maranacook* set sail for sightseeing tours around the lake.

On the evening of August 25th, as the *Maranacook's* captain steered near Craig's Point (Tallwood), he collided with a rowboat and its two passengers were thrown into the lake. One managed to swim to safety but as the other person went down for the second time young Boutwell sprung into action and saved her. He was hailed as a hero and a story appeared in newspapers the next day "BOSTON GIRL SAVED BY STEAMER PASSENGER". Festivities were planned for the evening of August 27th when the hotel management would present Boutwell with a plaque and recognize him as a hero, but it was not to be.

The evening of August 26th began uneventfully with dinner in the dining hall followed by adult conversation on the swings, in the lounge, at the water's edge or on the croquet court. Mattie Hackett's murder had to be fresh on the minds and tongues of these folks who surely thought they would be safe in Maine away from the throng of city life. They must have watched their children closely for there was still a murderer on the loose. Little did they know that hours later a perpetrator of another kind would invade their haven.

Most retired to their rooms at a reasonable hour and all were asleep when sometime in the night Boutwell and another employee were awakened by the sounds and smells of fire. Boutwell immediately ran through the hotel pounding on doors calling "FIRE! GET OUT NOW!" With his hands, face and neck severely burned he helped carry ladders and placed them as alternate escape routes. Guests fled down the stairs, jumped from the roof or windows and exited down the ladders. News reports from the time described the eighteen room hotel as 27 years old, nothing more than a shell and dry as a tinder box. Within 30 minutes after the alarm was put out the roof caved in. There were many injuries – three doctors were brought in from Readfield and Winthrop to attend those in need. Guest ledgers were destroyed so there was uncertainty about whether everyone had escaped. It was not until the next day, when the rubble had cooled enough to sort through, that three bodies were discovered.

Had it not been for the valiant efforts of Robert Boutwell, many more lives would have been lost. He did not know this because he had been transported across the lake to the Sir Charles Hotel where doctors were monitoring him closely for severe burns and inhalation of smoke and fire. The outlook was grim and his father was summoned to come from Malden posthaste! Mr. Boutwell arrived in time to hear his son's final words early the next morning - "Good bye father. God bless you and dear mother."

On the following day the *Boston Globe* and *New York Times* printed the headlines "HERO OF HOTEL FIRE SUCCUMBS" and "HERO'S DYING PRAYER".

The press coverage of the Mattie Hackett murder continued off and on for years. Elsie Raymond was brought to trial but found innocent. The crime was never solved.

Oral tradition has kept these stories alive over the years. A book titled "In Search of Mattie Hackett" was authored by Emeric Spooner and published in 2010. Readfield musician Ellen Bowman recently wrote a ballad in memory of Mattie Hackett which Bowman says pays long overdue tribute to Mattie's memory. On July 22, 2014 a cousin of Boutwell, Lois Buchan of

N.H., visited the current owners of Maranacook Hotel to share information about the young hero and to pay tribute to his memory. As others looked on she stood on the spot where young Boutwell had spent his last days and played *Amazing Grace* on her fife.

Left: Robert Boutwell Right: Miss Mattie Hackett

THREE ROSLINDALE VICTIMS OF THE HOTEL FIRE AT LAKE MARANACOOK

MR AND MRS EDWARD A MARTIN AND SON SPENCER MARTIN.

Edward Martin, 33, his wife Ellen, 29 and their only child 7 year old Spencer perished in the fire. The family hailed from Roslindale, MA. Their bodies were discovered eight hours after the fire. Sadly, they were to leave the Hotel that very morning.

Destroyed by fire on August 27, 1905

This reading room, located in the original Maranacook Hotel, gives some indication of how the entire structure was built.

Guests sitting on the upper deck of the original Maranacook Hotel, before the fire of August, 1905.

"Maranacook Bowling Party" at the turn of the century

New Maranacook Station, built 1915

Passengers waiting for the train at the original
Maranacook Station, built 1880

CAMP MARANACOOK (MORGAN'S) ~ 1907

Bill Morgan, founder of Maranacook Boys' Camp [273]

Bill Morgan was a 10th generation New Englander, born 1879 in Weld, Maine, and the elder of two brothers. His parents moved to Readfield in 1882 where they bought a 245 acre farm adjacent to the present day Maranacook Community School.

Bill was a go-getter from the start. He attended Kents Hill School and afterwards he went to New York where he served as head of a business college that turned out 1,500 students a year.[274] In 1905 he returned to Readfield and married Pearl Hannaford, who was also a Kents Hill School alumnus and daughter of Dr. Eli S. Hannaford, a well known Readfield physician.

By age 27 Bill Morgan owned Morgan's Business College in Waterville (Thomas College 2016) where he and Pearl taught and Bill was president. Advertisements of the day proclaimed Morgan's Business College as a "...high grade commercial school which secures employment for its graduates...and (featuring) special rooms for every department...on the highest standard of efficiency with all modern office devices, including billing machines, mimeographs, letter presses and other pieces of labor saving machines..." One promotion went on to say that "Under Mr. Morgan's management the college has been phenomenally successful from the first..."

Back in Readfield, Bill's parents sold their Readfield farm in 1906 and bought another house - also on Main Street but with frontage on Lake Maranacook. In researching various census records, directories and Kennebec County property deeds one can see Morgan's life story unfolding. His parents shared the lakefront home part-time with Bill and Pearl, who were living in Waterville at that time. Morgan bought Birch Island on Lake Maranacook in 1907 where he built a cottage that same summer. From there he began to develop Camp Maranacook, an eight-week summer adventure camp for young men ages six to sixteen. More than likely Morgan was inspired by John Chase, another Readfield native and educator who had established Camp Cebennek for boys on Torsey Pond seven years earlier. (see pg. 208)

William H. "Bill" Morgan

In 1911 Bill ran an advertisement in the Maine Chamber of Commerce Catalogue that included a picture showing large canvas tents set-up in a woodsy setting. The caption read "Real tent life at Camp Maranacook for boys, Readfield, Maine under the personal direction of W.H. Morgan of Waterville, Maine." Morgan, who was known as a suave and likeable people-person with drive, had simultaneously developed a second venture - this one to satisfy his ambition during the summer months. That same year Bill sold his school in Waterville to John L. Thomas, Sr., who renamed it, Morgan-Thomas Business College. In 1962 it was finally renamed Thomas College.

Morgan was also involved in the lumber business after he sold the college. In December, 1919 Charles Collins, Morgan's neighbor in Readfield and the former co-owner of the Maranacook Hotel, wrote about the Morgan family in a letter to his son Parkman. "Will has gone out of the lumber business entirely. I am afraid he lost money last winter, says he is going to strictly attend to his summer school business now..." [275]

After that Morgan was devoted fulltime to building Maranacook Boys' Camp into a successful business that served hundreds of young men from all over the country. He and Pearl continued to live in Readfield during the warmer months. In the wintertime they kept an apartment on Boylston St. in Boston where they could more easily meet and recruit campers.

As the Camp grew Bill accumulated two islands and one-hundred-eight acres with over a mile of wooded lakeshore. Fifty buildings were built on the camp property, plus athletic fields and a barn and a horse riding rink. He also owned a forty-three acre outpost on Tumbledown Mountain in Weld. Campers were exposed to every kind of outdoor adventure and athletic activity imaginable as well as photography, music, theater, woodworking, Indian lore and boat building.

Bill Morgan ran Maranacook Boys' Camp for thirty-eight consecutive years until he was stricken with heart disease and was forced to sell out. In 1965 Camp Maranacook's subsequent owners sold the camp to a Massachusetts developer, who subdivided all the land into cottage and year-round house lots. A few of the original buildings remain as the only reminders of what once was. Some old-timers say that if you sit quietly near the shore you can still hear the echoes of youthful voices drifting across the lake, from the direction of Camp Maranacook.

Morgan's home on Main Street (Henderson 2016)

Bill Morgan died suddenly in 1947 at age sixty-seven. His home on Main Street, Readfield eventually passed to his niece, Joanne Hunt, who owned it until 1974. In the meantime she subdivided part of Morgan's land into Hunt's Lane. Morgan is buried at Readfield Corner Cemetery with his wife, infant daughter, parents and brother along with Joanne and her husband Donald.

We were recently privileged to receive reminiscences from Gary M. Boone of Presque Isle, Maine, who attended Camp Maranacook in 1937 and 1938. What better way to convey the ambiance of a Camp Maranacook experience than directly through the words of one of "Morgan's boys"? We thank Mr. Boone for permission to include his account below, along with a photograph from his personal collection.

MY YEARS AT CAMP MARANACOOK
By Gary M. Boone

I was sent by my parents to Maranacook in July 1937, from my home in Presque Isle. I'd had almost no camping experience, and Maranacook was a good choice for a young and rather isolated young boy.

A very wise and sensible aspect of the Camp was that it was naturally divided into an island camp, and an adjacent mainland camp, separated by a narrow cove of the lake. There were 4 - 5 small sleeping cabins on the island for about 20 lads ranging from 7 to 8 years of age, together with a counselor or, in my case, a counselor and his wife, for each cabin. It was a fine and friendly way to introduce young boys to an organized camping life. I was assigned to the last cabin in the row, and Mr. and Mrs. Lynch from New Jersey were my counselors. They were very friendly and even-handed with us boys. Mr. Lynch always read a chapter of a "Hardy Boys" adventure story to us as we settled down for the night. I think I never did know their first names, nor do I remember the names of the other boys.

I turned 8 the middle of the month. It was a Sunday, during which there were no organized activities, and I walked to the end of the island and sat on some rocks and gazed into the clear water lapping onto the shore.

All the older boys, up to 16 or 17 years of age, were assigned to cabins on the mainland. But all of us ate in one large dining / cooking camp. Always following the main meal of the day, we sang songs. One or another counselor would play an accompaniment on an old upright piano, and the lyrics were projected from a large lantern-slide projector onto a screen for all to see. The songs ranged from well known college football songs ("Lord Geoffrey Amherst" was a favorite), to military ones such as "Anchors Away" and the Marines' "From the Halls of Montezuma." It was an effective, fun way to get the older boys and the younger ones together.

Swimming and canoeing were of course paramount for both safety and enjoyment. When the basics of balance and paddling got to be second nature, we also had to swamp a canoe and learn how to upright it, get back in, and paddle it to shore.

I loved the woodworking shop, of which elderly Mr. MacRae was in charge. I made a paddle, which is still in my family. Older boys even tackled making a wood-framed canvas-covered kayak. I also enjoyed target-shooting with a single-shot, 22 caliber rifle. I didn't enjoy group sports much and I was not pushed into them.

The following year, 1938, I returned to Maranacook and was assigned to a mainland cabin, of perhaps 6 - 8 boys. We could now take sailing lessons in the camp's cat-boats, coached by Stanford Hendrickson. But the biggest event for me was being part of perhaps a dozen boys who were taken in the camp's large caravans to Weld, some 50 miles NW of Maranacook. These large Dodge caravans had open truck bodies, lined with benches along the sides, and with canvas coverings to give some protection from wind and rain. We were headed for a fairly large screened in camp in a field at the base of Tumbledown Mountain, of roughly 3,000 ft. elevation, and a wonderful mountain, replete with a brook, side trail full of enormous glacial erratics, and a tarn near the summit. The southeast flank of the mountain was very cliff-like, and a narrow slot, dubbed the "Lemon Squeezer" allowed us, one at a time, to approach the end, which looked out on the cliff face itself. This was very exciting. [Note: I sent Aislinn Sarnacki (Bangor Daily News nature writer) a description of it, and she soon discovered what I had, so many years ago; only now the Lemon Squeezer is called "The Fat Man's Terror" or some such name.]

I vaguely remember Mr. & Mrs. Morgan, who always joined the entire camp for the main meal. My memories of Camp Maranacook remain vivid, and with great affection. I only realized in later years how well organized the camp was, both in its physical layout, and its seemingly laid-back organization of camp activities. How I wish young people today could have an experience, second-to-none, such as I had.

Some Camp Maranacook campers and counselors, in 1937
Photo courtesy of Gary M. Boone

This photo was captioned in a 1911 Maine Chamber of
Commerce catalogue advertisement: Real tent life at Camp
Maranacook for boys, Readfield, Maine under the personal
direction of W.H. Morgan, Waterville, Maine.

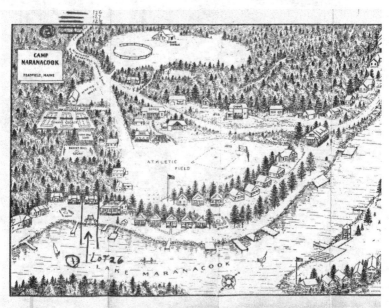

This 1948 map of the grounds at Camp Maranacook
includes the horse riding arena and barn;
the tennis courts; baseball field; and Birch Island

"Morgan's Island Summer School", Birch Island, 1910

Camp Maranacook truck loaded with canoes, 1948

Junior campers at Camp Maranacook, year unknown

Mabel (Mrs. James) Harvey of Readfield wrote this fable in 1907 in which an Indian named Haukeemah[276] was the male hero. [277] She and her husband founded a boys' camp by the same name in 1914.

ANNA BES' COOK? MARY NO COOK?

When Maine was a wilderness the region was inhabited by tribes of the Cushnoc Indians. And one of their favorite camping grounds was on that island in Maranacook Lake because of a certain spring that was there.[278] The spring can no longer be located, but there are men in Readfield today who remember fishing parties who camped at that spring to eat their lunches. An Englishman came to this region, bought a tract of land from these Indians and built himself a log cabin on top of Mount Hunger. He cleared some land, planted a crop and went away. When he returned he brought his wife and two little girls.

As time went on other settlers came in and built homes on the surrounding hills and prospered. They built frame houses with chimneys of brick from the clay of the bed in the stream just to the west of the Englishman's home. There are still traces of brick making to be found along that stream. An orchard was set out, a garden was made the like of which the Indians had never seen. The girls grew up friendly with the Indians and the few scattered white neighbors.

They were Mary and Anna and as they grew to womanhood they were sought as wives by the young settlers. There was one fellow who was very much in love but he did not know if it was Mary or Anna that he would rather have for his life companion. One day he arrived at their home at about dinner hour and was cordially invited to stop for the meal. He dismounted and entered the house. The girls were busy helping their mother prepare the meal and Mary took a pitcher and went to the well for water. On her return she was met at the door by Haukeemah, the son of the chief of the Indian tribe camped on the island nearby. He held out to her a large piece of venison but Mary felt there was something unusual in the eyes of the brave. She smiled and shook her head.

"You ought to give that to Anna" she said. "She's the best cook."

The Indian still held out the venison saying "Anna bes' cook? Mary no cook?"

Mary called to her father to come and see the fine piece of meat Haukeemah had brought. And the farmer came and took the meat, thanked Haukeemah, and gave him some food from his own table, and the Indian went away.

But the young settler who had heard the conversation said to himself "Anna's the girl for me" and he pressed his suit so ardently that he soon won Anna and took her away to live near the neighboring lake.

The year went by. Mary did not want for suitors but she never saw that look in their eyes like she had seen in the eyes of her Indian lover. And Haukeemah, though he never proffered her another gift, did not find a mate for himself among the dusky maidens of his tribe.

Among the claimants for Mary's hand was a man who was a stranger. He made his boasts that he would win her but Mary did not look on him with favor. He made up his mind that he would get her if not by fair means than by foul. And he laid plans to kidnap her. News of this came to the Indian tribe and Haukeemah and another brave took a canoe and came across to the settler's home in the dusk of early evening.

The Englishman was greatly startled when the two figures noiselessly appeared before him and he rather gruffly asked them what they wanted. The news greatly distressed him. They told him how this suitor had made arrangements with some Indians from the Androscoggin County to kidnap Mary; then he was to play the part of the gallant rescuer and claim the girl for his bride.

"Are you sure this is so?" inquired the father.

"Great Chief says so" answered Haukeemah.

The father went and consulted his wife and Mary. The Indians had invited the family to come to the island for the night but the farmer felt that he had better stay at his home. The wife thought it best for her to remain with him, but they both agreed that Mary had best go with her Indian friends. So, wrapped in a dark shawl Mary followed Haukeemah down the steep bluff and paddled across the lake to the Indian camp.

In the evening as the farmer and his wife sat by their open fire there came a knock at the door and the farmer, opening it, admitted the man they were expecting.

After a somewhat lengthy call, during which his eyes were constantly watching the inner door for the appearance of Mary he broached the subject of his desire to have Mary for his wife. The father told him he had better take her "No" for his answer. But the fellow insisted "I'd like to see Mary once more before I take that for my answer."

"Mary is not here" said her mother.

The fellow looked up surprised at the father who had his eyes fixed on the window behind him. Turning, he saw the faces of his Indian hires peering in. He knew his plan had in some way been discovered, and shouting "I'll get her yet" he went out slamming the door behind him.

The farmer barred the door and started to bank the fire when a terrible yell sounded outside the house. He and his wife tried to escape out the back door but they were struck down on the threshold and the house was set on fire.

In the morning the settlers who had seen the blaze from their homes gathered at the scene of the terrible deed. With one of the men came the cowed and shrinking suitor, and at the same time from the other direction came Mary accompanied by her

Indian friends. They came with her to the side of her parents and turned their backs upon her grief. The neighborly women did their best to comfort Mary and then up came the settler with the shamed suitor and tried to explain how the Indians had gone beyond his control. He told her how the thing had started through the love of her and concluded by saying that the young man was overwhelmed by sorrow at the way things had gone but that he would make the best home for her that he possibly could.

Mary was startled. She looked at the fellow with the greatest aversion. Then she read in the faces of those around her that they expected her to accept the guardianship of slayer of her people. She looked around in despair. It was simply impossible. Still, where would she go? She was homeless. Her gaze fell on the group of silent Indians, and from his place beside his father, a little in front of the rest, Haukeemah swung wide his arm in a gesture of invitation and Mary flew to him and his blanket covered them both. At the foot of Mount Hunger is a camp called after the young Indian Chief Haukeemah, and in front of it ripples the water of the lake named for his young bride, Maranacook.

Dead Stream Bridge looking north towards Readfield Corner. The Harvey's boathouse can be seen on the right.
Courtesy of Steve Johnson

Dead Stream outlet into Lake Maranacook. The Harvey homestead overlooked Lake Maranacook and Harvey Island. Their barn can be seen in the distance, on the side slope of hill. All of the buildings once located there were razed by the 1960s.

Dead Stream store, 1932. The child sitting on the steps is Angie Willard Harvey. Later this became "Angie and Billy's Bean Hole Beans" and still later "the Tackle Box". The sign atop the roof reads "Maranacook Lake Fish & Game & Tourist Information". *Courtesy of Vergne Harvey*

CAMP HAUKEEMAH BOYS' CAMP ~ 1914
CAMP HAUKEEMAH GIRLS' CAMP ~ 1920
JOURNEY'S END CAMPS ~ 1927

Harvey Island, which is fifteen acres in size, sits opposite the Dead Stream inlet into Lake Maranacook in Readfield.[279] Local lore says this island was a favorite camping and fishing spot for the Indians of ancient times. Besides the attraction of a clear and ample spring on the island, the white perch ran in great numbers there. Fish were much more plentiful when the Cushnoc people roamed this land than they are today. James E. and Mabel Harvey founded a boys' camp on Harvey Island which they called "Camp Haukeemah".[280] The name came from a fable written by Mabel about an Indian chief's son by that name whose tribe camped on the island. Imagine the romantic and adventuresome visions that must have appeared in the minds of young campers as they listened to Mabel's tale around the campfire?

The Harvey family first appeared in Readfield in 1839 when William Harvey, Sr. came from Portland and bought one-hundred twelve acres bordering Dead Stream and the western shore of Lake Maranacook. At one time the Harveys owned both Center and Harvey Islands as well.[281] Their large farmhouse and barns were located on a hillside overlooking the lake and stream.[282] A son, William Harvey II, was a successful businessman who owned Dirigo Salt Co. and was part owner of the North Wayne Tool Co. His home at Readfield Corner remains an ostentatious landmark to this day.[283] The Harvey's ancestral home on the lake remained in the family for several generations, James E. Harvey being the third generation to live there.[284]

The buildings for Camp Haukeemah were set up on both Harvey Island and on the mainland adjacent to 'Camp Maranacook'.[285] A grand-nephew, Vergne Harvey, explained that his parents met at Camp Haukeemah when they were both working there. Vergne's father, Jim, taught archery at Haukeemah and at Camp Maranacook. He and his wife Starr later owned the mainland section of Camp Haukeemah, while Jim's sister and her husband took over the island.[286]

Campers came to Haukeemah from New York City and the Washington D.C. area.[287] The campus consisted of a large lodge type building on the east corner of the island with a "crow's nest" where one could see a grand view of the Lake.[288] There were also two bunkhouses and an ice house. A boathouse sat on the mainland at the edge of the lake where the Dead Stream boat landing is now.[289] A sports field was located on the opposite side of the mainland where Lakeview Drive is today.[290]

Mabel and James' granddaughter, Marjorie Black, told of her grandparents' appreciation for nature saying "My grandmother knew a lot about the flora of the woods which she taught the boys, and my grandfather shared his love for fishing and hunting." There was canoeing and other activities that kids' camps of the day offered as well. Helen was their only child and when she became a young teenager Mabel thought it a bad idea to have all those teenage boys from New York City around, so they changed Haukeemah from a boys' camp to a girls' camp. "I think that was about 1920" Marjorie said with a chuckle.

The camp for girls continued until 1927 when the Harvey's niece, Asaphine Chappelle, and her husband bought it. Asaphine and Vergne Chappelle lived in New York City where they were ideally located for recruiting campers.[291] Unfortunately the timing was poor - on the brink of the Great Depression. "They had a full enrollment all signed up and for some reason everyone backed out on them and that was the end of it" said Marjorie.

Soon after the girls' camp failed the Chappelles created a resort for adults they called "Journey's End Camps".[292] That establishment was set up to accommodate twenty-five guests but nothing else is known about how it was operated. The island setting must have created some level of thrill and mystique for city guests. Charles Ricker, an owner of the famous Poland Spring Hotel, invested in the Chappelle's business in 1934. This was one of many significant investments that Ricker made in Maine hotels and resorts during the Depression era.[293] The Poland Spring Hotel offered outpost adventures to their clientele so perhaps Journey's End Camps was to provide some of those? One can only puzzle over Ricker's reason for this investment. Those years were tough on everyone involved in the tourist industry and the Chappelles were no exception. Sadly, Journey's End Camps did not pan out either but the family did keep the land. The Chappelles, Jim and Starr Harvey and their children, had wonderful summer vacations on Lake Maranacook until they sold the property in the 1960s.[294]

MORE ABOUT YOUNG JIM HARVEY

Jim Harvey was an ingenious mechanical engineer and created several inventions. For one, he converted a bunkhouse on the island into a power house that generated electricity to all the buildings.[295] His best known invention was a unique inboard canoe motor that he designed to mount just forward of the stern of a canoe. The "Harvey Inboard Motor Case" patent was adopted in December 1930 and it was expected to take off like wildfire.[296] The motor was distributed by the Kennebec Boat and Canoe Company of Waterville and the promotion touted unique features such as higher speed potential plus a quieter and less smoky engine. The motor was also proclaimed to be better balanced thus safer, making the vessel less apt to take on water. Again the Depression of the 1930s interfered and fewer than thirty engines were sold. When Fred and Nancy Hudon of Canton, Connecticut bought Harvey Island in 1981 a Harvey inboard motor was in storage on the island. The Hudons did some research to learn more about it and eventually they donated it to the Maine State Museum[297] where it remains to this day.[298]

Memories of the Harvey name and Camp Haukeemah have faded with time but... perhaps now when you drive over the Dead Stream Bridge, or stand on the shore near the boat landing, or hear the hum of a boat engine drifting across Lake Maranacook you will pause for just a moment to pay them homage.

Harvey Island, 1910 *Photo courtesy of Steve Johnson*

Harvey Island, 2016

Jim Harvey behind the wheel and beside him is his sister Asaphine. The boat is powered by Jim's inboard motor which is in the Maine State Museum collection as the only surviving example of Jim's patented invention. Passengers in rear are unknown. *Photo courtesy of Vergne Harvey*

The "Tackle Box" sat where the Dead Stream boat landing is today. In the 1950s Herbert and Lynn Stufflebeam ran an ice cream and fishing bait shop there which they sold in 1960 to the "Readfield Fish & Game Club". The club gave the land to the State of Maine Parks and Recreation Department in 1966 and the boat landing has been there since then.

"Mary Jane Richardson, the seer, made her annual trip to this locality last week." ~ Readfield Depot news, Kennebec Journal, August 1906

THE SUMMER PEOPLE'S FORTUNE TELLER ~ 1910

In 1910 when anyone rode from Readfield Corner to Winthrop, about a mile out, they saw a two room early settler's cabin that sat on a knoll in a lonely pasture. Just beyond that was the impressive farm of James O. Butman. Research reveals the log structure was built by Samuel Mayhew about 1760. The cabin and land it sat on changed hands several times over the years until it became part of Butman's holdings. By then all the cabin's windows were broken and some openings were boarded up to prevent tramps from intruding on its occupant. Furnishings consisted of one chair, four boxes, a trunk and a small kitchen woodstove.

Its' inhabitant might have gone unnoticed except for one thing; come summer a sign appeared outside the door that read "FORTUNES TOLD Poor People 5 Cents. Those with more money 10 cents." The fortune teller's name was Mary Jane Richardson. "The rent here is very satisfactory...nit a month...cheapest rent in town..." she told a newspaper reporter in 1910. She also sang songs to "make a little extree" she said pointing to a sign on an interior wall that said - "5 cents for 3 songs. 10 cents for 3 songs and 3 hims."

Richardson was born in Readfield to Asa and Sarah (Cottle) Richardson in 1828. She had become an eccentric old lady by the time that reporter discovered her. She refused to tell her age – perhaps she did not even know her age? After all, she had been the sixth child of thirteen born between 1815 and 1837 so her parents surely had trouble keeping all those birthdays straight. Survival was their major concern. Some of the children had to be farmed out or sent off to work in the factories in Massachusetts, including Mary Jane. She worked in the textile mills in Lawrence and also in Manchester, New Hampshire where she made enough money to dress well and participate in social activities such as dances and shows. "If I hadn't been so foolish as to try to keep agoing and wear so many fancy good togs when I was in the mills" she said, "I might have more money now. It cost money to swim in society."

She remained single – in fact she was reported to be a "confirmed spinster". Sometime after 1870 she returned to Maine and for several years worked as a housekeeper for prominent families in Augusta, Brunswick and Gardiner. Then she found herself temporarily out of a job and her life took a different direction. She met a woman who taught her how to tell fortunes with cards and the very first week she made a little money using her new found skill. After that she just kept right on reading cards as her livelihood, but she did not bring in enough income to live on. Mary Jane ended up living at the Readfield Poor Farm near Maranacook Lake, where she became well known to locals as a fortune teller.

In 1888 the poor-farm was sold to the hotel developer, David W. Craig, and Mary Jane was told she would have to live at the new one in the far western reaches of town. Enter George E. Coleman.

Two hotels sprung up on Lake Maranacook about that same time – the Sir Charles Hotel near the site of the original poor-farm, and Maranacook Hotel (see pg 74) directly across the lake from the Sir Charles. Maranacook Station was built nearby to accommodate the out-of-state vacationers who flooded in by railroad. Coleman was the station agent at Maranacook Station, and owned the aforementioned, uninhabited log cabin which was fairly near Lake Maranacook. The entrepreneurial Coleman must have seen Richardson's mystique as a potential attraction for summer visitors and he invited her to live there. She had never known anything but deprivation and hard work at the direction of hard task masters, so the idea of having her own house where she could also make a living, must have been a welcome relief. Richardson took Coleman up on the offer.

She lived very simply there, unlike her days of working in the textile mills. Richardson related that she ate little bread and subsisted almost wholly on crackers and water and occasionally some milk. She told the reporter she would not wear "boughten" stockings and knit her own hose and mittens. Come winter she sometimes returned to live in the shelter of the Readfield Poor Farm. A picture in the 1910 article shows Mary Jane standing in the doorway of her abode. Her face was serious and eyes glaring at the camera, one arm braced against the doorframe and the other at her side. She had large hands – like those of a working man one might say. Kerchief on her head, shawl over her shoulders, a checkered skirt covered with a tattered apron. One could almost feel her destitution while at the same time her contentment.

Word about the local fortune teller spread quickly among the summer people, with help from Coleman. They made their way to Richardson's cabin where they confided to her their innermost secrets. Richardson told them things like who they would marry, how they would get rich, and whether they would die in the poorhouse. According to her there were hobgoblins all around her cabin and at one point she shushed the reporter to listen for them, then went on to say "Do you know how much I made picking some people to pieces last summer? Well, I made $7.20. That ain't so bad. And I've got it all in a bag in that box over in the corner. I wouldn't put it into no bank. They break into banks, and the fellows in the bank run away sometimes." She lived the way she chose and, by all appearances, the townspeople respected her choices.

Three years after the interview Mary Jane Richardson died at the Readfield Poor Farm, of heart failure. One must wonder if she foresaw her own demise.[299]

MARTHA WASINGTON INN ~ 1924

"Did George and Martha Washington stay at the Martha Washington Inn on Lake Maranacook?" asked the third grader. "No they were alive a long time before the Martha Washington Inn came into existence" I answered, "but that is a good question."

It was 1924 when George and Carolyn Nobis bought an old Colonial house near the Readfield / Winthrop town line. Their acquisition also included 100 acres on both sides of the Winthrop Road and extensive frontage on the west shore of Lake Maranacook. Even though the property has no direct connection to the wife of our Country's first President that we know of, it does have a rich heritage.

James Craig was the first to settle on this land in 1765 – a 200 acre lot at that time - where he ran a ferry to and from Waugh's Landing. (see pg 59) Craig sold the southern part to Revolutionary War veteran Capt. William Armstrong in 1774[300] for twenty-three pounds six shillings. The Armstrong homestead remained in his family for five generations, until George Armstrong sold it to George and Carolyn Nobis in 1924. [301]

The Nobis family was living in the Bronx, where George was working as a mail carrier, when he brought his wife and their two young sons to Campers Point (see pg 62) for a vacation. Carolyn saw the Armstrong farm nearby and envisioned how desirable a place it would be to raise their boys. Armstrong agreed to sell it to them and on August 24, 1924 the Nobises signed the final papers and moved to Maine. They first tried to make a living by farming but learned that working the land was not one of their strengths. To supplement their income they rented spare bedrooms to summer visitors while Carolyn charmed them with her good cooking. They soon discovered their potential for running a successful tourist home.

In 1929 - 1930 the Nobises borrowed $18,000, Carolyn designed a hotel and they hired a crew to build the twenty-two room "Martha Washington Inn". Bill Wyman of East Readfield set up a portable sawmill on the west side of the Winthrop Road opposite the house and a crew began to harvest timber while Wyman sawed it into framing lumber. Roy Giles of Readfield helped build the hotel – said to be his first paid carpentry job – and he also built a massive fireplace in the hotel lobby. [302] Columns were added to the house to augment the ambiance of the grounds as well. Eventually more rooms were added making it a four-story structure with 45 rooms and 25 bathrooms.[303] During the off-season each year several of the guest rooms were given face lifts with fresh paint, wallpaper and new linens.

The new structure was constructed separately but the dining room and kitchen, complete with walk in refrigerator, remained in the original house. At dinnertime the tables were set with fine linens, silver and china. Guests dressed in their finery for the evening meal [304] but informality was encouraged for the rest of the time. Three meals a day were served in the dining room but when day excursions were planned the kitchen staff provided wicker picnic baskets packed with sandwiches and baked goods. A favorite tradition was lobster bakes prepared on the lakeshore when diners were also served complimentary beer and wine. In those days Readfield was a dry town so alcohol could not be sold.[305]

The Nobises also had a boathouse and docking area built at the water's edge. When they went into business guests were still arriving by train at the Winthrop and Readfield train stations and brought from there by steamer. By the 1940s the Nobises owned a woodie station wagon[306] and used it to transport their clientele from the local train stations. Some guests had also begun arriving in their own automobiles by then. At some point the boathouse was converted to a recreation hall that included a pool table and pin ball machines.[307]

Throughout the 1930s and 40s the Martha Washington Inn brochures promoted a vast array of activities such as swimming, diving, boating, water sports, dancing, ping-pong, billiards, croquet, badminton, tennis, woods trails for horseback riding and hiking. Road trips for a day of golf at the Augusta Country Club, a theatrical show, and shopping were also available. Stressed was the excellent fishing, with local guides, for bass, pickerel, perch and salmon. Amenities included a cocktail lounge, a gathering room with fireplace, and several large airy piazzas with rocking chairs and views. Soon after the Inn opened their brochure boasted guest rooms with hot and cold running water and private bathrooms for a daily rate of $22.50 per person. Accommodations without running water were also available for $2.50 less. The pamphlet also pointed out that all rooms had attractive color schemes and Simmons Beautyrest inner coil spring mattresses and that some were two room suites. All rates included three meals a day and charges were less for children. Near the lakeshore there were also several "modern three-room guest cottages with bathrooms and porches." [308]

Staff housing was located on the west side of Winthrop Road as was the laundry which was equipped with a mangle iron.[309] Employees were expected to live on site through the entire summer – even those who lived locally.[310] Many seasonal jobs were available including pastry cooks, chefs, launderers, waitresses, dishwashers, groundskeepers, chambermaids, boatmen, chauffeurs, carpenters and painters. The Nobis family was hands on and participated in much of the work and cooking themselves.

Understandably, during WWII business faltered and the Nobises were forced to close. In 1946 they sold the property and business to Chauncey and Phyllis Simmons of Brattleboro, Vermont for $15,000. Included in the transaction were the buildings and part of the acreage plus all the furniture, furnishings, plates and plated articles, linen, glassware, china, household items, boats, canoes, farming equipment and tools, office equipment and supplies and any other fixtures and equipment of any kind in operational use at the Martha Washington Inn. The Simmons remained in business for only one year and they sold to Louis and Pauline Prolman.[311]

The Prolmans were hard working Russian immigrants who had entered this country in 1908. They bounced from Massachusetts to New Hampshire to Florida and finally to Auburn, Maine where they were running a meat market when they purchased the Martha Washington Inn in 1947.[312]

The couple gained a reputation for their scrumptious dinner buffets complete with carved ice centerpieces. Their spreads included fresh vegetables, meats, milk, butter and cream from local farms. Unlike their predecessors they opened the dining hall to the public, rented space, and catered wedding receptions and other special events as well. Added to the classic sign at the entrance was another one that read "Fine Foods and Cocktails". The Prolmans brought a new persona to the Martha Washington Inn which they operated for about ten years, during its final heydays.

When Gerard and Noella Poulin bought this property in April of 1967 the sale included all the buildings and the contents. They rented rooms for a short time but the popularity of lakeside resorts such as this had passed. Vacationers were more interested in owning or renting their own private cottages or staying in modern hotels by then. The Poulins opened the lounge and offered live music and dancing but that only lasted a year because apparently the neighbors did not like the loud music.[313] After that all business ceased and by 1992 the Inn had fallen into disrepair, became unsafe and was torn down.

Today there is little left of the Martha Washington Inn – just the original house and remnants of that massive fireplace. But if you listen closely enough you may hear children splashing on the shore, the clomping of horse hooves on the woods trails and the laughter and chatter of guests as they arrive in that old woodie wagon.

The house with the addition of columns on the front,
a kitchen and dining hall. This and the next photo appeared
in the first brochure about 1930. Note the vintage automobiles.

The Martha Washington Inn sat adjacent to the house.
Landscape and trees had not yet been planted. The
Armstrong family had used this piece of ground as pasture.

This lounge was on the first floor inside the Inn. Note
the fireplace on the far wall. Today that fireplace is all
that remains of the hotel.

Barbara Fogg and the Martha Washington Inn woodie
wagon. She worked for the Prolmans in the 1940s.
Photo courtesy of Joanne Fogg Fournier

Louis & Pauline Prolman with one of their dinner buffets

KAMP KIWANACOOK ~ 1927

Elmer Ellsworth "E.E." Peacock was born in West Gardiner in 1873 into an old Gardiner family. He was industrious from the start and by age sixteen he was already publishing a semi-weekly newspaper called the "West Gardiner Observer".[314] When Peacock married Della Curtis of West Gardiner in 1896 both were teachers. He was living in Readfield by that time where he was the principal of the business school at Maine Wesleyan Seminary. In 1905 Peacock turned to studying law fulltime and within two years he was admitted to the Maine Bar Association.[315]

As a well known lawyer in this area E.E. Peacock's name appears time and again on legal documents and land transactions. The most significant, for the purposes of this book, was in 1925 when he bought 15 acres and a log cabin on the east shore of Lake Maranacook.[316]

In 1927 E.E. was a member of the Kiwanis chapter in Waterville when a proposal was set forth that the organization purchase a lakeside property and start a summer camp for the sons of Kiwanians. The membership body voted it down but E.E. was convinced there was great potential in such an enterprise. He later wrote *"…There are more than 100,000 members of the Kiwanis International. Surely these members have sons or grandsons whom they would like to send…from the hot and crowded cities into the country…to live the simple life…and study the wondrous lessons of nature…"* [317] E.E. went on his own to develop his Lake Maranacook retreat into Kamp Kiwanacook. In addition, he bought land on "Thundercastle Hill" near Torsey Pond, where his campers could trek for wilderness adventures.

Peacock wasted no time in adding buildings and planning details. Months after that proposal was turned down in Waterville he opened the doors at "Kamp Kiwanacook". A sixteen page brochure outlined his plans and expectations.

The original log cabin would be used for dining and general assemblies. Added were several 18x26ft.buildings with numerous screened-in windows and each with an 8ft wide piazza. Every camper would have his own locker and key, and a *"...spring bed and comfortable mattress and clean, adequate clothing..."* One counselor for every five campers would sleep in the same quarters.[318] It seems that Peacock left no stone unturned when he planned how his camp would function. The brochure gave details about how the staff would provide safety and discipline; foods that would be served; "sweetmeats" that would be rationed; and even the sanitary conditions the campground employed. Their methods for maintaining the boys' spiritual growth, good health and rest periods were also included. Under "Camp Improvement" Peacock wrote *"...each boy is expected to spend one day during the season (to) improve the camp or grounds..."* Peacock's approach was very thorough and would be defined as holistic in today's world.

The brochure also gives insight into what activities were available to the campers, as well as an understanding of Peacock's philosophy and standards.

"Within every boy there are many latent qualities which, on account of a lack of confidence and courage, never come to the front...One of the purposes of this camp is to bring out these latent qualities...Programs are arranged from week to week to meet the requirements of camp life so to keep the boys intensely interested in their work. A set program becomes monotonous."

The physical activities put forward at Kiwanacook were similar to what other kids' camps were offering such as, swimming, fishing, canoeing, tennis, quoits[319] and horseback riding. His equipment included canoes, a motor boat and several "Rangeley row boats".[320]

Fred E. Williams, Peacock's son-in-law, was the camp's Assistant Director. The brochure describes Fred in glowing terms as an all around athlete who took special interest in baseball.

"...For several years he was a pitching 'ace' of one of Maine's best semi-professional baseball teams and later became a member of the professional team in the Blue Ridge League of Tennessee. In addition to being a versatile athlete he is a great lover of boys and the boys love him. He is an ardent devotee of rod and gun and takes great delight in showing the boys where the deep pools are in which the big fish are hiding and how to find nests of birds and the lair of wild animals. He is also a nice singer and banjo player..."

One might think Fred received such high praise because his father-in-law authored the words, but that was only part of it. Fred died young in 1956 at age fifty-nine. He and his wife Evelyn, a Readfield school teacher, had no children nor did Fred's only sibling so there were no Williams' descendants. Memories of Fred could have easily vanished with time, yet his name has lived on. He built a fine reputation and he is remembered with fondness by those who knew him personally. Fred was a friend, baseball player, coach, trapper and overall sportsman who left his mark on a good many boys and men from both near and far.[321]

Peacock chose all his staff wisely – *"...men of age, experience and character...even temperament and pleasing personality (who) fully realize the responsibility that rests upon them...(and) bring out the best there is in (the boys)..."* In addition to coaching and other outdoor activities the Kiwanacook staff also helped campers expand their minds and talents. There was an organized music program and campers were encouraged to bring their own instruments and participate in Kiwanacook's orchestra. In a wood working shop the boys learned the use of simple tools and manufactured boats and other wooden creations of their choice. The weekly camp newspaper "Kiwanacook News" provided opportunities for budding authors and journalists. There was a reading room, a library, and a camp bank where the youngsters learned the life skill of money management. Tutors were available for the kids who needed extra scholastic help during their summer vacations. Scientific minds could enjoy *"the work of the Creator"* by studying birds, insects, plants and animals in their natural habitats.

Peacock's mention of nature as the work of the Creator was later followed by this personal description of his spiritual philosophy, also contained in the Kiwanacook brochure.

"This camp has no controversy over religion as represented by the various creeds and denominations. How we live, not what we think or believe, is the true scale in which to weigh our religion. The Golden Rule and the Lord's Prayer are the cardinal points of religion and point the way to right living. The aim of this camp is to impress upon each boy the necessity of keeping faith in himself, his parents, his fellow beings and his God; to be unselfish, kind, thoughtful, considerate, sympathetic and helpful; to be of real, heartfelt service to those with whom he comes in contact..."

Later in the brochure, under "Membership", a passage appears that is contradictory to his comments regarding the importance of extending kindness and consideration towards one's fellow man. In the midst of Peacock's criteria for membership he states:

"...The camp is conducted primarily for sons of Kiwanians but any boy of the WHITE race between the ages of seven and seventeen years will be received..." (Emphasis on "white" added)

This boundary was surely a testament to the times and not to the man.

Kiwanacook, like other kids camps, offered canoeing and camping trips that lasted for several days. Peacock hired Registered Maine Guides to lead the adventures, which were arranged according to the boy's ages and physiques. According to Peacock's brochure the older, more experienced boys could go on an extensive canoe trip starting on Lake Maranacook, on to Annabesasook then across Cobbosseeconte. From there they entered Cobbosseeconte Stream and paddled all the way to the Kennebec River at Gardiner; then upriver through Hallowell and Augusta to Waterville. From there, the description said, the paddlers entered Messalonskee Stream and made their way to Messalonskee Lake, then on to Belgrade Stream and into the Belgrade Lakes chain.

That would be quite a feat for even the most advanced canoeist but then E.E. Peacock always did set his aims high.

KAMP PEACOCK ~ 1931

It is an honor to include in this section some stories and memories shared by Evelyn Adell Potter, Readfield Historian and Readfield Depot native. She and her mother, Ruth Adell (Mullen), worked at Kamp Peacock for several summers in the 1930s and 1940s.

Having started Kamp Kiwanacook on the brink of the Great Depression it did not flourish as E.E. Peacock had hoped. But in his usual can-do style he converted the compound to rental cabins for adults and renamed it Kamp Peacock. He continued to use the log cabin as the dining hall where meals were served and special gatherings could be held. Case in point in 1933 a Kennebec Journal article related that more than one-hundred teachers from the Augusta Teacher's Association held their annual meeting at "Peacock's Camps on Lake Maranacook in Readfield".

A 1931 Peacock promotion[322] spoke of the quiet and restful atmosphere of his individual cottages; all equipped with electricity and the modern conveniences.[323] The ad suggested Peacock's was *"a delightful place to spend a honeymoon."* There was emphasis on dining by saying *"the dining room is very pleasing... the meals are well cooked, of good variety and served in generous quantity...Chicken dinner every Sunday."*

Ruth Adell[324] of Readfield Depot was one of the cooks at Kamp Peacock for several summers. Her daughter Evelyn Potter tells how Ruth's reputation as a good cook spread when she worked as a private cook for several summer residents within the kitchens of their rental cottages, such as at Pinerest.[325] Peacock called Ruth to cook at his establishment when he had "special guests who wanted to be served Ruth's meals in particular." She liked working there because Peacock's kitchen was state of the art for the times.[326]

Evelyn also worked at Kamp Peacock in various capacities as a young person and she recently shared memories of her own experiences. Evelyn was not much more than ten or eleven when she started to tag along as her mother's helper. "I washed the pots and pans. I was not allowed to wash the 'good dishes'. Peacock had nothing but the best china and glassware. Someone older was brought in to wash those." She also helped Nellie Wyman in the laundry. Nellie lived at Readfield Depot in the tenement house.[327] The laundry was a rather professional operation. "We used a washer and ringer and a mangle.[328] I had never seen a mangle work but Peacock's had one. We didn't do people's personal items but washed the camps' towels and an awful lot of sheets, I know that! I think the sheets were changed every day. He had chambermaids too and those cabins smelled so good. Mr. Peacock was awful fussy about cleanliness and he wanted everything just right. I think he had the inside of the cabins painted every year. They were kept immaculate."

The dining hall sat out over the water and there were windows facing on three sides towards the lake. By noontime the sun started streaming through the windows. "I really liked setting the tables in the dining room" says Evelyn. "I carefully put the dishes and silverware in their places – I was always taken by the utensils that were made of real silver. After I got everything all set I used to stand back in the doorway to admire my work. It looked so pretty with the sun sparkling on the silver and glassware."

E.E. showed up every morning to watch over things but Evelyn does not recall ever seeing his wife Della there. After lunch he drove to run errands and to pick up fresh vegetables. "He wouldn't let anyone else go because he wanted to check the vegetables himself and if they were not just right he would reject them. He brought fresh vegetables into the kitchen every single day." Peacock set-off about the same time Evelyn was done for the day and he oftentimes gave her a ride as far as South Road. "He was not a very good driver and one time he missed the turn by the railroad crossing above the camps. He always made me sit in the back seat. We didn't have seat belts in those days and I was thrown all around and the dust flew when the car tires spun. It scared me. When my father found out what had happened he said 'You are not to ride with Mr. Peacock again!' I walked all the way home every day after that." [329]

Della, E.E.'s trusted lifetime companion of nearly fifty years, died in 1944 which dealt him a great blow. Two years later he sold Kamp Peacock to Norman and Beatrice Chapman of Winthrop. He lived with one of his three daughters[330] near Readfield Corner during his final years, where he died in 1950 at age seventy-six.

CHAPMAN LODGES AND DINING ROOM ~ 1946

Norman and Beatrice Chapman took over on the heels of WWII and renamed the establishment "Chapman Lodge and Dining Room on Lake Maranacook". Their brochure highlighted activities such as tennis, archery, bathing (swimming), boating, croquet, canoeing, photography and weenie roasts. They also assured potential guests there was a golf course nearby.

Under transportation the Chapmans included a mention of passenger trains stopping at Readfield Depot as an option. This had been the primary mode of transportation to all the local camps up until that time. But the Chapman brochure goes beyond train transportation and reflects the progress of the times. Included are detailed directions by automobile, flights on Northeast Airlines into Augusta Airport, and the Greyhound Bus line. But what stands out in the way of progress is "planes with pontoons can land on the lake at Chapman's."

The Chapmans stayed in business for only four years and sold to Ruth Ehlert from Melrose, MA in September, 1950. She filed a plan with the Kennebec Registry of Deeds one month later called "Lazy Loon Colony on Upper Maranacook Lake". The plan included forty-eight individual camp lots, but development to that extent never came to fruition. Two months later Ehlert sold the entire property. The reason for her change of heart is not known.

DIXON'S LAKESIDE COTTAGES ~ 1950

Where better to learn about the years that Eugene and Carrie Dixon ran the camps than a firsthand account from their son Ron? He was five years old when his folks moved to Maine from New Jersey and from then forward he spent all of his childhood and teenage years living and working with his parents at "Dixon's Lakeside Cottages". We hope to do his story justice! [331]

"Gene" Dixon grew up on a farm in northern New Jersey until just before WWII where he ran "Franklyn Lake Dairy". His family would probably have stayed in New Jersey had his wife Carrie not developed respiratory problems from the poor air quality there. When her physician recommended she move for health reasons the Dixon family set off for a Maine vacation to take in the fresh air. They found their way to Lake Maranacook and Lazy Loon Colony. The beautiful location immediately won them over and they also recognized the business potential.

In 1950 Gene sold Franklyn Lake Dairy and moved his family to Lazy Loon Colony where they set up residence in the main lodge. At that point the "overnight cabins" were in the same rustic state as in Peacock's days and did not have indoor plumbing. [332] Guests were still being served three meals a day in the dining room. The Dixons decided to modify the cabins into housekeeping cottages which would eliminate the need for employees and reduce their workload. The conversion required a significant investment and up-front labor.

Gene went to work part-time for Howard Harriman of Winthrop as a plumber, and the experience he gained with Harriman was invaluable. When it came time to install bathrooms and kitchens with hot and cold running water in all fifteen of Dixons' cottages he did the work himself. As his son Ron became older Gene taught him about plumbing in addition to many other skills. Ron says "I learned an awful lot from my father that I have drawn from my whole life...He was an awful good father to me."

Renovations also took place in the main lodge. They did away with the dining hall and put up partitions to create private living quarters for the Dixon family and a workshop for Gene's tools. A small store was added where they sold staples such as milk and eggs to their guests. They also sold bait to fishermen and mixed gas for their motor boats. Their "Sealtest" sign was visible from the lake, which beckoned boaters into shore for ice cream treats at Dixon's little store.

Vacationers generally rented cottages for one to three weeks and they came in from all over the country. On Monday evenings they gathered at the recreation hall for a get acquainted time. The Dixons also held square dances on a regular basis. There were no other organized activities. A large sandy beach was available to all guests and each cottage had its own private lake frontage complete with a dock, canoe and swimming area. The cottages were also equipped with a sink, refrigerator and stove so guests could live independently. Drinking water was carried from a pure spring on the property while lake water was pumped to a large holding tank and gravity fed to the cottages for other purposes.

The Dixons faced a few drawbacks over the years. Their proximity to the railroad tracks was one. Gene always stressed to his guests that they should "Stop, Look and Listen!" In those days several freight trains, one-hundred or more car lengths, went through every day. As the train engineers approached Dixon's crossing they blared the warning whistle. Guests who found the whistle and clatter of the train on the rails disruptive also disliked the inconvenience of waiting in their automobiles when they got held up at the crossing. Occasionally someone would ask Gene for the train schedule so they could plan departure from their cottages accordingly. Gene would chuckle to himself and give them a piece of paper saying "You just write this down and put it on your refrigerator, it will only take me a minute to tell you." As the relieved guest stood poised with pencil in hand Gene told them "They can come anytime."

At check-in Ron was often the one to give guests a tour and camp orientation. Gene told them what rules to heed which included his warning to obey Maine's fishing laws. "DO NOT TOUCH your kid's poles" he would say, "unless you have a Maine fishing license because if you get caught you'll be fined." Not everyone listened and occasionally someone got caught red-handed by a game warden. Some became angry and Gene often took the brunt. A few of them even told Gene that HE should pay the fine. Once in a while someone would sign out and go home in a huff in spite of Gene's knack for handling touchy situations. But, says Ron, "It was not unusual for another car to be coming down the road, whose driver was hoping we had a vacancy, at the same time that mad man was driving away."

For the most part everyone banned together and helped the Dixons when there was a need. On several occasions hurricanes were forecast and all the guests helped button up the windows and pull the boats and docks onto safe ground. "We had some mighty high winds a few times" said Ron. But he does not recall any devastating and damaging storms like one that hit Tallwood in 1952.[333]

Proprietors of the other housekeeping cottages also helped each other. "They were competitors but good business people too and they referred guests to each other when their rooms or cottages were full." Ron remembers in particular Fred and Catherine Bliss at Pinerest.[334] Most businesses on the lakes were members of the Winthrop Lakes Region Association and each year the Association had a booth at the Boston Sportsmen

Show. Several local proprietors from around the Winthrop Lakes gathered in the same booth to promote their respective businesses. Ron went with his father a few times and was taken at how well spoken and congenial they all were. He also remembers fondly the time that baseball great Ted Williams, who was also an avid fisherman, was at the show giving fly fishing lessons, and Ron was given an autographed baseball by Williams. That is something a young boy would never forget to be sure!

Dixons had such a wonderful location Ron related. "We were on the east shore and looked west to Blueberry Island, south to Martha Washington Inn and north to the boys camp (Morgan's) and all the way to the Weathervane Restaurant. "We could hear the boys at (Morgan's) playing by the water and swinging off a rope swing. Sometimes they came down in front of our place in their boats. But they were never disrespectful or gave us any trouble. When a shower was in the air the loons cried warnings to each other to take cover and we could see a wall of rain coming across the lake. It sounded like a giant roar when it hit the surface. I would watch lightening storms from my bedroom window. It was something. And the sunsets were beautiful!"

Ron loved to fish and had his own two-man canoe. He oftentimes set out on his own but stayed within sight of Dixon's. On one of his paddling adventures he discovered a shallow spot out in the middle of the lake at what should have been the deepest part. He set down anchor, cast out his line and in no time the fish started biting. He fished there often after that and was sometimes asked "How come you anchor in the middle of the lake where it's so deep?" Ron remembered his Dad's advice. "Don't tell anyone your best fishing hole or the next time you go six other boats will already be there." So, Ron never told anyone why.

"My mother and father loved the lake and the camps" said Ron "but as the years went on the culture changed and people began to expect frills like room and maid service." Then there were others who were disrespectful of the Dixon's property and drank and partied like the Dixons had never seen before. This all added stress to the couple's workday. When Gene had a heart attack in 1961 the couple decided it was time to sell. Like several other similar businesses of the day they sold each of their cottages separately. The buyers formed an association and voted to name the colony "Lazy Loon".

Having visited Lazy Loon and met several of the current owners, this author knows they love and enjoy those shores as much as the Dixons did, and those before them. There are no more square dances in the recreation hall, or boaters coming in for Sealtest ice cream, or mad fishermen driving off into the night. But the loons still cry, the rain still washes its way down the lake, the sunset still glows in the west and if you listen closely enough I'll bet you can still hear the clatter of those freight trains and Gene Dixon saying "They can come anytime."

August 23, 1955
To: Mr. Thomas Griffin
Ardmore, Pennsylvania
We left at 9:30 Friday. Here 4:00 Saturday. Ran into flood areas in Massachusetts had to detour to R.I. Bobby is sleeping on the porch across the front of the (Beachmont) cottage. X marks the window of our room. The fishing is best early and late. It's very hot here... Swimming is perfect. Gets cold at night. Very quiet and peaceful. All well here.

Love to all, John, Emeline, Bert and Bob

Ellsworth E. Peacock, Owner and Director

Left: Kamp Kiwanacook founder and director, E.E. Peacock. Right: Kiwanacook assistant director, Fred "Gus" Williams.

Left: Ruth Adell worked at Kamp Peacock in the 1930s and 40s as the cook. Right: Her daughter Evelyn also worked at Peacock's then, in the dining room and laundry.

Note the old car – this photo was taken when people first started to arrive by automobiles rather than by trains. The owner of these cottages is not identified on this postcard.

The Birches, Peacock Camps, Readfield Depot

The Avalon, Chapman's Lodge, Readfield Depot

Beachmont at Dixon's Lakeside Cottages, Readfield Depot
(See postcard note on page 171)

The Trading Post, Dixons Camps, Readfield Depot

Recreation Hall at Dixon's Lakeside Cottages
Readfield Depot

NEWTON'S CAMPS ~ 1920 [335]

George Coleman, the founder of Coleman's Grove on Lake Maranacook (see pg. 44) was the one to begin developing this section of Maranacook's shoreline. At this location he invested in a 45 acre woodlot in 1911 and when he had harvested the timber to his satisfaction he began selling lots along the shore - the first one was conveyed to J. O. Newton in 1920.

On Main Street near Readfield Depot the street sign "Newton Lane" identifies a camp road. The cottages on Newton Lane do not stand out for any particular reason but the man behind that name does!

John O. Newton
1864 ~ 1958

John Orville "JO" Newton came from his native town of Andover, ME to Kents Hill as a student in 1882. After graduating from Wesleyan University in Connecticut in 1893 he returned to Kents Hill to teach. From there he became vice-principal in 1905 and in 1909 was promoted to headmaster. He remained in that role until 1923 when he and his wife went to California thinking they would remain there. The following year, when J.O. returned for the annual Kents Hill School reunion, he was persuaded by the trustees to return as head of the science department. He ultimately served as headmaster and teacher at Kents Hill School for 46 years and he filled various positions on the board of directors for 37 years. J.O. single handedly raised half the funds needed to build Newton Gymnasium in 1932 which was named in his honor. "Newton Hall" appears in large letters on that building to this day.

Community service was an exemplary part of J.O.'s life. He was the Readfield superintendent of schools for 6 years; a member of the Maine State Legislature; a Kents Hill Methodist Church trustee; and he served as Kennebec County Sheriff for 6 years. He also moderated Readfield town meetings which became a tradition for several Kents Hill headmasters after him. In 1946 his leg was broken in a car crash which slowed him down physically but he would not be stopped. He wrote *Kents Hill (School) and its Makers 1824-1947* while he was recuperating. J.O., it appears, was in perpetual motion and always looking for ways to make a difference.

J.O.'s life was not without trials. In 1893 he married Addie Denning, a Kents Hill alumnus. Ten years later she died in a boating accident on Echo Lake and he was left with three small sons – Max 8, Ronald 6 and Robert 5. Two years afterwards, at about the same time he became vice-principal, he married Louise Munroe, a nurse who was fifteen years younger than him. She took on the role of mother to his boys as well as "the first lady" at Kents Hill School; and later in life she stayed true to the school as alumni secretary. During WWI the influenza epidemic of 1918 struck; all three of the Newton children fell ill. Max and Ronald died within months of each other. Robert developed tuberculosis as a result and it eventually killed him too. J.O. and Louise never had children of their own.

Soon after the two older boys died J.O. and Louise bought waterfront property from George Coleman and had a cottage built. Perhaps during that time of deep personal grief they needed a retreat away from the hustle and bustle of the village and the Kents Hill School campus? After 1920 the Newtons spent summers at their getaway on Lake Maranacook.

Benjamin V. "B.V." Smith also worked at Kents Hill School as did his wife May (Williams), a Readfield native.[336] B.V. served as steward and May as school matron from 1911 until 1923. In reading *Kents Hill and its Makers* it becomes apparent that J.O. held Smith in high regard and they were, most likely, good friends. Newton wrote of "B.V." and May "…they were younger than most of their predecessors, and they entered heartily into school life… B.V showed excellent judgment in his duties, and took an active interest…he was a valuable man for the institution…"

Both men resigned their posts at Kents Hill School in 1923 and at the same time the Smiths bought a lake lot next door to J.O. & Louise. As previously mentioned the Newtons returned to the school a year later but the Smiths moved to Massachusetts and were never affiliated with Kents Hill School again. The couples did remain connected at a personal level.

In 1928 George Coleman put all of what remained of those 45 acres up for sale. J.O. Newton and Benjamin V. Smith purchased them all. They added cottages, improved the camp road, created a parking lot and began renting to vacationers. In 1939 the Kennebec Lakes Association published a promotional booklet which included listings for several Readfield rental cottages, kids' camps and other businesses. One entry reads "Furnished housekeeping cottages on Lake Maranacook, John O. Newton, Readfield Depot". Two years later Newton and Smith began to liquidate by selling small parcels of land and cottages. The last conveyance was made ten years later when J.O. was 87 and B.V. was 75. The Smiths were still residing in Massachusetts at that time and the Newtons were still calling Kents Hill their home.

In 1949 an 85th birthday party was held for J.O. at the Readfield Community House (Library). More than 100 people of all ages came. The guest list included several other couples who were running businesses similar to Newton's Camps including Mr. & Mrs. John Chase, Mr. & Mrs. Ralph Lane, Mr. & Mrs. Gene Dixon and Mr. & Mrs. Stanley Hight. A *Kennebec Journal* article written about the occasion gives a sense of just how much the man was loved and respected in the community he had called home for sixty-seven years.[337]

Although the Smiths lived in Maine for little more than a decade as a married couple they returned to Readfield in their final years to live on Church Road near her nephew Fred E. Williams.[338] May died in 1961 and B.V. in 1962 - both in their late 80s. They are buried in the Readfield Corner Cemetery. J.O. died in 1958 at age 94 and Louise followed him seven years later. They are buried in Kents Hill Cemetery with J.O.'s first wife Addie and their sons Max and Ronald. The third son, Robert, died in southern California in 1941 where he is buried. Neither couple had surviving children.

All these years later the name "Newton Lane" has endured. Nearer the lake Newton Lane extends into "Coleman Lane", named in honor of George Coleman who sold that very first lakeside lot to the Newtons in 1920.

Brown's Cove was known as "Sandy Beach"
by locals in the 1930-50s. Located south
of Newton's Camps, near Thorp Shores.

LANE'S COTTAGES ~ 1932

Have you ever noticed "Mildred Lane" when driving down Route 41 towards Winthrop and wondered how that name came to be?

For those who have lived in town for a long time the name Mildred Lane conjures up memories of the days when she and her husband Ralph ran the kitchen at Kents Hill School. He was the chef and pastry cook and "Millie" was his assistant. They worked there for nearly four decades and lived on campus during the school year.[339]

Millie and Ralph Lane, 1923.
Courtesy of Beverly Norton Newton

Ralph was a musician as well as a chef. With violin in hand he played solo for events and entertained as part of a group called "The Crusaders". The band appeared regularly at several halls in the area including "Island Park" in East Winthrop, "The Moon Glow" in Wayne, Manchester Grange Hall and at "Purgatory" in Litchfield.[340]

Millie was born in 1904 the youngest of eight children. Her father Nathaniel Adams was a farm laborer who moved the family from Penobscot County to Readfield before Millie was born. Ralph was born in 1898, a descendent of the Readfield pioneer, James Lane, who settled atop Kents Hill before 1770. Ralph's family lived on a large farm on Lane Road[341] for most of his youth. Mildred and Ralph were married in 1923 and never had children of their own.[342]

Between 1932 and 1936 Ralph bought thirty-five acres, and the right of way to it, on the west shore of Lake Maranacook in Readfield.[343] Ralph and his brother Carroll built two cottages there on the lakeshore. When the Kents Hill School kitchen closed for the summer Ralph and Millie moved into one of the camps and rented the other one to various parties throughout the season. Like other proprietors in this area's hospitality industry of the day, the Lanes soon developed a following and the same people came back year after year. Ralph's cousin Roger Lane related "We had neighbors in Livermore some years ago and they spent part of every summer down there at Ralph and Millie's camps."

The cottages were about 24x30feet with two bedrooms, a living room and kitchen.[344] Electricity was run to them sometime around 1948 and after that fully equipped kitchens and bathrooms were installed in each.

An interview with Emery Nason of Winthrop revealed that he built the access road into the cottages in 1973. "Before that it was just wheel tracks through the dirt down there" he said. "I rented a cottage there too for quite a few years. They were small but they had all my family needed. The Lanes were really nice people." Nason graded the Lane's camp road annually after he built it. "I was about the first one around here to do that kind of work" he said. "I had a little grader I pulled behind my dump truck. Didn't really do much more than push the dirt around a little bit and fill in the pot holes. Then later I bought a big grader and that did a better job. I graded about every camp road in Readfield and some in Fayette, Mt. Vernon and Winthrop too for quite a few years before Bill Rourke and John Cushing started doing it too." [345]

Ralph and Millie retired from cooking at Kents Hill School in the early 1960s. They bought a home on Winthrop Road, near their cottages, and lived there year round. "After Ralph died Millie kept the camps going. She was quite a trooper" said her cousin Roger. At age seventy-six Millie submitted a subdivision plan to the town of Readfield called "Mildred Lane subdivision; six camp lots on Lake Maranacook, formerly Lane's Cottages." [346] The year was 1980 when she began to sell off each of the lots; including the two cottages she had managed for almost fifty years. Millie died in 1993 having outlived Ralph by thirty years.

In 1999 the town of Readfield formed a committee to name all the roads in town for the new E911 system. At the end of one day that same year David Giroux and Evelyn Potter[347] were driving along the Winthrop Road with their assignment in hand – name all the roads that branch off route 41 in Readfield. As they passed where Lane's Cottages had once been David said "We still have to name that one." Evelyn responded "Yes, that is where Ralph and Mildred Lane's cottages used to be..." Without missing a beat David replied "Mildred Lane. That is what we will call that road. Mildred Lane." And so, with a quick stroke of David Giroux's pen the Lane legacy lived on.

In the early days men graded roads with horse drawn, handmade graders like the one pictured here. With the advent of motorized vehicles men like Emery Nason began pulling graders behind their trucks. By the mid 20th century special tractors were invented especially for that purpose. These men are grading Beaver Dam Road, Readfield

"...With its rich historical background, its lovely tree lined streets and winding lanes, its mellow old churches, its modern summer hotels, its fine summer camps for adults and sportsmen, its ideally located housekeeping camps, its splendidly equipped and staffed summer camps for boys and girls, Readfield offers a vacation to suit all tastes..." ~ Kennebec Lakes Association, 1939

MACES COTTAGES ~ 1937

In researching the families who owned this property, prior to the Maces, interesting discoveries were made starting with...

SPENCER'S LIVERY ~ 1871

Like "Hutchinson's Tavern" [348] this building sat on part of the original Daniel O. Craig homestead. (see pg 1)   In 1870 Frederick "Freddie" Spencer bought the entire Craig homestead, with all one-hundred acres, thanks to a loan from his mother Mariah (Smith) Spencer. A year later she extended Freddie a second loan and he built the structure we will call "Spencer's Livery". There will be more about that later.

Some members of the Smith-Spencer family were extensively involved in real estate investments and the hotel industry. To begin, Mariah Smith's father was Capt. John Smith who was a merchant, land speculator and attorney in Readfield.[349] His assets included vast land holdings. One of Mariah's sisters was Ursula Gile whose husband Asa was a local philanthropist, investor, and hotelier of the Elmwood at Readfield Corner.[350]   When Ursula and Mariah's father, died on December 3, 1860 he left them both a generous inheritance.

Mariah's husband, Maj. Frederick Spencer, was a merchant at Readfield Corner from 1845 until 1860 when he and Mariah moved to Belgrade. Maj. Spencer continued to operate a mercantile in Belgrade where their son Freddie worked alongside him. Sadly Maj. Spencer died a few months later, on the very same day that Mariah's father died!

Given the accumulated wealth of both men Mariah became a wealthy widow and heiress over night. That fact did not diminish her grief by any means nor did it help that, unlike her sister Ursula, she was essentially left to fend for herself. She seemed to cope by fleeing from the heaviness that surrounded her. She moved to Marlboro, Massachusetts where she lived for several years. By the time she returned to live near her son in Readfield he was in the process of buying the Daniel O. Craig homestead. She loaned him enough money to fund the purchase plus some extra to build "Spencer's Livery" across the road.

With that Freddie was set-up at an ideal location only a quarter-mile from the Readfield railroad station where "sports" and businessmen were arriving by train more and more frequently. His business also sat on the major land route from Hallowell to all points west that drummers and road travelers traversed. But that apparently did not meet his expectations. He soon set his sights towards another location.

In 1877 Freddie signed the lease on a boarding house and livery at the corner of Oak & Dickman Streets in Augusta, close to the Capital City's train station and Haymarket Square. In order to recoup the monies she had loaned him Mariah sold the Craig farm with fifty acres, plus a small land parcel with the livery to separate parties. Freeman A. Coombs, a "stable man" from Augusta bought the livery[351] on the very same day that Freddie signed his lease in Augusta. We must assume the two men had coordinated the transaction beforehand.

Freeman Coombs stayed in Readfield for six years[352] and returned to Augusta where he and his brother went into the livery and carriage making business as "Coombs Brothers". For years afterwards he was also the proprietor of the "Farmers Hotel and Livery" on Water St. in Augusta.[353] Coombs never returned to Readfield but kept his property there until he sold it to Jennie Brainard in 1890.[354]

By that time Jennie already owned fifty acres of property that abutted Spencer's livery. Her land included significant frontage on Lake Maranacook's eastern shore so the question arises... Did Jennie have plans to develop a lakeside resort at this location? Perhaps so, but it never happened because Cupid intervened.

Jennie Brainard married John W. Robbins of Augusta in 1893. Days before her wedding she sold her lakeside property and the livery to her father, Richard Brainard. Jennie moved to Augusta with her new husband where he worked as a baker and she ran a boarding house.[355] Jennie's sister Flora had married an Augusta man ten years earlier and she operated a boarding house in the city as well. All signs indicate there was significant interaction between Readfield and Augusta proprietors of such establishments during this era.

Although Richard Brainard was a tinware peddler by trade he converted the livery into a residence and rented it to one Jake Rogers. Brainard continued as a landlord until his death in 1904 at which time the rental and 50 acres went to his daughters, Jennie and Flora.

After Jake Rogers' death his step-son Freeman Galouch lived at the former livery with his family. It was always referred to as "the barn" by the Galouch children and grandchildren, although part of the inside had been converted into a pleasant residence.[356] Over time the building fell into disrepair and was taken down in a controlled burn in the 1990s.[357]

SOME SALTY OLD BRAINARDS

The first Brainard came to this area in 1785 but the name died out in Readfield many years ago. At this juncture we will share some tidbits about this family's contributions to Readfield "tourism" during earlier days.

Jennie Brainard's paternal grandparents were Benjamin and Mary Ann Brainard whose homestead (Collins 2015) was located in East Readfield. Benjamin's brother and wife, Asahel and Nancy

(Johnson) Brainard, lived next door as did their son Augustus (Vorpagel 2015).[358] A small body of water is nearby that was first called "Little Pond" but over the years its name changed to "Brainard Pond". Oral tradition says that Augustus and his wife Mary E. (Townsend) Brainard ran an inn at the larger of the two homesteads. Little is known of their operation except that Augustus used to pour bags of salt into Brainard Pond and then advertised "salt water bathing". [359] The success of his ploy is not known.[360]

In 1870 one Nancy Johnson,[361] age eighty-two, was living at the Benjamin Brainard homestead and taking in boarders. That year there were twenty men living there, most of them Irish and Canadian immigrants and all were laborers, carpenters and brick masons. The reason for such a concentration of these workers is a curiosity and the imagination goes towards wondering if there was a large construction project going on at the time, or a training program of some sort. There were several experienced masons, carpenters, housewrights and cabinet makers living in East Readfield around this time.

There is yet another connection to Mary E. (Mrs. Augustus) Brainard and to tourism in Readfield. Mary was a paternal aunt of Ernest Linwood Townsend, who owned and operated Townsend Farm. (see pg 98) She was an aunt to Nellie (Townsend) Collins and Lotta (Townsend) Collins whose husbands ran the Maranacook Hotel. (see pg 74) Suffice it to say the Brainard, Townsend and Collins clans were all interconnected and very much involved in the tourist industry of their day.

JENNIE BRAINARD'S DREAM ~ 1886

Jennie Brainard was twenty-one and single in 1886 when she paid Fred Spencer $250 for those fifty acres on Lake Maranacook. That was six years after Maranacook Grove opened so by that time activity on the lake was booming and Readfield Depot had become a bustling village. As previously mentioned, Jennie must have recognized how to profit from the opportunities before her and had set an eye towards the development of her own lakeside resort. Her marriage to John Robbins in 1893 changed any plans she may have had along that vein and she sold all her holdings in Readfield to her father, Richard.

Richard Brainard built a cabin on the lakeshore in 1894.[362] When he died ten years later the entire property went back to Jennie and to her sister Flora. It appears there were no further improvements made until after Flora's death in 1933 when her share was passed on to her son and daughter. Research indicates that Flora's son Merton built two more camps there[363] in 1934 and 1935.[364] Whether he constructed them for personal use or as rentals is not known but the family's reason for selling the property is known.

In 1937 Merton left Maine and moved to Rhode Island. By that time Jennie was in her seventies and obviously did not wish to maintain or keep the camps or the former livery in Readfield. Jennie, her nephew and niece sold everything to Roy Mace in 1937, including all fifty acres on Lake Maranacook.

MACES COTTAGES ~ 1937

"Mace's Cottages" sit on the eastern shore of Lake Maranacook one mile from the (former) train station in Readfield Depot village. Like the sites of the old livery and "Hutchinson's Tavern" this fifty acres was part of the original Daniel O. Craig homestead.[365]

Mace is a pioneer name in town. The first to come was Andrew Mace who settled in East Readfield before 1795.[366] Since then the family has maintained a prominent presence in this area as landowners, farmers, businessmen and in town government. Andrew's 3rd great grandson Roy and his son Everett owned several enterprises during their lifetimes including Mace's Cottages.

By 1937, when Roy Mace bought this property, housekeeping cottages had become popular among vacationers. Neighboring him to the east was "Brann's Camps" run by Bob and Eleanor Brann[367]; on his west J.O. Newton had built a group of housekeeping cottages; and a mile down the eastern shore E.E. Peacock's Kamp Peacock was in full swing.[368] It is not surprising that Roy and his wife Alice chose to take the same route.

The first thing Roy and Alice did was to name the existing three cottages "#1, 2 and 3". In the 1950s they added two more and later still they built a sixth which they named in succession as "Cottages # 4, 5 and 6".[369] Peter Mace, one of Roy and Alice's great-grandsons, owns the oldest camp on this property. He said in a recent interview "I was always told that my camp was over one-hundred years old. It's (still) pretty rustic" [370]

The railroad tracks do not intersect this property like they do at Pinerest and Lazy Loon further south. "Mace Cottage Road" extends from Main Street to the lake and along the shore. There is also a loop off Mace Cottage Road that is named "Alice's Way" in honor of Alice Mace.[371]

In 1939 Roy signed this property over to Alice - perhaps that was the same year she began renting the camps? Alice's name appeared in all their promotional materials as the proprietor. Many local people referred to this business as "Alice Mace's camps" but its official name was Mace's Cottages. Each of the six camps included private lake frontage, a dock and boat. Inside they were equipped with a heatilator, a full kitchen and bathroom with hot and cold running water. The "comfortable" living rooms had fieldstone fireplaces and on the front of each building a large piazza overlooked the lake. Five of the cottages had two bedrooms and "cottage #6" had four to accommodate larger parties. According to Mace's brochure the cottages were furnished with everything "except towels and dish linens".[372]

At the time of this writing Lenny and Sue Reay of Readfield own "camp #3". They knew Alice and her son Everett well having worked for both of them over the years and Lenny was raised by Everett from the time he was five years old. Sue speaks of how particular Alice was about how well the cottages were maintained and cleaned. She also had "camp rules" posted inside each building which she expected everyone to adhere to. "I helped with cleaning them for a while" said Sue. "The camps were completely cleaned after every (party) left. We had to wash every window between guests and Alice directed us what to use and how to clean them. It always had to be with vinegar and water and dry them with newspapers. There were so many windows in the big one (cottage #6) that we always dreaded cleaning that one. We had to defrost the refrigerators every time too. And if there were holes in the screens we had to patch those. Then Alice came and inspected them afterwards. At the beginning of the season a crew came in to rake all the grounds around the buildings and make sure everything looked nice and neat."

"The cottages were filled all summer" says grandson Peter. "Every once in a while there would be an open week and (our family) would stay down there but most of the time we just went down to rake the grounds and clean up between guests."

Reservations were made by calling Alice at her home in East Readfield, known to many as "the yellow house", and guests stopped at her house to pick up the key when they arrived in town. She continued to manage the cottages until an advanced age when she yielded to Everett in the 1980s. People continued to call "the yellow house" for reservations and for years afterwards they still dropped by there to say hello to Alice. She became an institution herself over the decades and many of her returning guests came to consider her a friend.[373]

Roy died in 1972 and Alice in 1991 at age ninety-six. Everett sold four of the cottages to people outside the family before his death in 2003, including cottage #3 to the Reays. The other two were passed on to his grandsons. Peter Mace now owns camp

#1 and his brother Larry owns camp #2. "My brother and I still rent ours out sometimes to people who have come here for vacations for years – since way back when my grandparents owned it," says Peter. "They come from all over – places like Pennsylvania, Colorado, New Jersey, Massachusetts and Connecticut. They love it up here away from the city. People have made a lot of good memories down there!"

Four generations of the Mace family in 1970. Sitting center is Alice Mace surrounded by her son Everett, grandson William and great-grandsons Peter and Larry.
Photo courtesy of Lenny and Sue Reay

CAMP KV ~ 1949

The land where "Camp KV" sits was originally part of Joshua Bean's 400 acre circa 1780 homestead. Bean's property bordered almost the entire northern end of Lake Maranacook in Readfield including where Tamsonhurst[374] (Millett Manor), Maranacook Community School, the Weathervane Restaurant, Readfield Town Beach and Camp KV are located today. When Lewis and Anne Millett bought Tamsonhurst in 1948 the Joshua Bean homestead had long since been subdivided but Millett's acquisition still encompassed the land where Camp KV is situated now.[375] The Milletts donated fifty-nine acres of their land to the Kennebec Valley Council of Girl Scouts (KVCGS) in 1949,[376] where the organization developed a day camp for Girl Scouts.

Mrs. Yvonne Turcotte of Augusta was the first director of Camp KV. She died in 2010 at the age of ninety-three after a long and active life. We were fortunate to speak with three of her children - Margaret Mast of Brunswick, Valerie Sulya of Bucksport and Jack Turcotte of Arundel. They all attended sessions at KV during its earliest years, when their mother worked there, and they enthusiastically shared some background and memories.[377]

Yvonne was an active Girl Scout leader in Augusta when Camp KV opened and someone from the Kennebec Valley Girl Scout Council asked her to accept the camp directorship. She hesitated at first but finally said yes when the Council agreed she could take along her three-year old son Jack and daughters Margaret, age eight and Valerie, age thirteen. All three described some of the positive effects KV had on their childhoods. Their father ran Turcotte's shoe repair shop in Augusta and they were a family of modest income who "didn't get out of Augusta too much" said Val. "Imagine what it was like for us to be able to leave the city every day and spend them at a place like Camp KV" Jack declared. "Some kids got to visit a camp on the lake for a week or two but we got to go every day all summer long." Val was thirteen when her mother accepted the job. "I was older so she put me in charge of the special unit for little kids which my mother named 'the Chickadees'. Jack was in that group and he was the only boy at our Girl Scout camp. We tease him about that to this day" she said with a chuckle. "Sometimes he acted out and I had to send him to the office – in other words to my mother so she could straighten him out." Jack doesn't recall that but did say "I remember we were proud of our mother – she was the 'the big shot' and she was a take charge kind of lady. She liked the kids but she wasn't shy about managing problems when she had to." Yvonne's children spent the day immersed in activities alongside the other campers. "She was busy at KV so we didn't see much of her when we were there." Val shared "Mother had everyone split into their own groups and lined them all up along the lake shore. We went into the woods and gathered pine cones and things to make arts & crafts. Mother had a strict schedule and lots of different projects planned for every minute and she kept the Scouts occupied all day long. She had several women helping her. Everything we did was towards earning our (Girl Scout) badges." Val learned to swim at KV relating "It was pretty shallow and mucky there but there was a nice swimming area all fixed up with a dock and we were given swimming lessons too." When asked what she liked most about Camp KV Val said "Setting goals and doing something together (with my family) during the summer instead of staying in the city."

Jack was quite philosophical in his memories about Camp KV. "It was a highlight of my growing up. I developed interest in the out-of-doors that has always stayed with me. We rode the bus which was a real social time for everyone. It seemed like 5,000 miles from Augusta to Readfield…that was really out in the woods for us back then. We sang songs on the bus and that is where I learned to like music. I played football and was in the band at Cony (High School) and I don't know if I would have if it hadn't been for (my experiences) at Girl Scout camp. We also learned the importance of ceremony and patriotism...We had very positive experiences at Camp KV and I made some long term relationships there too." Chuckling he added "but they were girls of course." With warmth in his voice Jack reflected "I still think of those times when I happen to drive by there."

Some Readfield natives also shared memories of Camp KV from the 1950s and 1960s. Joanne (Fogg) Fournier, age 65 of Saco was a seven year old Brownie when she attended. "I was a day camper and went on a bus. I remember that I loved it... We had to bring a sandwich but I think they gave us a drink and lots of s'mores. (It was the) first time I ever had s'mores and I loved them. I learned to swim, made lots of arts & crafts, and played field games. I can still weave a lanyard and swim!" Elaine Moore, age 69 of Wilton went as a Girl Scout and told how she made a square dancing outfit her last summer there and got her sewing badge for it. Dottie Macomber, age 62 of Woburn, MA says "The thing I remember most about Camp KV was the arts and crafts. I still have a clay ashtray (boy, that's a sign of those times!) that I made there – kind of a brick colored clay with a glossy blue glaze on the rim!" And finally, Wendy (Nett) Ross, age 64 of Fort Fairfield simply but powerfully pointed out "It was the best childhood experience ever!"

In the early 1970's financial strain forced the KVCGS to close the camp and the property went to public auction. Dr. Robert Mohlar of Readfield was a member of the newly formed Readfield Conservation Commission (RCC) at that time. He recounted how members of the RCC recognized that developers would no doubt buy and sub-divide the land. The group went to work immediately to raise community awareness in hopes the camp could be preserved for public use and continued as a summer camp for children. Donald Laubenstein and Jack Smart of Readfield and several other business people from the Augusta area led the charge and formed the Camp KA VE Committee. They managed to place the winning bid and signed the 59 acre Camp KV for Kids over to the Kennebec Valley YMCA in

March, 1975. When the KA VE Committee transferred it they stipulated the property should "not be used for any purpose other than for the benefit of youth of the area." [378] There was a great deal of community and philanthropic support behind this effort and by 1995 it was fully endowed.[379]

The Kennebec Valley YMCA has operated Camp KV as a state-licensed co-ed day camp since 1975. Children enjoy days filled with swimming, boating, arts & crafts, nature hikes, archery and field sports all the while learning to practice the YMCA's core values of caring, honesty, respect and responsibility.[380]

In 2012 Camp KV began hosting a one-week camp founded by Julia Clukey, an Augusta native and Luge Olympian. "Julia Clukey's Camp for Girls" is designed "as a place to develop self-confidence and a healthy lifestyle" for girls ages eight through twelve.[381] Additional to the activities offered by the YMCA's day camp Clukey's program includes theater, music, a rope course, gardening and fishing. She also provides educational sessions for the girls based on her own life experiences.[382] Enrollment increased exponentially as youngsters came from all over New England and New York. As of this writing Clukey's program can accommodate one-hundred campers at once.[383]

As Camp KV approaches its seventieth year it faces yet another phase of its evolution. In 2015 a 1,116 square foot director's cabin was added to the Camp KV facility, made possible by $100,000 in donations. The new building sits on higher ground than the original directors' cabin, which was built in the 1940s, so its wrap around deck provides a panoramic view of Lake Maranacook. The new building includes an improved kitchen, infirmary and more expansive changing areas. Perhaps the most progressive component however is a heating system[384] which makes Camp KV available for four-season use for the first time since it began in 1949.

To this day when Jack Turcotte and his sisters get together they sing old Girl Scout tunes. "We'll sing something like the round song Make new Friends but keep the old, one is silver and the other is gold" said Jack, "and then we'll just look at each other and say 'Do you remember'?"

In this vintage photo of the trestle note the difference in its structure. In those days the steamboat Maranacook had an articulated stack so it could be bent to create clearance.

The trestle over Lake Maranacook as it looks today. It extends over the narrowest point of the Lake commonly called by 19th century landowners "the narrows at North Winthrop Pond".

WIND STORM HITS LAKE MARANACOOK ~ 1952

WINTHROP… Hurricane like winds and a driving rain with hail in some areas lashed southwestern Maine yesterday, causing thousands of dollars of damage as trees fell across roads, homes and cottages and phone and light service throughout the state took a beating. Memorial Drive, on the eastern shore of Maranacook Lake at Winthrop, was one huge lumber camp today. Men from surrounding communities joined summer residents and cottagers in a gigantic effort to clear thousands of huge trees toppled and broken up like matchsticks by the brief powerful tornado which twisted through this section late yesterday afternoon. The point on which was formerly located Tallwood Inn, for many years a famous Maine resort, was a scene of devastation. The twister cut the trees there about 20 feet from the ground, just as if a huge sickle had been swept across the point. Several of the cottages were damaged by the falling treetops. This morning Tallwood looked like a no man's land. The huge pines which made it famous for the most part were ugly broken stumps. The eight minute storm happened here at 5:53pm yesterday afternoon. ~ *Lewiston Evening Journal,* July 29, 1952

Above and below are two more photos taken at Tallwood Peninsula after the twister of July, 1952. Several cottages were destroyed as well as the huge Pine trees that once graced the entire area. The Pontiac in the photo above belonged to Ruth Townsend. See the story on the previous page.

All three photos courtesy of the Townsend family

FOLSOM BROTHERS DAY CAMP FOR BOYS ~ 1961

"They had a real handle on a boy's psyche and excellent instincts" said Schuyler Ludwig of Vienna, a former camper at Folsom Brothers Boys Camp. "I was only there for two weeks one summer but it had a big impact on me" said Ludwig. "I went on to run track and field at Cony High School because of the confidence I gained there. Today I am 62 years old, in good shape and still able to work as a carpenter thanks to what I got from the Folsoms." [385]

This boys' camp, for first-grade through high school ages, was situated on fifty acres in a cove on the western shore of Lake Maranacook.[386] Part of the property had been owned by the Maranacook Hotel Company at one time.[387] Bob and Elaine Folsom were residing in Manchester when they bought the land in 1960 and by the following summer Bob had established the camp with thirteen boys in attendance. Enrollment increased to sixty-four campers by 1968.[388] Bob and his brother Bud ran the camp for fifteen years[389] and another brother, Bill, worked with them when they offered additional outdoor adventures.

The campground included an arts & crafts building called "aqua hut", a regulation little league baseball diamond; an 8,000 sq. ft. basketball court which was later converted for tennis; a "pee-wee basketball" court for the little guys; an air gun range; an archery course; and water frontage where swimming, lifesaving, rowing and canoeing were taught. Throughout the woods there were tents and teepees where the boys learned Indian and nature lore, camp craft, fire building, tent pitching, pioneering and knot tying.[390] A lodge, where members of the Folsom family lived during the summer season, was located near the water's edge.

When Skip and Joyce Adell first moved into their house on the Winthrop Road in 1962 the Folsom's camp road was uncomfortably close to it. Joyce recalled that when the school buses came and went from Folsoms Camp she watched very closely because her boys were real small then and she needed to keep them from harm's way. [391] That is no longer the case because the route, known today as Cove Road, was eventually moved.

Indeed, campers did come in by school bus from Augusta, Hallowell, Manchester and Winthrop. The Folsoms arranged pick-up points according to where their campers lived and provided transportation from as near their homes as possible.[392] Upon arrival at Folsoms there was first a ceremonial raising of the American flag and the boys were given their activity assignments. That varied on opening day when introductions were made followed by a review of the rules called "The Three NO's" – 1. NO matches; 2. NO leaving camp; and 3. NO unauthorized swimming or going into the water. At the end of each day military taps was played.[393]

It was 1965 and Schuyler Ludwig was a youngster living in Chelsea when he was first introduced to the Folsom family. "I took swimming lessons at the Augusta YMCA from Bud. He was larger than life". Bud told about the activities offered at the Folsom's camp and the stories caught Ludwig's interest. He asked to go and his parents arranged to send him. Each morning he boarded a school bus in Augusta with 50 to 60 other local boys – all with bag lunches, swim suits and towels in hand. They were not required to wear uniforms or bring equipment - T-shirts and sneakers were required garb. There were Folsom Brothers T-shirts available for sale but even those were not required.[394]

From all descriptions it seems this camp was more like a mission for the Folsom brothers than a way to significantly augment their livelihoods. They were educators and coaches in their "other lives". Bob, who was the camp's owner and director, was the father of five and assistant professor in charge of recreation and intramural athletics at the University of Southern Maine in Portland. It appears he and Bud simply wanted to touch the lives of boys in positive ways; especially those who would otherwise not have a camping experience, or opportunities to enjoy part of the summer on a lake. Bob sometimes accepted campers on the barter system rather than turn a boy away for financial reasons.[395] In spite of that he did not short-change the organization in any way, most especially with staff members which included teachers from area schools and college students who had years of camping experience.[396]

Come late August, after the final two week session of the summer, additional offerings were made available for older boys. These included overnight baseball and basketball clinics at Folsom's campground, and canoe and camping trips of several days duration. Jim Schmidt, who currently lives in Readfield, was one of Folsoms' earliest counselors. In 1965 he served as the director of one such excursion when boys ages 11 to 14 camped and paddled the Belgrade Lakes for four days.[397] Another trip, for 12 to 18 year olds, extended for five-days and fifty miles from Pemaquid Pond, through a chain of lakes to East Bristol, then up the Pemaquid River to the Damariscotta River and eventually to Nobleboro. Ever safety conscious, the Folsoms began those adventures at their campground on Lake Maranacook with a sunrise breakfast and a full day of safety training before they even got started. Folsoms' overall goal was "for campers to have a good time and at the same time enjoy the learning process."[398] In this case the boys were taught campfire cooking, map reading and camping as well as canoeing.[399]

Back at camp, four or more counselors worked with Bob and Bud to keep the boys engaged in activities for the entire day. Ludwig related stories of their playing baseball, basketball, swimming and arts & crafts. After lunch they enjoyed a round of "capture the flag". Other sports included soccer and volleyball, in addition to nature study, fishing derbies and canoeing.[400] They were also given some free time and a movie titled "The Big Adventure" was shown in the event of rain.[401] Some activities were not planned ahead but added spontaneously such as making totem poles, building dams, or constructing a pioneer village deep in the woods.[402] An Indian named "Wasagumpi" also visited the camp several times each summer to introduce stories and crafts from his culture.[403]

Ludwig stressed that safety was always an important part of the Folsom experience. They were given demonstrations on how to carefully use an ax and split firewood, and target practice with air guns was done under close supervision. A highlight was the water safety course. "Bob and Bud had us watch for mistakes while they gave us canoe lessons. They always ended up in a Charlie Chaplin like slap stick comedy skit that made us all laugh while we were learning."

At the finale of each two-week session an overnight jamboree was held. There were no bunkhouses so the boys pitched tents in the field and roughed it. They built a campfire and experienced some other typical evening pastimes.

"I didn't hold back" said Ludwig "and I became more advanced because the Folsoms encouraged us so much. After that I never went back to Folsoms' Camp because my parents sent me to a different camp" said Ludwig. "But nothing there ever compared to what I learned from Bud and Bob Folsom."

The Folsom Brothers Boys Camp was discontinued in 1975 but some Folsom family members still own the property. Bob and Elaine's daughter, Deb Harvey, is the keeper of their scrapbooks and mementos. "I am thrilled that what they did here is going down in history in (this) book" said Deb. More importantly the Folsom brothers' legacy lives on through men like Schuyler Ludwig, their children and by now, no doubt, their grandchildren as well.

Bob Folsom (kneeling center) with four of his counselors and the campers in 1971. Counselor Jim Schmidt is standing far right.

Bob Folsom with "Wasagumpi"

The Folsom brothers of Augusta, Bill, Bud and Bob have scheduled a regional basketball clinic Aug 30-Sept 5th at their camp on Lake Maranacook, Readfield. If it is successful it will become an annual occurrence. (K J caption, date unknown)

The lodge where members of the Folsom family lived when camp was in session. 2015 photo

LAKE MYRA (CRAIG'S MILL POND)

On the stream that runs from Torsey Pond into Lake Maranacook in Readfield there used to be a mill pond on "Factory Square". A "new" stone dam replaced the old one in 1845 which created a fairly significant reservoir. Its purpose was to generate power for several mills and factories that existed around it. Over the years the pond was also enjoyed by fisherman, skaters, swimmers and young explorers. When the dam was breached in the "500 Year Flood" of 1987 there went the mill pond. Today the Readfield Trails Committee is developing a trail system at and around the old dam site.

For several of the years between 1865 and 1949 the mill pond was called "Lake Myra" by Mrs. Myra Mitchell. She and her husband owned the "Gov. Hunton house" nearby which she named "The Larches". (Harris 2016)

THE LARCHES ~ 1870

Any memory of the Mitchells, the Larches and Lake Myra had long ago vanished until an old photograph was presented to a Readfield Historical Society volunteer several years ago. Subsequent research revealed this story.

Dr. Joseph and Myra Mitchell were natives of Newfield, Maine who moved south to Jacksonville, FL in 1852 due to the strain of winter weather "up north". When the Civil War erupted Dr. Mitchell bought a house in Readfield from Gov. Anson P. Morrill and he moved his wife and sons there to safety. Mitchell then joined the Union Army as a physician surgeon, serving with the 8th Maine and later with the 31st Maine.

Their house in Readfield was known as the "Gov. Jonathan Hunton house" when the Mitchells bought it because Hunton and his wife had previously owned the property. The story goes that Hunton had planted several Larch trees near the building which provided blessed shade when they matured - thus Myra named the house "The Larches." After the war Dr. and Mrs. Mitchell returned to Jacksonville but continued to summer in Readfield where they also offered accommodations to summer visitors. This gives us the justification for including their fascinating story in our book.

Soon after their return to Jacksonville Dr. Mitchell built a 50 bed hotel called "The Union Hotel". He did this so any Union soldiers who wanted to experience recovery and respite in a warm climate would have this place to stay. Dr. Mitchell's hotel was the impetus for the northern Florida tourism that began and evolved after the Civil War. It was not until years later that tourism spread further south in that state.

Myra was equally as ambitious. For one, in 1872 she and two other women from Jacksonville founded St. Luke's Hospital. At that time the capacity of local hospitals was inadequate and non-residents were turned away. Myra and her friends were adamant that sick tourists should receive necessary medical care. St. Luke's Hospital was the result of their convictions.

Like their father, both of Dr. Mitchell's sons, Sollace and Neal, were successful physicians in northern Florida. Neal was also involved in the hotel business. He and his wife Mary owned the Aragon Hotel in Jacksonville along with other properties. After Neal died his wife continued to operate the hotel with her second husband, calling the business "Trail's End Co".

Dr. Neal Mitchell bought the Asa Gile mansion on Main Street (see pg 37) in Readfield in 1905 from Mrs. William Harvey. He had plans to open that to summer tourists like his mother had at the Larches. Neal died an untimely death however, in 1911, so plans along those lines never materialized.

The patriarch Dr. Joseph Mitchell died in 1893. Myra made her annual treks to Maine, where she continued to welcome visitors at the Larches until her death in 1915. After that her son Sollace used the house as his summer home and later on his son Sollace II lived there year-round with his family until he sold it in 1949. Today Will and Bonnie Harris call the Larches home.

The Larches in 1914 with Myra Mitchell (left) and
a guest sitting in that blessed shade of the Larch trees.

Looking east on Old Kents Hill Road, Readfield near
The Larches. On the right is the mill pond that
Myra Mitchell called "Lake Myra".
A guest cabin can also be seen near the water's edge.

The camps described on pages 209-228 were built on Torsey Pond

TORSEY POND

The lower end was called "the swamp lot" by those who settled in Readfield in its earliest days. Running through the swamp lot there was a stream that was fed by a subterranean flow and from springs on the surrounding highland. The stream's drop of forty-one feet from the origin and southeast towards Chandler's Mill Pond (Lake Maranacook), was significant enough to supply power to several mills. But no one paid it any particular mind until James Craig built his grist mill and saw mill further downstream. Soon after that Robert Cornforth built a woolen mill near Craig's establishment and that section of town became known as Factory Square.

There was still water power to be had further upstream though, which Joel Bean finally tapped into ten years later when he built his own saw mill, grist mill and fulling mill. A small basin at the headwater could, with some human ingenuity, generate additional power. Bean rigged up a crib dam at the stream's outlet adding boards that he could set in place or remove to control the flowage and water power to his mills. That dam increased the size of the basin enough that people started calling it "Bean's Mill Pond" and the stream was dubbed Bean's Mill Stream as well.

Joel Bean and his sons came to own nearly the entire east side and the southern end of the pond in Readfield and Mt. Vernon. At least five Bean farms sprung up along what we now know as Stonewall Drive, Torsey Shores, and Old Kents Hill, Thundercastle and Chase Roads. After Joel Bean died in 1828 his family was no longer engaged in the mill business. By then there were four dams on Bean's Stream between his mills and Factory Square. Thereafter businessmen clamored for the water rights on the full length of the waterway whenever the sale of mills on Factory Square transpired.

In about 1872 a new and more substantial dam was built adjacent to Bean's mills (on Old Kents Hill Road). By 1879 the swamp lot had completely flooded which doubled the size of Bean's Pond. The man responsible for building the new dam was named Greeley so now people started calling it "Greeley Pond". The remains of Greeley's dam, which the road from Readfield Corner to Kents Hill once passed over, is still there as are the foundations and sluiceways for Bean's mills.

Dr. Henry Torsey

Dr. Henry P. Torsey was a Monmouth native who attended several terms at Maine Wesleyan Seminary (Kents Hill School). Then, in 1844, he became the headmaster at a time when the school was on the verge of financial ruin. Through hard work and personal sacrifice he nearly doubled enrollment in one year and remained devoted to the school as headmaster for thirty-eight years. Torsey gained the respect of people throughout this area and beyond, including that of Maine Gov. James Blaine and President Abraham Lincoln who offered Torsey the governorship of one of the U.S. territories. He declined that and other opportunities and remained steadfast to the school and the Kents Hill Methodist Church.[404] Torsey was an avid fisherman and especially enjoyed fishing on Greeley Pond where he spent many hours in solitude and contemplation. After he died, in 1892, the townspeople showed their admiration for him by renaming the church and Greeley Pond in his memory.

CAMP CEBENNEK ~ 1900
CHASE LODGE & COTTAGE COLONY

From the author: Chases Camps on Torsey Pond was not far from my childhood home and since my mother is the Readfield historian[405] I grew up hearing that it was the first camp for boys started in Maine. When the time came to learn more through research a challenge ensued for neither of us knew it was also called "Cebennek". Research indicated the first session was held in 1900 not in 1898 as first thought. The land for Chases Camps was carved out of the Albert and Franklin Bean homesteads. The Maine Youth Camping Foundation was unable to confirm when the first kids' camp was established in Maine.[406]

The founder of this camp was John A. Chase, the oldest child of Rev. A. Fitzroy "A.F." and Louise (Allen) Chase. John came from a line of educators, clergy and scholars on both his mother and father's side of the family. His maternal grandfather, Rev. Stephen Allen, served as headmaster and trustee at Maine Wesleyan Seminary (Kents Hill School); and he was one of the founders of both Bates College in Lewiston and the University of Maine at Orono. He also authored several scholarly works including the *History of Methodism in Maine.*

John Chase's father and paternal grandfather were both teachers. By the age of three his father, A.F., had already developed a passion for literature and throughout his childhood he read and retained everything within his grasp. Both A.F. and his future wife Louise Allen attended Kents Hill School in the 1860s. After that he went on to Wesleyan University in Connecticut and then returned to Maine and married Louise in 1869. Two years later they returned to Kents Hill School where A.F. joined the faculty and served as the librarian and head of the mathematics and literature departments for twelve years. There he earned the reputation of brilliant scholar, strong leader and adept orator. The Chases had five children, four of whom survived to adulthood, and all were born at the Chase's home on Kents Hill, which they named "Jollity Manse".[407] Their children were - John A., Crystal M., Joseph C. and Louise S.[408] Some of A.F.'s and the Allen's genius was inherited by John and his siblings.

In 1883 the Chase family moved to Bucksport, Maine where A.F. taught advanced math at Bucksport Seminary Preparatory School for the next fourteen years. John Chase's grandaughter, Stephanie Wilson Hatch, related this story. The first year that A.F. was teaching calculus in Bucksport he was stricken with diphtheria. There was no substitute to take his place. John was a brilliant mathematician by then even though he was only eight years old so he filled in for his father. He had to stand on a box in order to see the students over the instructor's desk.

As a young man John became very ill and was told by the family doctor that he needed to spend more time outside in the fresh air to fully recover. "He knew how to mix paint colors" said grandaughter Hatch "so he became a painter." Perhaps he learned about paints from his younger brother Joseph, who was an artist? Through that work, tells Hatch, John gained a fondness for the out-of-doors. With his love for nature said another grandaughter, Dorothy (Wilson) Crockett, John became quite an expert at identifying flowers and birds. He also became skilled at building and repairing things such as canoes. He enjoyed working with his hands. Those abilities would serve him well.

In 1897 A.F. was offered the position of headmaster at Kents Hill School and the Chase family enthusiastically returned to Readfield. Across the street from the main campus they had a twenty-five room house built which is known today as "Chase Hall". According to grandaughter Hatch the Chases had the largest personal library in the State of Maine at that time and it filled twelve or thirteen of those rooms. Most of the books were first editions.[409]

John attended medical school but instead of entering that field he accepted a teaching position. He got the idea for Chase's Camp when he was teaching at the prestigious Haverford Preparatory School for boys in Philadelphia.[410] He soon observed that come summer vacation his students and their parents were at a loss for where the boys could go and what activities would keep them entertained for two months. John came up with the idea of opening a summer camp in Readfield for boys ages 9 through 12. They would spend a few weeks living in tents on Torsey Pond near his native Kents Hill, followed by an extensive canoe trip in the wilds of Maine. His idea was well received and enough boys signed up to make it a go.

Over the years John had business partners. First, one of his colleagues from Philadelphia and later he brought on a Greenville man with knowledge of the big woods who had guide experience. According to grandaughter Hatch, the campers came by train from Pennsylvania to Boston where they joined others coming in from Connecticut, Rhode Island and the Boston area. From there they continued their journey together on the "Downeaster" into Readfield Depot. In early July of 1905 the Kennebec Journal (KJ) reported "A party of twelve boys arrived from Philadelphia, Thursday, and will pass the summer at Chase Camp under the direction of John Chase, who will be assisted by Arthur Palmer. The culinary department will be in the charge of Thomas A. Dow, chief (cook) of the seminary (Kents Hill School)…" The following summer the KJ reported "Camp Chase has about 25 boys who are spending the summer there. This is a much larger number than usual." In August of 1916 Chase and his partner Robert Meade Smith, Jr. of Haverford, PA incorporated as Camp Cebennek Company.[411] Five years later a *Harper's Magazine* ad read "Camp Cebennek, famous Allagash canoe trip. Twenty-first season, boys 12 to 16. One month at main camp, one month on canoe trip. Best of equipment. All land and water sports. Junior boys ages 9 to 12." Some ads also touted "Best fishing and photography of big game" as additional camp offerings. A 1939 advertisement read "Camp Cebennek for Boys…two weeks on Torsey Lake, seven weeks on Allagash Canoe Trip…"[412] Eventually Chase's Camp was in operation four months of the year, from May to October, said grandaughter Stephanie Hatch.

John married Irene Drisko in 1904 and their only child Dorothy, whom they called "Tommy", was born the following year. Interestingly she was also an avid reader from an early age, noted Hatch. "By the time my mother was 9 yrs old her favorite book was *Vanity Fair*." Irene and Tommy did not go to Philadelphia to live with John during the school year but they remained at Chase Hall on Kents Hill. Irene was an independent woman to be sure – some might say a woman ahead of her time. Hatch told of the dances her grandmother held at Chase Hall which were frowned upon by the old-fashioned women in the neighborhood. But Irene enjoyed entertaining and paid them no mind. "My grandparents kind of did their own thing" said Hatch, but as she talked on it became apparent the couple was also an effective business team.

Tents were in use at Chase Camp for a short time before John started building bunkhouses. The first one he put up was 'Brookside" and others soon followed until there were eleven[413] in addition to a lodge and dining hall. The cabins were empty while John and his campers were away for their month long canoe trips. At that point thirty to forty Chase family members and friends moved in for their summer vacations. "They liked the fishing and the food" said granddaughter Crockett. Irene realized there was a business opportunity there so she organized "Chases Camps and Cottage Colony" and began taking reservations from paying guests. As with most summer resorts and rental cottages they built up a following and the same city dwellers returned year after year. A fully staffed kitchen, dining room, office and grounds crew kept the camp running smoothly with Irene's adept guidance. Crockett told of the French Canadian lumber camp cook who her grandfather hired for the Allagash trips. His name was Henry Beaulieu. Irene liked Henry's cooking so she "hired him away" from John. She gave Henry her own recipes which he prepared with finesse and he continued working at Chases Camps for years. When it was time to retire Henry trained his son Bernard to carry on. After Bernard went into the Army Irene hired local cooks.

Cebennek ceased operating soon after the onset of WWII. Transporting the boys from the city became problematic, and most of the older boys joined the service so John couldn't get counselors. "But the wealthy people who were accustomed to vacationing in Europe could not go overseas during the War so they started coming to us" said Hatch. "So the War gave the cottage rental end of our business a bit of a boon." Many of those prestigious guests, from New York City and "main-line Philadelphia" had sent their sons to Cebennek in the years prior.

Dorothy Chase Wilson
Courtesy of Stephanie Hatch

The Chases' daughter Dorothy participated in running the camps as well. She married Dick Wilson of Brooklyn, NY in 1928 and they lived in New York until they retired. At that point they bought a house on Kents Hill and moved there permanently. Dorothy and Dick took over Chases Camps when Irene became older but as they got older themselves it became necessary to sell. In 1972 they subdivided the property and sold the camps to individuals. Most of the original structures remain to this day. In walking the grounds, one can still see signs on some of the buildings and byways that reflect the past such as "Tree Top",

"The Birches", "Rose Point", "Pine Point", "Wilson Way" and, of course, "Chase Road".

Rose Point, Chase Camps, Torsey Pond, Readfield, Maine

Ralph Ives designed his bunkhouses at
Camp Thunderbird (see pg 225) after "the Birches"
at Chases Camps, pictured above

Irene Drisko Chase
1882-1974

Kennebec Journal, June 1964:
John A. Chase, 89, died Sunday at Chase's Camp on Torsey. He was born at Kents Hill on May 15, 1875... He graduated from Ohio Wesleyan College in Delaware, Ohio and Columbia University School of Physicians and Surgeons. He operated one of the first boys camps in the state and was originator of the Allagash canoe trip for camp boys... He was a member of Layfayette Lodge AF&M... He was also past patron of the Layfayette Chapter OES. He has lived at Kents Hill for 60 years...

CHASE LODGE and COTTAGE COLONY

on Torsey Lake, Readfield, Maine

Offer in beautiful woodland setting, unexcelled smallmouth black bass fishing, land and water sports, games and music in recreational lodge, central dining-room, charming modern cottages along the lakeshore. American plan. Special rates June 20 to July 31. *Booklet and rates.*

MRS. JOHN CHASE

Readfield   Maine

This ad appeared in "Field & Stream" in 1955

Hirundo was a boys' camp that existed for only seven years. After that the cabins were rented out to summer guests. It was located on the lakeside property of John and Abby Coryell and was founded by one of their four sons. In 1915 the "Handbook of Private Schools for American Boys and Girls" published an entry for Camp Hirundo which read: "This boys' camp established by Harold H Coryell (is) to provide an environment (that makes) the summer profitable as well as pleasurable. The boys are encouraged to develop hobbies, to build dams etc. There are one hundred acres of woods meadows and pasture."

CAMP HIRUNDO ~ 1915

John Russell "J.R." Coryell of New York City and his wife Abby, an Augusta native, bought land on the north end of Torsey Pond in Mt. Vernon in 1907. There they built a house that was fit for year round living but they never did live there through all four seasons. J.R. was a prolific dime novel author who wrote under several pseudonyms including Nicolas Carter and Bertha M. Clay. Local lore says the couple planned to use the Mt. Vernon home as a summer retreat where J.R. could sink deep into writer's mode. Their great-grandaughter, Susan Roberts, explained there may have been more to it than that.

In New York City the Coryells were friends of the well known anarchist Emma Goldman. J.R. was a collaborator and contributor to Goldman's controversial magazine "Mother Earth" which was first published in 1906.[414] Goldman wrote of the Coryells in her autobiography saying "I came to know many persons of advanced ideas...among them were John R. and Abby Coryell...John possessed exceptional depth of mind...had travelled extensively (which gave) him a wider outlook on life and a deep understanding of human beings...He was one of the most generous men I have met. His writings had brought him a fortune, of which he kept almost nothing, giving lavishly to those in need...His greatest charm lay in his sense of humor, no less incisive because of his polished manner...The Coryells were (among) my dearest American friends..." [415]
"I think they may have actually gotten into some trouble (with Goldman) in the city" said Susan "and I think my grandfather

may have even been arrested at one point. Some family members believe they actually left New York City to escape escalating troubles there." [416] Indeed, Goldman wrote of such events: "We organized a 'Mother Earth Club' giving weekly lectures on various topics...The police were furious, they had been hounding us for nine weeks...and still we would not be put down...Something more drastic and intimidating had to be done to save the sacred institutions of law and order. The next move of the authorities took place at a meeting that was to be addressed by Alexander Berkman, John R. Coryell, and Emma Goldman. They arrested all the speakers..." [417] This was in late May of 1906 and the following May the Coryell's bought the property in Mt. Vernon, Maine.

Thus it is understandable why some of their family members believe that J.R. and Abby Coryell's winter-worthy house was built in the woods of Maine, in virtual obscurity, in 1907.

J.R. died in 1924, Abby outlived him by thirty-three years. She sold some of the lakefront to her three sisters soon after J.R. died and they had a cottage built which was fully enjoyed every summer by "the Aunties". The rest of the Coryell homestead was retained by J.R. & Abby's sons - Harold, Roland, Hubert and Russell. They all attended college and pursued careers out of state and never lived in Mt. Vernon fulltime. Hubert became a teacher and author and his accomplishments were many. Russell was also an author and a world traveler. Their brother Roland became an osteopathic physician. Harold, the eldest, was a real estate agent and salesman as well as the founder of Camp Hirundo. His granddaughter Susan, her twin brothers David and Harold Roberts, and several other family members own the Coryell property to this day. "From what I understand Hirundo is an Indian name for swallow and we do have a lot of swallows around here" said Susan.

At Camp Hirundo's outset a large platform was built where tents were set-up for the young campers until cabins could be constructed. The platform later served as the foundation for a two-story lodge complete with a dining room and working kitchen. There was no running water in the early days so they had to carry drinking water in from elsewhere. The cabins were "built by master carpenter Roy Giles of Readfield" said Susan "and they are very well made!" The boys' camp was short lived for reasons unknown. After it ceased operations Harold, his mother and wife Rose rented the cabins to summer guests. According to advertisements from the late 1920s they continued to call their establishment Hirundo.[418] Abby Coryell cooked on a woodstove in the lodge and served guests in the dining room there. "She was a legendary cook from what I hear" said Susan.

Most of their summer guests were artists and authors from New York City so the Coryell compound essentially became an artist's colony every summer. Susan related a story told to her by artist Ina Tillman, now in her 90s and living in Los Angeles. One summer during WWII Ina was the only guest who could make it there from the Bronx and the experience was life-changing. Shortages of fuel, supplies, food staples and fresh meat forced them to use their ingenuity. One evening, after dark, a local farmer brought them a freshly slaughtered chicken. In order to conserve lamp kerosene they gathered in front of a car's headlights to pluck the chicken feathers. Ina returned to Hirundo the following year, after the war had ended, but there were more people there and it was not the same.

In driving about the compound today one sees several arteries extending off Coryell Lane that are named in honor of the four sons – Harold, Roland, Hubert and Russell. The fourth generation of the Coryell family now owns and occupies Hirundo's lodge and cabins. They treasure the property and its' history enough to have preserved the character of each building.

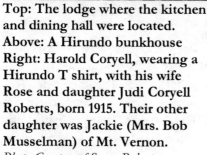

Top: The lodge where the kitchen and dining hall were located.
Above: A Hirundo bunkhouse
Right: Harold Coryell, wearing a Hirundo T shirt, with his wife Rose and daughter Judi Coryell Roberts, born 1915. Their other daughter was Jackie (Mrs. Bob Musselman) of Mt. Vernon.
Photo Courtesy of Susan Roberts

ARMSTRONG'S / FIVE SEASONS ~ 1919

The year was 1919 when George R. Armstrong of Belmont, Massachusetts purchased an eighty-acre farm from the widow Mrs. Frank (Kate) Brown of Mt. Vernon. The conveyance included "…Land with buildings (and) all personal property on the premises owned by the grantor excepting two incubators, one brooder, one stone lifter, a parlor organ, and all clothing, ornaments and jewelry worn by said grantor.." In 1885 a deed for the same property stated it was located on "the stage road leading from…West Mt. Vernon to Cobb's Hill…" The east end of that stage road is discontinued now and what remains, on the west end, is called "Five Seasons Road".

Armstrong was the owner of G.R. Armstrong Manufacturers Supplies Inc. which he founded in 1916.[419] Five years later the *Iron Age*, a manufacturers' publication, reported "The Standard Metal Products Co Boston has been incorporated with a capital of $100,000 to manufacture metal goods. George R Armstrong is president…" Armstrong also dealt in mill works, manufacturing products and tools. He acquired the property on Torsey Pond with plans to create a remote lakeside retreat for his customers.

Some of the land and the existing farm buildings were soon after sold by Armstrong. On the remaining acreage he built a fourteen bedroom inn that included all the comforts anyone of that time period could hope for. He also developed walking paths and some of the lakeside frontage into a beach area where visiting customers could enjoy swimming, fishing and boating. He provided canoes and at some point he also brought in a mahogany hulled Chris-Craft. He had a boathouse constructed that extended over the water's surface far enough so the Chris-Craft could be driven directly into it from the lake. That elaborate a water craft was an anomaly in this area in those days so it became the talk of the town!

Stephanie Wilson Hatch, whose family owned nearby Chases Camps, tells the story of when Armstrong dammed up a section of Torsey Pond and stocked it with trout for his customers' fishing pleasure. Torsey Pond had always been known for its pickerel, perch and bass but never for trout. That changed when, during an ice out, Armstrong's dam breached. "Guests at Chases Camps were mystified about why they were catching trout all of a sudden until they figured it out" said Hatch. Armstrong was wealthy and he reportedly carried a lot of clout so nothing ever came of his actions except chatter among the summer residents.

The lodge at Five Seasons
Courtesy of Linda Butman Kinney

Bob Rooney was Armstrong's protégé and worked for his company in Boston. Every summer Armstrong sent him to Mt. Vernon to manage the resort. Rooney and two partners bought it from Armstrong in 1971 and renamed it Five Seasons Resort and Campground. Peter and Diane Gerow have been the owners since 1998 and currently promote their facility for events such as weddings, family and class reunions or company picnics. Today it is known as Five Seasons Family Resort.

"Where was Captain Bishop's building located" I asked my mother, Evelyn (Adell) Potter, as we drove along Thundercastle Road. She pointed to a break in the stone wall on the west side of the road, slightly north of Torsey Shores Road. There I could easily see a leveled place where a building once sat. Several months before another Readfield native, George Allen, had told me about that same building and how it had been moved by the Bishop family to the spot where it remains to this day. [420]

GIRL SCOUT TROOP #1, CASTLE HILL FARM ~ 1930

Capt. Ethel Bishop was not a military person as the title might indicate, but the Girl Scout leader of Troop #1 in Readfield in the 1930s and 40s. "I always called her 'Captain'. She was so good to us and she did a lot with us Girl Scouts during the World War II years" said Evelyn Potter of Kents Hill.[421]

The Bishops moved to Readfield from Townsend, MA in 1930 and Ethel began volunteering with the Girl Scouts soon afterwards.[422] She had three daughters, Naomi 17, Olive 14 and Alice 13 at the time but whether they were also involved is not known. In a 1936 *Lewiston Daily Sun* article there is mention of a campground set-up at Bishop's home on Thundercastle Road. The article relates an outing whereby Doris Dow, Phyllis Dow and Dorothy Carson of Kents Hill attended a Girl Scout Council meeting then accompanied the troop on a hike. Ethel Bishop led the way as they trekked from the Readfield Methodist Chapel[423] to the campground.[424] From there they followed a paper trail to Sturgis & Elizabeth Coffin's camp on Torsey Pond for a day of swimming and exploration.[425] In June of 1937 another article stated "The Girl Scouts of Troop #1, Readfield are camping at the King mansion at North Monmouth. There are 12 girls in the troop with Capt. Ethel Bishop of Readfield and Lieut. Lyle Withers in charge." The girls were taught swimming and life-saving on that outing.

Evelyn Potter went on to share that Girl Scout meetings were most often held at the Bishop home which that family called "Castle Hill Farm". In addition to working on badge-earning projects the girls enjoyed snacks and sing-a-longs around the Captain's piano. When special events were being planned and presented they met at the Readfield Grange Hall or Giles Hall – two in particular being a WWII Victory Dance and a play the Girl Scouts presented for the community called *Seein's Believin'*. They also went Christmas caroling as a group each year. "We always had projects going on" said Gloria (Bryant) Clark of Readfield. "One I remember was when Mrs. Bishop brought shells back from Florida and we made gifts for Mother's Day with those." Annual outings at the Martha Washington Inn were a highlight when the girls enjoyed swimming and a picnic at the beautiful resort. Money was tight during those years so in most cases the mothers made uniforms for their daughters. Gloria Clark and Betty (Giles) Bailey of Wayne both recalled Memorial Days when they proudly marched in their uniforms from the Readfield Corner Cemetery to the Union Meeting House for remembrance ceremonies.

Overnights were spent at Castle Hill Farm too, remembers Gloria's sister Midge (Bryant) Potter of Kents Hill. "I recall when I was really young and went there to spend the night (with Girl Scouts) and I got homesick and (my) Dad had to come get me." Gloria told of camping there also. "We slept in big Army tents in the field behind the farmhouse." Sometimes the Kents Hill School Outing Club was made available to the troop for overnights but those best remembered were held at Roy Gile's camp on Lake Maranacook. "We spent a week at a time there" said Gloria. Roy's daughter Betty cooked meals for them with help from her friend Priscilla (Ladd) Bruen. Gloria told how they swam and did projects all week. She also recounted that her older sister Gladys (Bryant) Libby and fellow scout, Faith (Wills) Rourke, rowed across the lake at least twice during that week to Dead Stream landing. From there they walked up Butman Hill to the Bryants' family farm to get fresh milk for the campers, returning with it to the Giles camp by foot and boat. Evelyn recalled that both she and Captain were early risers. "Before everyone else woke up we would take a walk in the woods together and Captain would point out different wildflowers and animal tracks and things like that to me. She was a very smart lady." During WWII, when this troop was at its peak, gasoline was among the commodities that were rationed. In spite of those restrictions Captain Bishop somehow managed to transport the entire troop to Augusta for a sightseeing tour of the State House, Governor's mansion and suite of offices, the YMCA and the County Jail. "We had some good times, we really did" said Gloria. "It was wonderful of (Mrs. Bishop) to give so much of herself and to take a bunch of us girls for weeklong overnights. We learned a lot!"

Readfield Girl Scout Troop (by then the Readfield Troop was #22) in 1949. Front L to R - Brenda Boutilier, Donna Lee McCormick, Lillian Gilman, Annabelle Bailey and Patty Smith Standing L to R - Verna Piper, Mona Little, Nancy Pendleton, Marjorie Little, Irene Fogg and Natalie Giles

The next generation of Readfield Girl Scouts included Belinda (Potter) Burke (L) and Dottie Macomber. Belinda's mother is Midge Potter and her aunts Gloria Clark and Gladys Libby. Dottie Macomber's mother Jean (Wills) Macomber and her aunt Faith (Wills) Rourke. By the time Belinda and Dottie became Girl Scouts in 1963 Camp KV and Camp Kirkwold had been established in Readfield.
Courtesy of Dottie Macomber

The Bishops called this "Castle Hill Farm" when they lived there 1930-1956. The current owners, John & Marjorie Tyler, continue to call it by the same name.

"The Thunderbird is a mythical Native American creature that dominates all natural activities; the Thunderbird symbolizes protection, provision, strength, authority, and indomitable spirit. This cross-cultural symbol is found among the plains Indians as well as the tribes in the Pacific Northwest and Northeast, though its meaning may vary across different groups." ~ Native American Symbols (www.ancientsymbols.com)

CAMP THUNDERBIRD ~ 1945 [426]

In 1945 Ralph F. Ives and his wife Ruth of Darien, Connecticut bought the 160 acre Albert Bean homestead on Chase Road. This land bordered Chases' Camps in Readfield. They had one son, Ralph Jr, who was grown and had joined the military by that time. With their acquisition the Ives became owners of fields, woods, a farmhouse and barns in addition to frontage on Torsey Pond. Also included was a cottage which a previous owner, Sturgis Coffin of Boston, described in his memoir as "a comfortable camp down on the lakeshore".[427] Both the Coffins and the Ives chose this place as their families' summer retreat but the Ives took it a step further.

Ralph Ives was an electrician as a young man who became a recreational director in later years and still later a teacher. He also held a great interest in American Indian culture and lore which led him to founding Camp Thunderbird on Torsey Pond.

His grandson, Ralph Ives III of Washington D.C., shared [428] that he is too young to remember Camp Thunderbird but he clearly recalls his grandfather's extensive knowledge and affection for the American Indian. "He had an Indian head dress and an acoustic walking stick with symbols. He never treated those or anything he owned like a costume but with great respect, and he told us we must do the same. I never even realized that anyone else ever had anything but the highest respect for Indians because of my grandfather's teachings; at least not until I got older and studied American history." Ralph also shared that his grandfather was particularly enthralled by the Indian symbol, the Thunderbird. "He drew and painted them and told stories about them all the time. I never knew why but now I wonder why a man with a name like Ives was so interested in the American Indian."

Stephanie (Wilson) Hatch, whose grandparents ran Chases Camps, remembers the Ives family quite well. "Ralph Ives", said Hatch, "entered contests to earn some income. "There were always boxes of items that he had won stacked up in the farmhouse." She once asked him why he entered all those contests to win things to which he replied "You have to learn how to win things first in order to know how to win money contests." That aside, she agreed that Ives was interested in Native American culture and he saw this Readfield property as an ideal location to share that interest.

The exact years Camp Thunderbird existed are not known, but we do know the Ives owned this property from 1945 until 1952 and the camp was in operation for about three years within that time frame. The Ives catered to boys ages 8 to 10 for one or two week sessions. Generally there were at least six campers at a time but when enrollment was lower Hatch and her sister Dorothy were invited to join them. "The activities were based on Indian folk lore," said Hatch, so Ralph gave the campers the tribal name of Unka Inka. There was an initiation but the only part I recall was the requirement to learn a saying and we were supposed to figure out what it meant – 'ow-wah-ta-gu-si-am'. I was good at words puzzles so I figured it out right away and Mr. Ives had to make up a new one" Stephanie said with a chuckle. When asked what it meant she chuckled again saying "Oh what a goose I am".

The grounds included a small beach near the original cabin which Ives used as a recreation hall. Near that he built two bunkhouses using the same design as the "Birches" at Chases'

Camps. (see pg 214) There was also a fire ring for toasting marshmallows and outdoor cooking. Ruth Ives did all the food preparation and meals were served at the farmhouse. "We rarely saw her except at mealtime" said Hatch.

The Ives owned a woodie station wagon, like the one at Martha Washington Inn (see pg. 159), with seating enough to transport all the boys on outings. They left it in Readfield during the winter months when they returned to their home in Connecticut. "One winter" said Hatch "some porcupines ate right through the wooden doors and frame of that car. They got into the bunkhouses and made a mess in there too. That may have been their undoing. The camp did not last for very long after that."

Ralph and Ruth Ives sold their Readfield property in 1952 and continued to live in Darien, CT until 1961 when they moved to Tarpon Springs, Florida. She died there in 1973 and Ralph died in 1977; they are both buried in Tarpon Springs. Their one child, Ralph Jr., served in WWII and the Korean War as a Lieut. Colonel in the US Air Force. He died in 1997 and is buried in Arlington Cemetery, VA.[429]

The Albert Bean farm was owned by Ralph and Ruth Ives.
This house no longer exists.

The final section of this book describes kids' camps and resorts that were established on Echo Lake and Lovejoy Pond, part of the "30 Mile River" waterway.

30 MILE RIVER ~ ECHO LAKE ~ LOVEJOY POND

The 30 Mile River Watershed is 200 square-miles and encompasses twenty-two lakes and ponds, many of which form a chain referred to as the "30 Mile River." The chain runs from Kimball Pond in Vienna south towards the Androscoggin River, and includes some of the more pristine lakes in Central Maine.[430]

The first mention of the 30 Mile River in the history books is in reference to some timber hunters who paddled north up this waterway from the Androscoggin River. They did so before anyone had settled in this area – perhaps in the 1750s. When they reached the northern end of Crotched Pond in West Mount Vernon they climbed a nearby mountain to view the landscape. By then they estimated they had traveled about 30 miles. After that the waterway became known as "30 Mile River" and that mountain was named after one Mr. Bowen who was among those explorers.[431]

When the first survey was done of this area in 1771 a strip of land approximately one mile wide was omitted. This parcel stretched from the southern tip of Mt. Vernon to North Wayne. The surveyor reported "...there is a large proportion of pond in this tract of land that we have not surveyed..." [432] That tract of land came to be called the "30 Mile River Gore". It was divided between the towns of Mt. Vernon, Readfield, Fayette and Wayne in 1795.[433] Some early settlers had already taken stake in the land more than a decade before, so when the 1790 U.S. Census was taken a separate count for "Gore of the 30 Mile River" was done of those residents. For the purposes of this book Echo and Lovejoy are the two lakes that fell within the Gore. When traveling west from Kents Hill to Fayette via route 17; or on the

North Wayne Road towards Kents Hill, one passes through a section of the 30 Mile River Gore.

Echo Lake covers 1,109 acres and has a mean depth of 21 feet and a maximum depth of 117 feet. Some of the game fish that have historically appeared in Echo are salmon, brown trout, togue, brook trout, perch, smallmouth and largemouth bass, rainbow smelt, splake, pickerel and hornpout.[434] Echo Lake was originally known as "Crotched Pond" because of its shape. In viewing this body of water on a map one can easily see two branches at the south end that resembles the crotch of a tree.

Lovejoy Pond covers 379 acres and has a mean depth of 16 feet and a maximum depth of 22 feet. The variety of game fish includes rainbow smelt, smallmouth bass, largemouth bass, white perch, yellow perch and pickerel.[435] Lovejoy has been known by other names as well. Initially it was Jones Pond which may have been for the early surveyor John Jones. Next it was known as Lane Pond after the Lane family that settled on Kents Hill. In the early years locals also called it "Haynes Pond" and "Ford Pond" after families who owned land along its eastern shore in Readfield. It was also known as "Sleepy Hollow Pond". Finally it was named after the Lovejoy family who settled on the western shore in Fayette.[436]

Industry was prevalent on both bodies of water from the late 18th century into the early 1900s. Mills were located in West Mount Vernon, Fayette Mills - also called Foord's Mills - and at North Wayne. Seasonal homes, summer resorts and kids camps now dominate both Echo and Lovejoy.

Since 2009 the "Annual Paddle Trek" has been hosted by the 30 Mile River Watershed Association. [437] The trip encompasses 15 miles from Minnehonk Pond in Mt. Vernon to Pocasset Lake in Wayne village. Surely the explorer Mr. Bowen, and the early surveyors and settlers of long ago would marvel that such a trip could be completed in only eight hours.

Bowen Mountain can be seen in the distance. Taken in 2014 in Fayette, beside Echo Lake near Camp Winnebago

The Underwood (Mayo) farm in Fayette became a familiar landmark to summer campers who accessed their cottages via the drive that passed between this house and barn. Another (Mayo) camp road has been built now, further west. The Underwood farm was built in what was "30 Mile River Gore". It became situated in Fayette when the Gore was split between Mt. Vernon, Readfield, Wayne and Fayette in 1795.

"This plan describes a tract of land lying westerly of the town of Readfield in the county of Lincoln (Kennebec) on the thirty-mile river in the Plymouth Patent. And I judge that there is about one half of (470 acres) good land and the other half the greater part waste land." ~ Jedediah Prescott, surveyor, Winthrop April 23, 1794

BODGE CAMPS ~ 1891
SANBORN CAMPS ~ 1932
TWIN SPRINGS CAMPS ~ 1946

Twin Springs and Echo Lake Lodge and Cottages (see pgs 249 and 258) on Echo Lake in Fayette are both located within the tract of land described above. In our time it certainly would not be considered a waste land but a setting for serene, attractive summer retreats. In this immediate area the first lakeside structures were built by Frank Bodge about 1891. These were rustic fishing and hunting camps.[438] Leon and Mavill Sanborn of Fayette bought the camps in 1932 and changed the name to "Sanborn's Camps". They sold fourteen years later and it has been known as "Twin Springs" ever since.

The Foord family was the first to settle this acreage where they owned and operated mills.[439] Sitting on the lawn near the water's edge at Twin Springs is an ancient grinding stone from Foord's mills.[440] The sight of it exudes a connection to the past but that is not the only thing at Twin Springs that conveys that sense.

According to the Twin Springs' web site, Stanley and Mary Konieczko knew they had found a paradise when they purchased the camp property in 1946. At that time there was no plumbing or electricity so kerosene lanterns provided light; and outhouses, wash basins and the lake filled other needs. Ice was cut from Echo Lake and packed in sawdust in an ice-house, for use in ice-boxes during the summer. Wood stoves were used for heat and cooking. Stanley and Mary worked together and made improvements while raising a family of six children.[441] The description on the web site lured me in and I wanted to see Twin Springs firsthand. One of the Konieczkos' daughters, Judy Whitten, graciously met me there to give a grand tour and share stories.

Upon leaving route 17 to cross the threshold onto "Echo Lodge Road" I encountered a narrow dirt camp road lined by old trees and stone walls. This passage was described in the old deeds as "the cow lane" meaning it was used to drive cattle from field to field or to the lake. In travelling that road I could almost envision the wide open pastureland that existed here in those times. From there a road branches off and leads to Twin Springs where the character of the early 20th century cottages has been preserved. There is more. Twin Springs has been in the Konieczko family for seventy years and holds many precious memories for them all!

Stanley Konieczko was a Connecticut native who met his future wife Mary Sulya at a family wedding. He was stationed at Fort Belvoir, VA and Mary was living in Monmouth, Maine when they married in October, 1942. Mary traveled with him while he was in the Army. They were both of Polish descent and Stanley spoke that language fluently - a skill he put to good advantage during WWII. He enlisted in the U.S. Army in 1941 and trained as a paratrooper. When his superiors learned that he spoke a second language they recruited him to work in espionage for the Office of Strategic Services (OSS) under "Wild Bill Donovan".[442] "We never even knew that as kids", said Judy with pride. In the three years that followed, Mary worked and Stanley sent his service pay home to her. She saved as much as she could from both of their earnings. One job she took, at Sunset Lodge on Damariscotta Lake, proved to be invaluable later on because there she learned how to run a summer resort.

Mary and Stanley lived in North Monmouth after the War and they both wanted lots of kids. "They felt it was important to keep them off the streets in the summertime" related Judy. "My father was raised in the city so he did not realize what a small town North Monmouth is" she said with a smile. Mary's nest egg was used to purchase the camps on Echo Lake from Leon and Mavill Sanborn. The transfer papers were signed on March 13, 1946.[443] That same year the Konieczkos first child was born and five more followed. By 1958 they had three sons and three daughters.

There was no road leading directly to the cabins at that time but they had one built later. When Stanley and Mary bought it there were six cabins – four on the lake and two in back – and they needed a lot of work. Most likely the previous owners had suffered a financial loss during the Great Depression and WWII and were unable to maintain them. Stanley and Mary spent the next year or more fixing and rebuilding. "No one wanted to rent the two back cabins so my parents tore them down and used the wood to make additions to the other four" Judy related. Their first guests came in 1947 and "we have never needed to advertise" exclaimed Judy. The first clientele came from Stanley's contacts in Pennsylvania, Connecticut and New York and it grew from there. Judy mentioned one (of many) return customers - a group of physicians who attended medical school together, but live in various parts of the country now. They spend a week in the camp called Cedar Crest every summer, where they have left mementoes of the big bass they have caught over the years. The other camps are named Driftwood, Birchwood and Ash Haven. Each one sleeps six people comfortably and they all have fully equipped kitchens. There are no outhouses or ice boxes any longer. "Roy Giles (of Readfield) built fieldstone fireplaces in them sometime in the 1960s" said Judy, "which provides warmth on cooler summer days".

In listening to Judy's descriptions and detecting her passion for Twin Springs it became apparent that Stanley and Mary instilled their strong work ethic, exceptional hosting abilities and love for this place in their children. Judy and her five siblings spent magical summers on Echo Lake throughout their childhoods and the third and fourth generations are now doing the same. Both parents are gone so things are different for Judy and those of her siblings who are in charge. But the magic is still there as evidenced by the gleam in Judy's eye and the warmth in her voice as she tells the stories about summers on Echo Lake.

The Konieczko family has preserved the original Twin Springs road sign. In 2001 Mary Konieczko wrote on it "I hope you enjoy Twin Springs as much as I have for 53 years and still enjoying it as much as <u>ever</u>."

← Roy Giles of Readfield built many of the bunkhouses, cottages and stone fireplaces in this area. His name came up often in our interviews. At Twin Springs he built the fireplaces in four of the cabins.

Photo courtesy of Betty Giles Bailey

Stanley Konieczko
1914-1978

Mary Konieczko
1920-2013

Mary and Stan's oldest sons Peter and Danny with the
Wood brothers, the three sons of an early guest.

"Camp Mowana is situated on Echo Lake near Readfield. It is a small camp for younger boys established in 1912 by Mark HC Spiers. Since 1915 it has been conducted by A.R. MacMahon of the Cleveland public schools with whom is associated WD Gerken of Stamford Military School. A Canadian camp for boys over thirteen is maintained during August at Lake Croix." ~ The Handbook of Private Schools, Volume 7, 1922

MOWANA ~ 1912

Camp Mowana was first established where Camp Skoglund is located today (see pg.265). In 1910 Melzar Fish[444] sold 1.2 acres of Echo Lake frontage, from his West Mt. Vernon farm, to George Cushman, a farmer living in Mt Vernon. When Cushman sold the property to Mark H.C. Spiers of Wayne, PA in 1914 it was already identified as "Camp Mowana" and some buildings had been constructed. Cushman had returned to live in his native Massachusetts by that time.

Spiers was from a "mainline" Philadelphia family and a Haverford College alumnus, class of 1908. There is little doubt that, as a student, he would have attended John Chase's Cebennek on Torsey Pond. (see pg 209) Perhaps that is where he met his future wife, Faith Randall of Augusta, because the Chases did hire local people to work there. At any rate, Spiers was a teacher at the William Penn Charter School in Philadelphia when he and Faith married in 1910. Camp Mowana would provide seasonal employment for Spiers as well as a means for Faith to return to her native Maine in the summertime.

The same year Spiers bought Camp Mowana he established the "Spiers School" which was a "…country day and boarding school 'A B C' to college entrance…" His school was located on a twenty-five acre estate in Rydell Hills[445] eleven miles from Philadelphia making it easily accessible to boys from "mainline" families. Surely Spiers took the lead from John Chase and looked to his own student body to feed Mowana's enrollment, like Chase had from Haverford.

Finding male counselors and campers became very challenging for most camp proprietors during WWI and it is likely that Mowana suffered financial hardship during those years as well. Spiers sold Mowana soon after the war, in 1919 for $2,400+ to Mrs. Clark (Sarah) Merchant, a 75 year old socialite from Philadelphia. Why Mrs. Merchant made this acquisition at her advanced age is mystifying. It is known however that any transactions associated with this property were thereafter conducted by her daughter and trustee, Estelle Evans. Merchant may have purchased it with the intention that Estelle would operate the camp; she may have seen Mowana as an investment; but it's also possible that the Merchant family planned to use it as a summer vacation compound.

Deeds reveal that Mowana continued to operate from the same location for two more years after Merchant bought it, and then it was moved to where Camp Laurel is located today. (see pg.251)

Estelle (Merchant) Evans sold Mowana in 1932. Perhaps hers was one of the wealthy families that suffered great loss during the stock market crash thus explaining her decision to sell at that juncture. She let it go for one-fifth of what her mother had purchased it for thirteen years earlier. Interestingly Evans sold Mowana to Charlene (Folsom) Tebbetts Adams of Readfield, she being a sister-in-law to Mowana's director at that time, A. R. MacMahon.

New Brunswick Canadian[446] born A.R. MacMahon had married Charlene's sister Marian on December 22, 1916. The girls' father, Charles R. Folsom, was the owner-manager of "Echo Lake Lodge" (see pg. 249) at that time so most likely they all met through their similar business ventures. When the MacMahons married he was a teacher at Peekskill Military Academy in New

York but had already summered in Maine for two seasons as Mowana's director.

The campground at Mowana was restricted to a little more than an acre and as enrollment increased more space was needed. In 1920 A.R.'s father-in-law helped him acquire a large property known as the "Mitchell farm" in West Mount Vernon where A.R. established a new Mowana. By then he and Marian were living in Cleveland, Ohio where he carried on his career in education. They continued to summer in Maine where A.R. was owner-director of Mowana until 1938.

In 1933 MacMahon published a twenty-two page promotional booklet[447] that included many photos and detailed descriptions of the activities, history, rules and the physical plant of the new Camp Mowana. This would have been no small expenditure during those difficult financial times. Below is a brief representation of the booklet's contents.

CAMP SITE: One-hundred twenty-five acres...partly covered with spruce, pine, birch, cedar and oak. Slopes gradually to the lake...A beach of fine white sand, free from pebbles, extends almost the entire length of the shoreline, sloping gradually to the deeper water...The athletic fields include ball diamond, tennis, basketball and volley ball courts and track...

BUILDINGS: The dining hall, kitchen and supply rooms are contained in a large building thirty by sixty feet... Commodious glass-enclosed room with open fireplace, accommodating eight tables. The kitchen twenty by thirty feet has complete modern equipment including hot and cold running water, built in refrigerator and supply room. Other buildings contain the ice and wood supply, the garage and workshop, the sanitary system, pumping engine, help's quarters, office, store, stable and infirmary.

SLEEPING CABINS: Of which there are eight, are arranged in the shape of a crescent set in a cedar grove...fronting an open space that serves as a playground and a place for the morning set-up exercises preparatory to the morning dip...The cabins are sixteen feet square, open on three sides, screened, and equipped with canvas drop curtains for damp or rainy weather. Each cabin is designed to accommodate five boys and a counselor...Tents and cabins are allotted in the order of application...

CAMP FLOTILLA: Consists of four twenty-foot White cruising canoes, twelve seventeen-foot Old Towns, three eighteen-foot Kennebec Guide canoes, two twenty-five foot War Canoes, two Cape Cod sailboats, a sponson,[448] motorboat and rowboats... Immediately in front of the cabin row a seventy-foot slip connects to shore with a floating anchored dock. Thirty feet beyond there is a forty-five foot diving float equipped with graduated high dives, springboard and slide.

CANOEING TRIPS AND CRUISES: Younger boys take trips to Parker Pond, Minnehonk, Flying Pond, Belgrade, Androscoggin, Kennebec and Cobbosseeconte...Older boys (have gone on) the Canadian Cruise; the Grand Lake Stream and Machias River Cruise; the Rangeley and Quebec Hike; the Quebec City Excursion; The Penobscot-Katahdin Cruise; the Allagash Trip; the Canadian Fishing Trip; and the Katahdin and Mt. Washington climbs.

CAMP SEASON AND TERMS: Opens July 3 and closes August 26...The camp fee for the season is $225...covers all necessary expenses...with the exception of railroad transportation, purchases and laundry authorized by the parents...charge to employ a team or truck for trips.

The next section describes the point system that Ruth Cohen Steiner, Camp Vega, made mention of in her memoires (to read more see pg 253).

THE MOWANA POINT SYSTEM: A record is kept of the activities and progress of each camper from the time he enters camp until he leaves. Points are awarded for work done in all land and water activities, in nature work and in citizenship; and these points are entered daily on the individual charts of campers. The senior emblem, the "M," and the junior emblem, the "CM," are awarded at the close of the season on basis of points earned.

After twenty-three years as the director of Mowana A.R. MacMahon sold it to one Henry Tise of Hawthorn, NY. The records show that Tise then sold the camp to George and Ruth Cohen in 1943, in the midst of WWII. Perhaps the Cohens rented the facility for a few years first because Ruth's memoires indicate they opened Vega Junior at that location in 1939. She briefly made reference to Mowana in her memoires saying "...we purchased another but smaller disused camp on the opposite side of Echo Lake...The population (at this camp) was held to sixty-five." (see pg.251)

To read more about the next phase of this property see the chapters on Camp Vega Junior and Camp Laurel. Also see Camp Skoglund.

One of Mowana's large canoes with ten boys on board, 1932

"I have a conviction that a few weeks spent in a well-organized summer camp may be of more value educationally than a whole year of formal school work." ~ Charles Eliot, 1922, former President of Harvard

CAMP WINNEBAGO ~ 1919 [449]

"Some of the activities are timeless and have endured since Camp Winnebago began 95 years ago", Lynn Lilienthal pointed out. She and her husband Phil had agreed to meet with me to share stories about their long history at Camp Winnebago on Echo Lake in Fayette. On a muggy late August afternoon we sat around a table in the Camp museum, developed by Lynn more than twenty years ago. "There were artifacts all over the property" said Lynn. "Pieces of Winnebago's history had been scattered throughout the grounds in closets, attics and underneath porches." Things were disappearing, and Lynn knew the importance of preserving what was left, so she convinced Phil of the need for a building to house it all. Fittingly, the museum was built by the caretaker David True, whose maternal grandfather, Howard Gray, was Winnebago's first caretaker. He had built all the original buildings at Winnebago in the early 1920s. David constructed the museum in time for Camp Winnebago's 75th anniversary in 1994. Lynn catalogued and displayed pictures, artifacts, and documents; and she recorded oral histories. The Lilienthals discovered some items themselves, and others were donated by staff, alumni and townspeople. The result of those efforts surrounded us as the Lilienthals began to share their personal stories and special memories of Camp Winnebago.

It has been nearly a century since Frederick "Chief" Guggenheimer, a lawyer from New York City, founded Camp Winnebago for city boys ages 8 to 15. "In all those years the Camp has been owned and operated by two families" said Phil. His father Howard Lilienthal was hired by "Chief" in 1942 as head counselor and in 1956, when Chief died, Howard took over. Phil ran Winnebago for 30 years then his son Andy took the helm in 2003. The Lilienthal men have carried on Chief's philosophy that reaching the "whole boy" is important. They continue to provide a wide spectrum of life-enriching activities, as well as an array of sports. "Enrollment does not exceed 140-150" said Phil. "More campers would mean increased administrative time for the director. We feel strongly it is more important for the director to have personal interaction with the boys and counselors."

Phil's passion for Winnebago and the campers' wellbeing came through loud and clear as he explained further. Offerings include "take away occupational and life skills activities that are meaningful." Some of those offerings include radio, videography, stagecraft, riflery, archery, photography and working on the camp newsletter WAG. A variety of sports are included as well as river and mountain adventure trips, but Winnebago is "not a sports camp where the focus is on winning games." All the boys are paired with other kids their own age regardless of their skill levels. "We often sacrifice opportunities to win by doing that, but we feel it is more important for the boys to learn (age appropriate) socialization, good sportsmanship and to develop athletic skills without a lot of pressure. We want them to learn that losing does not equate to failure. Kids can be kids here, in nature and away from today's trappings such as electronics and trendy clothing." Lynn explained that men often return 30, 40 or 50 years later wanting to visit Winnebago and to reminisce about their accomplishments here as young boys and teens. Phil and Lynn agreed that they feel rewarded with that kind of feedback. These two remarkable people have many reasons to feel rewarded. In one way or another they have both devoted more than fifty years to impacting the lives of children – not just at Winnebago but in their home state of Virginia and globally as well.

It was June 1944 when 4 year old Phil Lilienthal came to Camp Winnebago for the first time. His father Howard had come for the 1942 and 1943 seasons to establish his interest in continuing as head counselor. The following year he brought his wife and two sons along on the two day road trip from New York City to Maine. "Chief" was the driver and in the co-pilot seat was "Mrs. Chief", Rose Guggenheimer. Phil does not remember much about his first reaction to Camp other than a raging case of allergies, but he soon came to love Camp Winnebago as his father and Chief had before him. He returned every summer – first as the head counselor's son and from 1947-1956 as a camper. Then it was off to college and law school during which time he married Lynn his high school sweetheart. "It was ingrained in me as a child to give back" said Phil so the newlyweds joined the Peace Corps and went to Ethiopia. "I went there as a lawyer" said Phil "but I ended up starting a camp there." He went on staff for the Peace Corps and accepted assignments in the Philippines and finally in Thailand. "Lynn has always been at my side no matter what I do" Phil added. During those years they visited Maine when they could but did not stay at Camp Winnebago all summer like Phil had in his younger years.

Phil planned to return full time as Winnebago's director at some point but it came sooner than expected when his father was stricken with cancer in 1974. Phil assumed the director role after an absence of 11 years. "I didn't know the people here anymore which made for a tough transition" said Phil. Enrollment dropped to a dangerous level of 120, and this on the verge of an economic recession. "We had trouble making ends meet for a few years and worked hard to increase the number of campers. At the same time I was setting up a new law practice in Virginia." Lynn was busy too – she co-founded the first licensed infant day care in Virginia. "In the early 1970s women were entering the workplace but there were no organized day cares" said Lynn. The need was great and the daycare capacity grew to a whopping two-hundred fifty.

To build camp enrollment, Phil saw advantages to bringing in more international campers and "traveled at the drop of a hat during those years". Campers started applying from Europe, Russia, Asia, South and Central America as well as the United States. The Lilienthals also made some major capital improvements and by the 1990s Camp Winnebago was back on its feet and doing well.

In 2001 Phil started mentoring his son for the directorship, and Andy took over in 2003. Phil and Lynn retired or, as Phil says "We went on to our next project." I discovered how humble he is when I asked what that next project was. In 2003 Phil and Lynn founded Camp Zizanni in the mountains near Johannesburg, South Africa. The 8-day camp is offered three times a year to children of South Africa's poorest townships hardest hit by the HIV/AIDS crisis. Thus far 7,000 children have attended. Both Phil and Lynn chimed in "It is a very powerful experience!" So what is next I ask, to which Phil casually replied "We just spent the summer in China helping two friends start a camp there… I hope it gets off the ground by next year." [450]

Asked if they see a fourth generation of Lilienthals running Camp Winnebago in their future Lynn said "Who knows what the future will bring?" Phil thoughtfully pondered for a moment then said "If I were going to make a bet, I bet there will be, but like Lynn says, who knows?" Likewise, who would have known that the little guy riding to Maine in the backseat of Chief's car in 1942 would have gone on to direct Camp Winnebago one day and touch the lives of tens of thousands of children from all over the world through the camp experience?

Left: Fred "Chief" and Rose "Mrs. Chief" Guggenheimer
Right: "Uncle Howie" Lilienthal arriving at Readfield Depot

The first year of campers at Winnebago, 1920

Swimming and canoeing, 1921

1940 truck used to transport campers to and from Readfield
Depot and on field trips. It was retired in the late 1960's

Abstract of a plaque on display in the Winnebago museum:
"Uncle Howie" Lilienthal ~ 1909-1974
Whose spirit and presence at Camp Winnebago from 1942
to 1973 was enjoyed by so many. "Winnebago is not only
for the boy who can, but…especially for the boy who will"
"Uncle Howie's Message" in the 1959 Echo (newsletter)
Gift of Winnebago alumni and friends at the 60th reunion,
1979

Left: Lynn and Phil Lilienthal at Camp Winnebago in 2015.
Right: Phil surrounded by campers at Camp Sizanani in Africa

Andy Lilienthal is the Winnebago director now, following
in the footsteps of his grandfather Howard and father Phil.
His wife Laura is a board certified pediatrician and serves
as the Camp Medical Director. Also pictured are
their two sons Levi (center) and Rafe.
Photos courtesy of Camp Winnebago

"View from Echo Lake Lodge"
In comparing this photo with one on page 257, Camp Vega
you can easily see that it and this photo were taken from the
same vantage point. A vintage postcard of "Camp Macaska"
also exists that was taken from the same exact location.
Photo courtesy of Ronnie Hewett

ECHO LAKE LODGE	1900
ECHO LAKE GIRLS CAMP	1920
CAMP MACASKA	1935
CAMP VEGA	1936

All four of these establishments were / are at the same location, on Echo Lake in Fayette, but little to nothing was known until now about those existing prior to Camp Vega. Thanks to Ron Hewett of Fayette we know the camps did exist at various times by the names listed above. Ron owns four vintage postcards, each taken from the same vantage point, and each captioned with one of the property titles above. Research helped sort out the years for each owner operator.

This property got off to a rocky start and it's no wonder having somehow survived WWI and the Great Depression. In 1881 Charles and John McInnis of Fayette bought the land, established a saw mill, a lumber camp and constructed two private residences for their own families. Surrounding this property was woodlands owned by two major lumbering companies of the day. The McInnises had operated successfully for eighteen years when they went bankrupt and their entire property went on the auction block. Long story short, in 1899 Charles R. Folsom of Readfield bought the saw mill, dwelling houses and other buildings plus the 12+ acres they sat on for about $1,400. Within two years he was operating a summer boarding home here that he named "Echo Lake Lodge".

In 1915 Folsom sold his operation to William R. Scott of Arlington, MA who, it is believed, also operated it as Echo Lake Lodge. Morris and Lenora Stark of New York City became the next owners in 1920 and it is believed that Lenora was the one who started Echo Lake Girls Camp. Ten years later they sold to a young attorney named Solomon Rogers and his wife Stella of Baltimore, MD. She died unexpectedly in January, 1935 and Solomon sold it less than a month later to Edwin and Dorothy Lindman of New Milford, CT.

The Lindmans bought the entire establishment and its contents for $4,000 - except Rogers' reserved his guns, fishing gear and his Cadillac "with extra seats". The Lindmans also borrowed $150 to build two bunkhouses, using these assets for collateral: "...a certain Reo Speed Wagon, a station wagon and a motor boat located at Echo Lake Camp..." They also changed the camp's name to "Macaska". After two seasons the Lindmans reneged on their mortgage, Rogers reclaimed it, and sold it a year later as "Echo Lake Camp" to "Vega Inc" aka George and Ruth Cohen. Camp Vega has changed hands twice since 1936 but the name remains the same.

Model Bungalow   Echo Lake Camp for Girls - Maine

"Indeed, on a bright Maine day, with the infirmary empty of serious concerns, the sense of my huge family, busy and content in the cool sun and shade of the grounds, or on the blue, pine-fringed lake, could produce in me a euphoria that was in large part sheer thankfulness." ~ Ruth Cohen Steiner

CAMP VEGA SENIOR ~ 1936
CAMP VEGA JUNIOR ~ 1940

Much of this chapter was garnered from memoires [451] written by Ruth Cohen Steiner in 1976, twenty-two years after her retirement. This describes how she established two camps for girls on Echo Lake. She and her first husband George Cohen bought an existing camp in Fayette in 1936 called "Echo Lake Camp for Girls" which they set-up for campers ages 8 through 15. Three years later they bought Camp Mowana in West Mt. Vernon to accommodate the younger girls and called it Vega Junior. Camp Vega Senior in Fayette is still known as Camp Vega. The West Mt. Vernon location is known today as Camp Laurel. We wish to extend a very special thank you to Kyle Courtiss of Camp Vega in Fayette for sharing Ruth's story for the purposes of this book.

The year was 1934 and Ruth (Heller) Cohen of New York City was a social worker on hiatus when her husband George was stricken with a severe heart attack. He survived but the doctors told him he could have another attack anytime which would most assuredly take his life. The Cohens, who were parents to two young daughters, knew that Ruth needed to secure a means for income in case she should suddenly become widowed. At the time she was volunteering for a two-week long summer camp for underprivileged children in the City. That experience led her towards thinking she could run a summer camp for girls. This all occurred during the Great Depression making such a venture less than wise. Ruth wrote "…an endless procession of doubts marched through my mind night and day. To start a private enterprise in the midst of the Great Depression? To compete with old, established camps…? To work, for the first time, with children of well-to-do families? Above all, to attempt promotion and selling, when I had never sold even a raffle ticket?... However, the die was cast..."

The following summer Ruth worked at an 8-week camp in New Hampshire as the co-director. The arrangement was that she would invest in the camp with the owner if she chose to do so at the end of the season. If not she could not return the following year. She did not agree with how the camp was managed so she and George set out to find a camp in "...Maine with its heaven-sent combination of lakes, rivers, sea-coast, forests, hills and mountains..." A real estate agent led them to Echo Lake Camp for Girls in Fayette. Ruth described it as "distressed property". Although some of the buildings were decrepit and had to be torn down, some were usable and the location was ideal – "surrounded by 300 acres of woods, on the edge of the pristine Echo Lake." The Cohens changed the named to "Camp Vega", meaning "brightest star in the summer sky".

They refurbished the buildings and also made a large expenditure to rebuild the public dirt road that cut through the middle of the grounds. To do so they had to get permission to move a "tiny, ancient burial ground" to Mt. Vernon five miles away. Ruth was relieved to do so saying "I could well imagine the ghoulish comments the children (would have made) strolling past..."

Next Ruth set about recruiting campers by mailing letters out to friends all over the United States asking "...in a most tentative fashion if they would be willing to give a tea for their possible interested friends to discuss camp for their daughters..." Camp Vega would be different from the other camps promised Ruth. In those days camps tended to break campers up into two teams which received points "not only for athletics but in correct bed-making, neatness of cabins, campfire 'sings' and all else that could foster comparison and incidentally produce tension..." Vega campers would not have that kind of pressure placed on them and activities would be planned to best fit the talents and nature of each girl. (see pg.241 for example of a point system)

She delivered as promised. Campers with interest in tennis tournaments, swimming meets and horse shows were given opportunities to compete in those. Other campers could participate in what appealed to them such as hiking, softball, canoeing, art and nature study. Trips to Mt. Katahdin, the White Mountains, shooting rapids on the Allagash and Kennebec Rivers and chartered schooner cruises on Penobscot Bay were also enjoyed. The girls were coached in conflict resolution when tempers arose from living in close quarters with each other. Ruth believed in community service and helping their neighbors in various ways. Some of those projects included painting a school and a church; collecting books for the local library; and producing a play to raise donations for a local scholarship fund.

Camp Vega's capacity the first year was fifty campers but only forty girls signed up. Some of Ruth's friends convinced her to make up the difference with ten boys ages 8 to 10. "It worked out well enough" wrote Ruth "but I had two older brothers and

**Ruth Heller
Class of 1918
Tulane University**

daughters and had never known small boys before…I had a couple of surprises coming. The ten (boys) could make far more noise and preempt more attention than could the forty girls. One gentle, forgiving mother told me, on a parents' visiting weekend, that we must never leave them alone in their cabin without a counselor." When Ruth asked the mother why she discovered "they had been lining up on both sides of their cots in order to see who could pee across the cot to the floor…" After the first summer Camp Vega took girls only.

Three summers later Ruth realized that the special needs of the younger girls were overlooked by their being integrated with teenagers. She and George bought Camp Mowana in West Mount Vernon and made it Camp Vega Junior for girls ages 8 ½ to 12. "Thereafter" related Ruth, "I drove around the end of the lake on bumpy dirt roads, sometimes twice daily, rather than disturb the lovely quiet with a motor boat." With that additional facility their enrollment increased to sixty-five campers at Junior and one-hundred ten at Senior plus sixty employees that included counselors, staffing for the infirmaries, offices, kitchens and maintenance crews. Ruth's campers and staff came to lovingly call her "Rufus".

Ruth shared several stories – some humorous and some not so much. During WWII finding experienced staff members became challenging – especially medical personnel - so she hired a married doctor-nurse couple who were German refugees. Both were temperamental and gave Ruth a run for her money that summer. One time in particular the doctor demanded the office secretary be fired because "She didn't giff regarts to my wife. She leafs or ve do!" Then there was the assistant cook at Vega Senior who went after the chef with a butcher knife. The dietician saved the day by grabbing his arm and told him to go pack his suitcase. Another time the very large English cook threatened to leave mid season. All Ruth could think to say was "Edith, an Englishwoman <u>never</u> walks out on children! "She straightened her tremendous shoulders, looked thoughtful, and stayed." Ruth mentioned more hairy stories about adult staff than the children, but come to think of it, one would consider it less remarkable for children to act out.

Husband George was an attorney and he gave Ruth "expert guidance and help with a myriad of executive and financial procedures" through the years. So after he died in 1945 Ruth was able to "carry on alone…because of (his) guidance…" Every summer "Rufus" remained at Vega into September, after the staff and campers had departed, to transition back to being Ruth again and to supervise repairs and new building construction. She related "The greater need was for quiet and solitude, recharging with inner strength after such intensive consciousness of the needs for so many…"

In 1951 at age 54 Ruth found the second love of her life - Albert "Al" Steiner. They married and started a new life in Cincinnati, Ohio. Ruth had come to love the camps like a third child so before she would move on she insisted on finding just the right person to take the helm at the Vegas. Neither of her daughters were interested so she interviewed a few eager would-be buyers. She found them "wanting in relative experience or a more serious lack in fundamental attitudes." Then she remembered a young woman named Mary in New York who she knew as a child and was very fond of. They had stayed in touch. "Here it is" she told Mary "you (and your husband) can work together summers and plan together winters." She offered them a financial arrangement that fit their budget and the rest is history. Matthew and Mary Penn became the owners of Camp Vega Senior and Junior in 1954.

After that Ruth returned to Vega only one more time. She wrote of that occurrence with the same sense of humor she conveyed in her other stories. "…It was ten years since the change over and Al and I were spending two weeks in Maine…I phoned and then drove over, and as I arrived at the top of the slope I saw a group of girls. Of course I knew none of them but I heard them calling 'Rufus, Rufus'. How lovely (I thought) the Penns must have alerted them to my coming so that I needn't feel so strange. Getting out of the car, I took in the whole scene (and) it became obvious that they were calling a little brown cocker spaniel." Life goes on at Camp Vega…

RUTH HELLER

Alpha Epsilon Phi; Class Basketball Team (1, 2, 3, 4); Varsity Basketball Team (3); Class Secretary (1); Class President (3); Class Poet and Historian (1, 2, 3, 4); Secretary Debating Club (1); Debating Council (2, 3, 4); Alternate Varsity Debate (1); Varsity Debating Team (2, 3); Nixon Debate (2, 3); Secretary Student Body (3); Vice-President Student Body (4); Student Council (3); Secretary Menorah Society (3); Executive Committee (3, 4); Student Fund Committee (3, 4); Student Summer Committee (3, 4); Delegate to S. I. A. S. G. Convention (4); *Arcade* Board (1, 2, 3, 4); Editor of *Arcade* (4).

Clearly, Ruth was already demonstrating strong leadership skills as a college student at Tulane University, 1915-1918

Matthew and Mary Penn sold Camp Vega Senior to Richard Courtiss in 1974. It has been owned and operated by the Courtiss family ever since, the current directors being Kyle and Emily Courtiss. Vega's motto is "The Most Exciting Thing a Girl Will Find at Vega Is Herself". Camp leaders strive to assure the campers are emotionally and physically safe; they have fun and develop skills; build strong relationships and friendships with peers and other members of the community; and connect with the Vega's history, traditions and values. A museum is maintained on the Camp Vega campus in Fayette. The web site provides photos and extensive information about today's Camp Vega. ~ www.campvega.com

CAMP LAUREL in WEST MOUNT VERNON

Mel and Bette Archard bought Camp Vega Junior from Matthew and Mary Penn in 1965 and changed the name to Camp Laurel at that time. Ron Scott began working for Camp Laurel in 1974 and four years later he and the Archards' daughter Ann began as Directors. They bought the camp and continued as directors until 1994 when Keith Klein became the owner and director. Jem Sollinger joined Keith as co-director in 2002. In 2007 he and his wife, Debbie, assumed the directorship. Camp Laurel is currently coed and accommodates 240 campers from all over the country. More than 40 programs are offered in six core areas: Athletics, Waterfront, Inter-Arts, Tennis, Adventure and

Equestrian. The web site provides photos and extensive information about today's Camp Laurel. www.camplaurel.com

We extend sincere appreciation to Ron Hewett of Fayette for sharing these and other photos from his collection.

**Offices and Director's Residence
Camp Vega Senior, Echo Lake, Fayette**

View from the dining hall at Camp Vega Senior, Fayette

This resort is not to be confused with Echo Lake Lodge that later became Camp Vega. (See pg 249)

ECHO LAKE LODGE AND COTTAGES ~ 1937

Joan was a teenager when her parents, Bill and Hope (Parker) Pfaffle, drove her and her younger brother Jim from their home in Westfield, New Jersey to scope out lodges in various parts of Maine.[452] The year was 1960. Bill and Hope had come to love Maine through summer camping trips to "Vacationland" so they decided to become the proprietors of a real, Maine lakeside vacation resort.[453] Their life took a very different turn with this decision but it was not the first time.

Hope was a Utah native where she earned a Bachelor's Degree in a college there. Bill spent his childhood in the Bronx. He developed an interest in aircraft mechanics in high school and went on to study engineering in college, eventually becoming an experimental aircraft engineer. As a younger man he worked as a lifeguard at summer resorts in upper New York State where he gained a love for the out-of-doors and photography which led him to becoming a professional photographer later on. Hope moved from Utah to Manhattan where she and Bill met at a youth church group. They were married in 1941 and the next year, soon after Joan was born, they moved to Westfield, New Jersey. Jim was born there in 1948. Hope started a nursery school and Bill opened a photography supply shop and studio they named 'Howill'.[454] She was a teacher but she was also an artist. Joan proudly shared that her mother could paint anything - portraits and landscapes. Bill and Hope worked together in their studio. He took pictures and developed them and Hope touched them up or painted them when they needed it.

"It probably wasn't a good time of year for them (my parents) to be looking for a place (in Maine), it was winter when we came up." said Joan "We looked at different places until they finally found Echo Lodge and bought it." By then Hope was the vice principal at Tamaques Elementary School in Westfield. Within a year she resigned and Bill closed their studio. They bought land on Norton Road in Fayette and built a house there.

Echo Lodge had been in existence for 23 years when the Pfaffles bought it. Charles J. and Matilda H. Lundvall of Bronxville, NY acquired the land in 1937 and constructed the lodge and six small cabins. The lodge was situated in a grove of trees about 100 feet from the shore. It held six guest rooms, the cook's kitchen, a summer kitchen, dining room, a gathering room with fireplace and a screened-in porch that overlooked the lake.[455] This establishment was a sporting camp when the Lundvalls owned it but the Pfaffles soon began marketing to an entirely different clientele.

After Bill and Hope had owned Echo Lodge for about a year he came up with the idea of creating some movies of the gorgeous scenery in the area, and showing the film to clubs and such in New Jersey. He thought people would flock to the lodge once they saw the beauty of Maine and Hope agreed it was a good idea. With her support Bill spent most of his spare time during the next year taking pictures around central and coastal Maine. This resulted in beautiful images of bubbling brooks, apple trees in blossom in the springtime, weddings, summer greenery, mountains, lakes, coastal scenes, fall foliage and fresh winter scenes.[456] Every winter Bill trekked to New Jersey with the film in hand where he showed it at various senior citizen meetings; then each group appointed leaders who organized bus tours. Before the Pfaffles knew it they were fully booked, for ten weeks of the summer season, with a new group of forty-eight senior citizens each week.

The guests arrived on a "Transport of New Jersey" bus on Saturday afternoon and left the following Saturday. The same driver brought them just about every time. He was provided with a room at the lodge and stayed for the entire week while he piloted them on daily outings. On Saturday he drove them back to New Jersey. "We fed them breakfast every day and sent them with picnic lunches on the half days. The other days they ate lunch in restaurants" said Phyllis (Nason) Hewett, a Fayette resident who worked as the cook at Echo Lodge for thirteen years.

Trips included a three hour cruise on the "Cap'n Fish" and a lobster feed in Boothbay Harbor; as well as sightseeing, shopping and fancy dining in Camden, Rockport and Lincolnville. They liked the coastal trips the best but Bill took them to see the mountains and rivers up north too. On Mondays the bus took them to Winthrop or Augusta to do some shopping and they usually came back with the makings for a week's worth of totties. Every day they returned from their excursions by dinner time to a meal prepared by Phyllis. "I cooked things like baked ham, fish or chicken. Sometimes I made beef bourguignon or spaghetti and meatballs and I found ways to use leftovers. One time Phyllis made a baked ham for a new group on Saturday night and they told Bill they would not eat ham. Phyllis recalled that Bill was beside himself saying 'what will we do?' She took a big can of tuna fish, mixed it with mayonnaise and plopped it onto a bed of lettuce. Phyllis chuckled saying "They loved it. But you know it's funny because all that week they ate more bacon and sausage for breakfast than any other group we ever had!" Thursday was BBQ night when Bill cooked steaks and "hamburgers as big as a plate" on the outdoor grill. Phyllis also made a birthday cake those nights. One time it fell apart when she took it out of the pan and she had to make another one in a hurry. She didn't want to waste the first one so she mixed the crumbs with some walnuts and whipped cream and put another dab on top. "They were crazy for it and asked what it was" Phyllis recalled. We told them it was 'crumb pudding'. I never had to make it again."

The Pfaffle's recruitment plan worked so well that Bill soon decided to push his idea along elsewhere. In early 1962 he made a proposal to the Maine Department of Economic Development (ME-DOD) about his idea for promoting tourism in Maine. Ironically the ME-DOD had already been talking about making a film similar to Bill's but the cost to have one made commercially was so prohibitive they had nixed the idea. Bill had already made a narrated film and he suggested the State buy the rights to reproduce it. His proposal was accepted, at considerable cost savings to the State of Maine, and he was commissioned to produce four more in various parts of the State. A detailed article about this appeared in the ME-DOD newsletter that May.

Bill and Hope had four additional cottages built to make a total of ten but one of them later burned. There were usually forty-eight guests because that was the capacity of the bus. At camp they enjoyed shuffle board, croquet, swimming, campfires and row boating. In the evening or on rainy days they played cards, board games and visited by the fireplace in the lodge. "Bill had a big motor boat and offered them rides around the lake" said Phyllis. "They really liked that."

Not to be forgotten are the people who kept the wheels turning behind the scenes. Bill took care of the finances and Hope was in charge of housekeeping. "Lil LaFlamme was the cook from the beginning" related the Pfaffle's daughter Joan. "She was the chef at a women's college in Massachusetts and worked at Echo Lodge during the summers until she got too old." Joan also worked at Echo Lodge throughout the years her folks owned it and when her daughter Linda became old enough, she joined in. "We remade forty-five beds every Saturday" said Joan. Hope washed all the towels and kitchen linens with an old wringer washing machine and hung them out to dry but the sheets got sent to a laundry in Augusta. Two chambermaids came in every morning to freshen up the sleeping quarters and on Saturday three or four did the changeover. Two uniformed waitresses served breakfast and dinner daily. An older man named Ernie Grover[457] was the caretaker. Some local men did repairs and construction jobs too. Harold Kent and Clyde Wyman of Mount Vernon installed a shuffle board court on the grounds. Joan recalled that she was eighteen that summer saying "That is when I met Clyde. He and I got married in front of the fireplace in the Lodge."

Hope died of cancer at about the same time that Lil LaFlamme retired. Understandably Bill became distraught about how he would manage the business without either of them. He happened to be visiting Phyllis Hewett and her husband Fred one evening and told them about his dilemma. Phyllis offered to help him out until he could find another cook but he expressed his doubts about the idea. "I told him that isn't any different than cooking for fifty of my father and grandfather's (Nason Farm, Kents Hill) family and crew." Bill wasn't totally convinced but he hired Phyllis for one summer anyways. She ended up staying there for thirteen years. Bill let Phyllis' family stay in one of the cabins during the summer. They lived on a dairy farm about a mile away so it was convenient for them to go back and forth to take care of their animals. "I worked seven days a week starting at 6 a.m. with a few hours off at lunch time while the guests were gone. I only missed one day when I had the flu." When asked if she enjoyed working there Phyllis said "I loved it, I still miss the people. Some of the same ones came every year and I got acquainted with some of them."

Subsequent owners of Echo Lodge have been William & Kristine Hutson of Katy, Texas 1982-1989; Ted Wiederhorn & Alison Reich of Readfield and Hallowell 1989-1994; James & Eleanor McKay of Norridgewock 1994-2005; Glen and Sandra Craig 2005-2012; and most recently James & Evelyn Feagin. The lodge was destroyed by fire in September 2013 and was rebuilt by the Feagins. Fortunately all the cabins were spared. The replacement lodge includes eight guest rooms with extra bathrooms, a gathering room and a commercial kitchen. The new structure is also energy efficient and suitable for winter lodging. Prior owners offered guests the "American Plan", which included three meals a day in addition to lodging, but that is no longer the case. All nine of the rental cabins have kitchens as well as the lodge so people can prepare their own meals. The Feagins do offer catering.[458] They started accepting online registrations recently, including for shorts stays of two or three nights, which appeals to Maine residents. This allows for weekend gatherings such as family reunions and weddings. "Last year" said Jim "a Maine family booked the entire place for their reunion. We must have had two-hundred people pass through here that weekend." Operating Echo Lodge is still a "family affair" as it has been with some past owners. The Feagins have three children ages 10 through 16, who all attend local schools. There is still a "changeover day" on Saturdays which their children give a hand with; and now that Echo Lodge offers shorter stays the entire family pitches in to help with housekeeping duties on weekdays as well.

Guests who visit Echo Lodge and Cottages these days do not come by charter bus but as individuals and families in their own cars. They still enjoy some of the same activities that those New Jerseyans did during the Pfaffle era; but since the new lodge is suited for cold weather business the promotions now laud opportunities for hunting, ice fishing, skiing, snowmobiling, snowshoeing and sledding. Modern times have brought more options, different clientele and new memories but the ambiance of recreating at an old resort on a pristine lake in Maine remains.

The original Echo Lodge, built in 1937 and burned in 2013
Jim and Evelyn Feagin, owners since 2012, replaced it with a
year-round facility per current codes and as close to the
original as possible. *Photos courtesy of Jim and Evelyn Feagin*

The original gathering room at the lodge. The fireplace
survived the fire and was incorporated into the new lodge.

CAMP SKOGLUND ~ 1957

Soon after the close of WWII Wilbur Nelson, a young Navy veteran from "the Garden State," entered the New Jersey State Teachers' College. At about the same time he was hired to work for several summers as a counselor at Camp Winnebago in Fayette. He expected to become a teacher but little did he know that owning his own boys' camp was also in his future.

In the years that followed Wilbur and several other people he knew from New Jersey enjoyed annual vacations on Echo Lake. From the mid 1930s into the 1950s some of them bought camp lots and built their own cottages. As an educator Wilbur was able to spend two weeks to a month of each summer in Maine which gave him ample time to explore and become familiar with the area. "During all the early years of me coming here" related Wilbur "the (original Mowana) camp site stood idle. I asked around about it and someone told me to go see Charlene Adams in Readfield; she owned it but I was told it wasn't for sale" said Wilbur. He found out from Charlene it could be and the two of them struck a deal.

Wilbur went on to describe the property's attributes in 1956 when he bought it. "It was a small piece of land a little over an acre with 350 feet along the shore. All there was for buildings was a two story house with a walkway down the middle. There were rooms for the kids upstairs, the mess hall was downstairs. There was a big rock there too that we moved down the shore to (my sister Ingrid) Singers' camp." That same summer Wilbur bought some abutting land to increase the size of his camp's grounds to twenty-eight acres. The expansion provided space for an athletic field and more buildings.

During the spring of 1956 Wilbur took the existing structure down and burned it. Then he stayed with the Singers while he cleared an area and built four 15x15 ft. sleeping cabins that could accommodate six to eight boys each. He put up an A Frame recreation hall which also served as the lodge. Then he named the camp Skoglund which is Norwegian for "Woodland" explained Wilbur. "Both of my parents were born in Norway."

Skoglund opened in 1957 with twenty-five boys in attendance. Enrollment gradually increased to seventy-five and ultimately to one-hundred campers ages 9 to 15. At first they came from New Jersey but as word spread campers also came in from Sweden, Germany, Mexico, Japan and other parts of the U.S. All of the counselors had been campers themselves at one time or another which helped assure smooth operations.

Jesse Welch of Sadie Dunn Road in Mt. Vernon cooked at Interlaken Farm so Wilbur knew firsthand about her culinary skills and he hired her at Skoglund. She worked for him for twenty-five years and he still talks about her pies and donuts with a gleam in his eye. Readfield native Ronda Luce was Jessie's assistant for a period of time. "Aunt Jessie was a little bit of a thing so I did the lugging and tugging for her" said Ronda. "We used to make up special meal trays and deliver them to "Uncle Will's" parents at their cabin when they visited." [459] The campers and younger employees all called their elders aunt and uncle at Skoglund, as was the case in several other kids' camps.

Activities included athletics, water games, canoeing and swim meets. Campers also trekked to the Rangeley area and Moosehead Lake for canoe trips; and to the White Mountains and Tumbledown Mountain for hiking and climbing. More locally an annual canoe adventure down "Thirty Mile River" was enjoyed. Each morning the boys were provided with music books and they joined together in song. This author, who once lived a short distance from Skoglund, well remembers hearing their bugle reveille every morning through most of July and August. It was a welcome sound that cast the vision of a group of hearty, smiling boys who were eager to begin their day on the lake.

When asked if he had any humorous stories to share Wilbur told about his strategy when the boys got rowdy in their cabins late at night. "We had midnight rides. I loaded them up in the camp truck and drove them out to the Armstrong (Five Seasons) Road and dropped them off. They were ready to sleep by the time they walked back to Skoglund." The "night walkers" did not know that adult eyes were watching from a distance to make sure they safely returned.

"Uncle Will", as his campers called him, soon gained a reputation as a "second Dad" – for some he was the only Dad they ever knew. Many of the boys worked through problems and gained self-confidence at Skoglund according to Wilbur. One former camper explained that Uncle Will liked the lost cause kids. "He took them under his wing, turned them around and had a big impact." Another revealed that if it had not been for Wilbur he probably would not be here today. "I was an angry

Wilbur Nelson with his daughter Rondi in 2014

kid. My father had just left... Coming to Skoglund was a make it or break it for me" he said with a quiver in his lip. He made it! One camper described his experience as "empowering". And yet another related that his years there were the happiest in his life and that he still thinks about the camp all the time. In hearing a dozen or so former campers speak about Skoglund and Uncle Will their love and admiration is undeniable! One remarked "He commanded respect and you gave it without question. Wilbur Nelson is the best human being I have ever met".[460]

Nelson is the late comer compared to other camp founders included within the pages of this book. But unlike most of them who kept up the fast pace of running a kids' camp for fifteen to twenty years at most, he did it for thirty-three years! Skoglund ceased operating as a boys' camp in 1990 but Wilbur wasn't done yet. He and his daughter Rondi converted Skoglund into a family summer resort. "I'm so happy that Rondi is interested" he said "and that it will still go on." Since they converted to rental cottages many Skoglund alumni return to stay there with their families during the summer. "I can still hear the kids playing on the waterfront" said Wilbur. "I like that."

Wilbur is still going strong at age ninety-one - six decades after he founded Camp Skoglund for boys. Today he and Rondi work long and hard, with nary a complaint, to keep things going. They do it for love of the place and the people who return year after year to claim their vacation haven at Skoglund. These words on their web site convey their sentiments well — "We want to continue sharing our idyllic summer home…"

The old Skoglund truck heading out for one of their canoe trips *Photo courtesy of Wilbur and Rondi Nelson*

INTERLAKEN FARM AND COTTAGES ~ 1931

This property originally encompassed 200 acres which extended westward from Torsey Pond to Echo Lake, thus the name "Interlaken Farm". Several people who have lived there tie in with other kids' camps and summer resorts in various ways. Originally settled in 1820 by an affluent farmer named Benjamin Davis, Sr. it remained in his family for four generations. From the patriarch it was passed on to his son Benjamin and next to his grandson Simeon Davis in 1885. Simeon was a resident of Winthrop by then and running the steamboats *Annie* and *Amarascoggin* on Lake Maranacook. (see pg. 21) He passed the farm on to his unmarried niece, Emily Isabel "Belle" Stanley. She had yet more connections to this area's hotel and sporting heritage. Emily was a cousin to the sportsmen Henry O. Stanley and George S. Page[461] mentioned earlier in this book (see pg.11); and she was related to Kate Stanley who ran the Stanley Hotel on Lake Maranacook in Winthrop (see pg. 42).

Belle's intentions for the future of this farm are not known. Given her family ties to this industry one must wonder if she was actually the first to offer lodging and meals at Interlaken Farm, but we will probably never know. It appears that Emily became ill or incapacitated at age 32 because she sold her farm to Melzar Fish in February of 1890, only one month prior to her death. Interlaken Farm remained in the Fish family for ninety-five years; the last to live there was his daughter Mrs. Stanley (Ruth Fish) Hight. After Ruth died it was sold by her heirs to Peter and Rebecca Halliday who remained at Interlaken Farm for ten years until they sold it to Edward "Ed" Voynik in 1995.

Ed's roots to Echo Lake and Interlaken Farm reach further back than his 1995 purchase. His maternal grandparents, Edward "Ted" and Mildred Cooper, were both educators from Linden, New Jersey and the first of Ed's family to summer on Echo Lake. "They knew they wanted to own a cottage on Echo" Ed related. "So they camped around the lake to find the right spot. When they stayed here (at Interlaken Farm) they knew they had found it." The Coopers bought a waterfront lot from Stanley and Ruth Hight in 1954 as did some other educators they knew from New Jersey – one being John Kuhlman from Rahway. Ed spent every summer at Echo Lake from the time he was 9 months old and he grew to love it there. Just one day after his 1987 graduation from Trenton State College he moved to Readfield and he has continued to live in this immediate area ever since. In addition to Interlaken Farm Ed owns his grandparents' cottage and the one previously owned by Kuhlman.

Returning to Stanley and Ruth Hight, they subdivided most of their water frontage on Echo and sold several camp lots in addition to selling larger parcels to Wilbur Nelson where he built Camp Skoglund. (see pg. 265) They also conveyed some road frontage lots along route 41, and land to George Armstrong which became part of Armstrong's Camps (Five Seasons) on Torsey Pond. (see pg. 220) With those sales this property shrunk to 45 acres from the original 200 but it still falls on both sides of route 41 as it always has. The house sits on the west side of the road and the barn, which has been nicely restored by Voynik, sits on the opposite side.

Ruth Hight in her kitchen at Interlaken Farm in 1956

In 1955 Ruth Hight was one of seven Maine women featured on a popular Maine radio show called "Ways of Earning Money at Home". She was also featured at the University of Maine "Farm and Home Week" that same year. In 1956 she wrote an article about Interlaken Farm for the "American Agriculturist".[462] Through that article, we are able to share some stories about Interlaken Farm as a business, in Ruth's own words.

"Catering has been done at Interlaken Farm for at least sixty years.[463] Mother used to set her heavily laden tables for summer boarders or hungry road workers,[464] and now I set my tables in the same dining room for a dinner party of twenty guests…About twenty-five years ago when Echo Lake was really opened up by summer campers we began selling farm produce, berries, milk, cream, eggs and chicken to the campers. In fact, we had quite a little roadside market. I can't remember when the first call came for a cooked chicken, but it really started something. Soon we were preparing entire dinners completely cooked to take out. I hate to think how hard we worked in those days, we couldn't do it now, but then we gloried in it…It was twenty years ago that we began taking house guests. Across Echo Lake from us a large girls' camp (see Vega Sr. pg. 251) was started…and the owners needed rooms and meals for their help until the place was ready. Then after the camp got going they needed a place for the parents to stay when visiting the camp. We had no electricity on our road then and no plumbing in the house – but we did have two sons (Rolfe and Robert)[465] who wanted to go to college, and this seemed to be the opportunity we were praying for. We bought a gasoline pump, installed two bathrooms, acquired a cottage for an extra bedroom, and we were in business. In a few years electricity went in and we were able to buy the appliances we so desperately needed. Then the picture changed. The war (WWII) came. My husband sold our cows and hens and went to work in the shipyards on the Maine coast. Our boys went to war as soon as they finished college and I stayed home to run the guest business. Since gas was scarce I got many calls for meals and thus I got into the business of serving dinners to the public as well as to our house guests. After the war we continued to do this...Our house and guest house accommodate ten people for sleeping, but the dining room sits twenty easily...not (enough) credit can be given to my helper Jessie[466]. She couldn't be more interested if the business were hers. She comes in each morning at 8:00 and stays until all the dishes are done each night...occasionally a local girl comes in to wait tables...The prices of our meals range from $2.00 to $3.00 - $2.00 for chicken, turkey, lamb and roast beef; $2.50 for lobster; and $3.00 for a steak dinner. We serve two vegetables, salad, a relish tray, hot rolls and a choice of dessert and beverage. No cocktail, as that is something I refuse to serve. Our deserts always include one homemade pie or pudding and ice cream...For us, the vision has come true. We are able to live where we want to live, on our farm and among lifetime friends. We constantly meet new and interesting people in our business. We keep the home place as a mecca for the roving ones in the family whose work takes them afar. We are not getting rich but we are doing what we want to do." [467]

Stanley, who was a skilled carpenter, eventually built three cottages on Echo's shoreline. The first one, known as "Gray Cottage", was rented out but they continued to take lodgers at the farmhouse and in the small guest house adjacent to it. They also added a dock near Gray Cottage so roomers from Interlaken Farm could enjoy access to the lake.[468] The other two cottages, which are named "Hemlock" and "Spruce", went to their sons Rolfe and Robert. They married and settled out of state after WWII but continued to travel "home" in the summer with their wives and children in tow. "I've been going there all my life and still have a camp on the lake" said Rolfe's son Gary. "It is a special place that holds many memories for me." Like his grandparents did before him Gary rents his cottage – at least for part of the summer when he and his family are not enjoying it themselves.

Stanley died in 1974 and Ruth in 1983 and although Interlaken Farm is no longer in the family the cottages are. Thus a portion of the Hight's property has remained in the Fish-Hight family for more than one-hundred and twenty five years - a fine legacy of family, hard work and good plain living indeed.

John Kuhlman (left) and a friend sitting
on the front lawn at Interlaken Farm
Note the sign and also that route 41 was not yet paved.
Photos in this chapter courtesy of Ed Voynik

Interlaken Farm and the guest cottage which sat beside it
Rooms were rented in both buildings and meals were served
by Ruth in the farmhouse dining room pictured below.
Photos courtesy of Ed Voynik

Vintage photo of "Echo Lake near Kents Hill, Maine"
Photos this page from the collection of Jean (Wills) **Macomber**

SLEEPY HOLLOW, KENTS HILL, MAINE.
Published by Miss C. M. Brown.

Lovejoy Pond was also known as "Sleepy Hollow Pond" for
some period of time. This is thought to be the location of Kents
Hill School's Outing Club. In 1881 the school trustees bought
the original 85 acre Nathaniel Ford homestead. It was used as
headquarters for the school's Outing Club to provide students
with opportunities to enjoy water sports, overnights and a wider
variety of natural areas in the immediate vicinity of campus.

Kents Hill Outing Club clearing land for Kents Hill School's
ski hill, 1947. Torsey Pond is in the background.

Photos this page courtesy of the Kents Hill School Archives

Kents Hill School students at the school's
Outing Club on Lovejoy Pond, 1966

Pumping station, Lovejoy Pond, Kents Hill, Maine
The card says Echo Lake but that is an error. This is the water
pumping station that Kents Hill School had near their outing
club. From there water was pumped to a water tower on campus.
From the collection of Jean (Wills) Macomber

Fayette Country Store in 1970 when owned by Walter and Jean
Hewett. This store has been an icon for Kents Hill students
and the campers on Echo and Lovejoy Lakes for decades.
Courtesy of Ron Hewett

MORE ABOUT LOVEJOY POND...[469]

After the Revolutionary War Lieut. John Lovejoy placed his belongings, which consisted mostly of a wife and nine children, in an ox cart and moved in that manner to Fayette, Maine, from Amherst, New Hampshire. He bought 200 acres of land for $30.00 and a small frame house for $12.00. Closely adjoining the land is a pond, long known as "Lovejoy Pond." In late years it has been rechristened as "Sleepy Hollow," by students from Kent's Hill Seminary. Mrs. Lovejoy would sometimes get lonesome and homesick and would go to the shore of the pond and call to a woman who lived on the other side who could hear. She would answer and they would both go down to their respective sides of the shore and visit in that manner.
~ *Sprague's Journal of Maine History*, 1915

Taken on the annual 30 Mile River Paddle Trek on July 30, 2016, near the portage at the north end of Lovejoy Pond, Fayette Mills.
Potter-Clark photo

KENNEBESCOGGIN CAMPS ~ 1904
TALL TIMBERS ~ 1946

"Crosby was already pretty old when I was a little fella" said Andy Knight, 85, of Wayne. "He lived next door to us. His niece (Lura Wells)[470] was living with him then." [471] Ellsworth Crosby was a Wayne native and a laborer at the North Wayne Tool Company in 1904 when he bought "Canwell's pasture".[472] The property had passed through several hands over the course of one-hundred years and an Evergreen forest had grown to dominate the landscape by then, but Canwell was a local legend so the land that was once his was still called Canwell's pasture.[473] Crosby built several sporting camps there and opened for business. His brochure makes mention of the land's heritage saying guests could "… roam at will to the graves of the first settlers, through the black depths of the Hemlocks…or over the hills to the ruins of the pioneer's home…" The same brochure described a spring that provided pure, clear, icy water no matter how hot the weather.[474] To this day signs point the way to that very spring!

The property was located on the eastern shore of Lovejoy Pond in a section of what had been the "Thirty Mile River Gore" in earlier days. Crosby chose to name his business "Kennebescoggin" because of its location between the Kennebec and Androscoggin Rivers. "The camp road went right in close by Crosby's house back then" said Knight. "So he could watch people coming and going pretty close." Crosby erected seven log structures – one had five rooms and was used as the dining hall, for dancing and other gatherings – and the other buildings were identified as "cottagettes". Each of those held a sitting room, an open porch and one double bed. Unlike other proprietors who tended to name their guest cottages after trees Crosby chose the flowers - "Woodbine", "Sweet Pea", "Sunflower", "Golden Glow", "Cyprus" and "Nasturtium". He assured that meals would be made with the freshest of vegetables, eggs, chicken, and butter from local farms. Guests traveling in from Boston to Winthrop via the Bar Harbour Express could make the round trip for $7.20 and New Yorkers could get here for $9.30.[475] They were picked up at the Winthrop train station and driven to the camps from there. Some stayed at Kennebescoggin for the entire summer for rates starting at $15.00 a week. There were hammocks, swings, croquet, dancing and boats for the guests' amusement. Travel arrangements were made for those who wanted to go on shopping or sightseeing excursions. Fishing, of course, was touted as an attraction "on nine lakes within a ten mile radius." [476]

Andy Knight described some of the camps' features, which were typical of all such establishments of the times. The road was primitive; there was no electricity or plumbing; they used kerosene lamps and outhouses and carried buckets of water from the lake. A couple of women came up from the village to clean them in the spring. In Knight's memory families usually rented the camps for a week at a time in the summer. He does not remember back to when they were sporting camps. Knight told with a chuckle of a Massachusetts family that used to rent the largest camp for the entire summer. "Crosby charged them by the person so they signed up for the mother, father and three or four kids. Then before you knew it there were eight or ten kids in there."

During the years that Crosby built the camps he went through a career transition. In 1906 a news article reported that he had resigned from his job (as a laborer) at the North Wayne Tool Company (NWTC) and was moving to New York to take a better position.[477] He either never went or did not stay long because he was back in North Wayne and working as a mechanic at NWTC from 1907 until 1910.[478] By the following year and thereafter the town directory listed his occupation as painter, which leads us to another side of Ellsworth Crosby.

Both Ellsworth and his niece Lura were artists and craftsmen. Neither of them ever married. In addition to painting Lura co-owned "The Green Dragon Gift Shop" in New York City. She and her business partner, Betsey DeWitt, sold items such as handmade jewelry, baskets, lamp shades and unusual dolls for children.[479] Each summer Lura, who was called "Aunt Lullie" by the family,[480] returned to North Wayne and the ancestral home[481] that she and Ellsworth shared.[482] Ellsworth had a talent for wood carving in addition to painting. He created extraordinary sculptures of animals - some of which have been on display at the Cary Memorial Library in Wayne village for decades. [483] At the North Wayne schoolhouse in 1917 Lura and Ellsworth hand-painted a stage curtain because they wanted local children to be introduced to original art.[484] It deteriorated with time so in 2005 some experts from Vermont, in collaboration with conservators from the Maine State Museum, worked for a week to repair, clean and mend it. The impressive curtain depicts a scene from Ben-Hur[485] and is large enough to cover the entire back wall of the school's second floor stage.[486] Most people are not aware that some of Crosby's earliest creations exist in the cabins he built on Lovejoy Pond. "All the hardware on the doors in his camps were carved out of wood and not made of metal" said Knight. This author remembers, from working there as a teenager in the 1960s, the cabin named Crosby - which was also known as "Indian Lodge" - and its uniquely crafted wooden door handles. Old pictures of the interior also show some of his bird carvings mounted over the mantle.

In April of 1946 Crosby's four camps and sixty-six acres were sold to Bob Nelson and his twin brother Harold of New Jersey[487] . They were later joined in business by Harold's son Kenneth and Bob's foster son Gordon Rutherford. Soon afterwards Bob moved from his hometown of Harrington Park, New Jersey to Maine to manage the cottages. Seven years later the partners changed the name of the business to "Tall Timbers".[488] They also built a better camp road, away from

Crosby's house, to where it remains today. Bob was also a carpenter and constructed two tent platforms to accommodate additional renters until he could add three new cabins.[489] Added to those was a storehouse and office that also served as the owners' living quarters.[490] The camps at Tall Timbers were named Maywood, Tamarack, Tall Pines, Crosby, Loon Lodge, Woodsman and Lovejoy. Loon burned but all the others still exist.

Andy Knight worked for Nelson the summer of 1949. "My Dad died that year when I was a senior in high school. Lloyd Beach was (Nelson's) maintenance man and he knew my family could use the money so he hired me. I carried ice for the ice boxes, hauled rubbish and helped do repairs." Nelson had brought in electricity by then so each cabin had a hot plate to cook on. They kept shorting out. It's a wonder there wasn't a fire." Knight recalled that guests were still using outhouses and carrying water in buckets then. Nelson eventually installed indoor plumbing and fully equipped kitchens so, unlike in Crosby's day, guests were responsible for preparing their own meals.

Brian and Caroline Donohue of New Jersey own a cottage at Tall Timbers. Brian has been summering there for seventy-one years, first coming with his aunt, uncle and cousins, the Alleborns. "I was 7 years old the first time I came. We were from the same town as Bob Nelson and he told my aunt and uncle he had bought some camps in Maine and they should come up." Donahue also recalls when people living on the lake still had ice boxes saying "When I was a teenager I used to help Andy Weymouth deliver ice… we went along the shore in a boat to do it." Caroline lamented there are no longer camp kids on Lovejoy and told some of what she and others miss. During the day they used to enjoy watching the kids from Menatoma and Kirkwold in canoes and sailboats and Menatoma's bugle calls in the mornings and evenings. Even more enjoyable was the sweet sounds that came from Camp Don Bosco (see pg. 296) when the

Nuns sang hymns during their evening worship. "Their voices drifted all over the lake. It was beautiful" said Caroline. Brian's cousin Rick Alleborn agreed with Caroline saying "Every night when it was time for the Don Bosco kids to sing around the campfire my mother would drop everything and go sit on our porch to listen." The lake is quiet now – blessedly peaceful some might say – but the sounds of the camp kids' laughter and singing will always be missed at Tall Timbers.

In 1988 Bob signed over the business to his nephew Kenneth Nelson, who still owns a cottage at Tall Timbers. Bob died six years later at age 95. The property was subdivided and the camps sold to individuals[491] – some who had rented camps at Tall Timbers before. Most of the cabins still have their rustic appeal.

Ellsworth Crosby (left) posing with some of his wood carvings and a young lad.
Kennebescoggin and Crosby photos are
Courtesy of Brenda (Wells) Joseph

Ellsworth Crosby with his niece Lula Wells
Name of child unknown

Ellsworth Crosby's home in North Wayne that he
shared with his niece Lula Wells. It has since burned.

From Crosby's brochure: "The Main Cabin, built with primitive style logs, has five rooms the largest used for Dining Hall, dancing and general gathering place. There is a quaint fireplace whose chimney is also built around the logs old-fashioned cob style. The furniture is mainly of 'ye olden days'. Screen piazza on three sides affords fine views of lake and hills. Kitchen and cook house being detached insures coolness and quiet."

Inside the "Main Cabin" called "Crosby". Door handles and the bird carvings hanging over the mantle were carved by Crosby himself. The lady is Beulah True.

CAMP ABENAKI ~ 1919 [492]
CAMP MERRYWOLD ~ 1927
CAMP KIRKWOLD ~ 1951

Like nearly every other camp and resort discussed in this book, Camp Abenaki was built on the land of a lakeside farm. In this case 100 acres, the farmhouse, pasture and orchard were included. Dr. Emma Greene Wood was a forty-nine year old widowed osteopathic physician from Maplewood, New Jersey when she bought this property on Lovejoy Pond in Readfield. [493] It was October 1919 and times were tough. Only eleven months had passed since the WWI Armistice; the 1918 influenza pandemic was still raging; and women had not yet been given the right to vote. That Dr. Wood took on this endeavor alone at that time in history speaks to her courage and ambition and tells us that she was a woman ahead of her time! Beyond that she was remarkable in both her personal and professional life.

Emma Greene Wood and her husband Otis were both natives of Surry in downeast Maine. They moved to Portland as young people where he operated an apothecary. Perhaps Emma's exposure to Otis' work as a druggist led her towards becoming a doctor after his death in 1908. Newly widowed, at age 38 Emma took her two young daughters to live in Philadelphia. There they boarded with another family while Emma attended the Philadelphia College of Osteopathic Medicine[494], graduating in 1911.[495] Immediately after Emma earned a D.O. she and her girls moved to Maplewood, New Jersey where she was that city's first Osteopathic physician. In treating patients during the devastating 1918 influenza pandemic she surely thought about ways her own daughters and other children might live a healthier lifestyle away from infected cities. Perhaps those thoughts helped her recognize an unfilled niche in the realm of kids' camps.

In December of 1920 "The Osteopathic Physician" printed a brief that read "Dr. Emma Greene Wood is planning to open the first Osteopathic Camp for Girls in the world next year. It is to be opened in Readfield, Maine..." [496] Another article described the camp in more depth and identified it as "Camp Abenaki". It further related, "Dr. Wood's policy is to give the girls (ages twelve to fifteen) a healthy, happy summer which will involve a sane use of their youthful energy, but which will not allow a nervous strain...caused by competitive athletics...The regime is flexible and is to be adapted to the needs of each individual ...The girls will have osteopathic attention during their sojourn at the camp..." [497] Abenaki was the first girls' camp established on the four lakes in this area but bear in mind that in 1919 girls' summer camps had existed in the entire country for only seventeen years. [498] The concept was still being met with some hesitancy and one as specialized as Camp Abenaki would have given rise to additional concerns. In spite of all that, fourteen families entrusted Dr. Wood with their daughters that first summer.

At the time of Dr. Wood's purchase there was a swath through the woods that extended from the North Wayne Road through the property to the lake. It was far from adequate for summer use as local farmers had utilized it only during the winter months for hauling logs and their ice harvest. Dr. Wood borrowed $1,000 right away to improve it as a road and to build footpaths and a combination lodge and arts & crafts building. In 1924 and 1925 she borrowed another $1,500 and added two bunk houses, a dining room called "Forest Hall", a tool shed and garage. Dr. Wood developed an illness and sold Camp Abenaki two years later to Marjorie Kirk. [499] One wonders if Marjorie had been an Abenaki girl.

Miss Marjorie S. Kirk was born in 1898 into a wealthy family from Syracuse, New York. Her father, George C. Kirk, was an executive with several cereal companies during his career including the Kellogg Corn Flakes Co. Marjorie graduated from Syracuse University in 1921 where she served on the Athletics Governing Board. She also excelled on the swim team, in tennis, archery and basketball. After graduation she refereed the University women's basketball games while working for the city of Syracuse as assistant supervisor for the Department of Recreation. Her world travels included trips to Asia, the Hawaiian Islands, Africa and the west coast about which she gave presentations to local assemblies. The Kirks were also heavily involved in scouting. Marjorie's father was president of the Eagle Scout Court of Honor in Syracuse and a benefactor of the Onondaga Boy Scout Council. Marjorie was an executive with the Girls Scouts of America and also volunteered for her local council. Contacts made in those activities as well as her memberships in the Professional Womens' League, The Republican Women and attendance at the National Girl Scout Conventions made Marjorie highly visible in the society pages. This exposure helped Marjorie secure her first camp enrollees.

From her first season in 1928 Marjorie called it Camp Merrywold, meaning "Happy World". That year she had eight campers ages 16 – 18 and two adult counselors. They established a theme of "Merry and Robin Hood old England" that included archery, a Robin Hood banquet and underground cookery. As enrollment grew over time the girls were split into three groups named the "Highlanders", "Hikers" and "Seahorsemen". Sessions lasted for eight weeks each summer. Activities were added to include horseback riding

Miss Marjorie Kirk

and canoe trips on Echo, Pleasant and Damariscotta Lakes and the Kennebec River. Marjorie's kayak was a familiar sight at

Merrywold and was used often by Marjorie as she accompanied the girls on their canoe trips. Campers hiked Mt. Blue, Saddleback and Bigelow Mountains in Maine as well as Mt. Washington in New Hampshire. The array of in-camp activities included swimming, nature exploration, silver and copper work and various arts & crafts. All the while Marjorie continually expanded the campus.

In 1928 Marjorie hired Roy Giles of Readfield to build "the Dingle", a building that sat on 32 concrete posts set four feet deep. Her father, George Kirk, built a fireplace in the infirmary which reportedly contained spikes from the USS Constitution in Boston and also from the historic Methodist Meeting House in East Readfield. The following year a water tower, toilets and a wash house were added. In the 1930s a fireplace was built in Forest Hall, and a building called "Treasure Trove" was constructed. The following features and structures (in addition to those already mentioned) were included on a circa 1930 map of the camp's grounds: an athletic field, camp farmhouse, fresh vegetables storage house, BBQ area, "the outpost" infirmary, tennis courts, the common so called "hamlet" and flag pole, "the Tavern" (wash house), an archery range, bridges over the two brooks on the property, several pathways, and several nature nooks with fanciful names such as "Fairy Pool" and "Wishing Rock". Along the shore there were areas designated for tenting, a swimming area, rowboat dock, the "Pirates Den" with canoe racks, a fire ring and the water pump house.[500]

Camp Merrywold survived the Great Depression and was operated successfully through the 1930s. Food and gas rationing were initiated during WWII and Marjorie was forced to close the doors in 1941. She offered Merrywold for sale through the rest of the decade to no avail. Given her family's lifetime commitment to scouting it is not surprising that in the end she donated Camp Merrywold to the "Tri Area Girl Scout Council (of Maine)". The Council held a celebratory banquet at

Skowhegan High School in 1952 which Marjorie Kirk, 275 Girl Scouts and their leaders attended. Marjorie spoke eloquently to the group saying "The camp belongs to you and becomes a part of your fun and adventure in Girl Scouting. Camp Merrywold belonged to scores of fine girls who (have left) their spiritual values lingering… (for) the Girl Scouts along with the natural wonders of the camp itself…The real worth of a camp is a combination of high spirits, good humor and thoughtfulness (towards) others augmented by a good camp program…Have fun, success and happy days at (Merrywold)."[501]

The Girl Scout Council renamed the camp "Kirkwold", in honor of Marjorie Kirk, and held the first session as such in 1952. It remains open today as one of four Girl Scout camps in Maine.[502] Camp Kirkwold has provided a "Happy world" to young girls and women for nearly a century thanks to the courage, foresight and generosity of Dr. Emma Greene Wood and Marjorie Kirk.

Fire building at Camp Kirkwold in 1955

Raising the American flag at Camp Kirkwold in 1955

In 1941 Marjorie Kirk and Gilbert Friedenwald bought this dam at North Wayne with the water rights. They could then raise or lower the lake level to meet the needs of their camps.

CAMP MENATOMA ~ 1926

A significant part of this chapter came from Dirk Peterson who interviewed Jim Lawrence in 1999. Peterson was a camper and counselor at Menatoma 1969-1975. Currently he is a physician living in Fort Myers, Florida. His son was a camper at Winnebago in Fayette for several years. Jim Lawrence was the director of Camp Menatoma for 25 years and a son of Menatoma's founder Gilbert Friedenwald.[503]

Dr. Gilbert Friedenwald was from Baltimore, Maryland where several of his family members were physicians at Johns Hopkins University. Friedenwald was an osteopath himself, a graduate of Jefferson Medical College in Philadelphia. "I understood that he had never graduated from elementary school and how he got into college I'll never know" said his son Jim Lawrence. "He liked tennis better than medicine and used to play at the 96th street armory in New York City. He would take my brother John and me in for an occasional lesson."

In the early 1920s Friedenwald and a friend decided to start a boys' camp but the friend dropped out before they even got started. Friedenwald carried on alone. Most of the early counselors and campers came from Baltimore because Friedenwald had gained the trust of so many parents through his medical practice and family connections. He also tied in with several men who led after school groups in New York and some of the boys came through those contacts.

For the first two years, in 1924 and 1925, Friedenwald rented Camp Minewawa on Panther Pond in Raymond. There were council fires at Minewawa and smoking the peace pipe and praying to Maka-ina, Mother Earth. Indian ceremonies were always a part of Friedenwald's camp experience. He later brought all that to Camp Menatoma.

After two seasons at Minewawa, Friedenwald decided to search for a camp facility of his own. He happened to be on the road from North Wayne to Readfield when he gave some boys a ride and asked them if they knew of a good place for a camp. They pointed him towards a 90 acre parcel on Lovejoy Pond in Readfield which he bought from Charlie and Hattie Ladd for $5,000. The only structure there was an old garage. Friedenwald had everything built from scratch.

A man named Weston Bishop was in charge of constructing Menatoma. Bishop had designed several other early camps using typical architecture. Jim discovered that when he became a camp standards evaluator for the American Camping Association and visited other facilities. There were no contractors - all the buildings were built with local help. When a particular job needed to be done, someone in town would know who could do it and it was easily arranged. Many were part time farmers who would do their chores in the morning and work out in the spring and summer for perhaps a dollar a day. Jim recalled riding in Calvin Norton's horse cart and watching him move earth with a horse and scoot. Walter Nickerson was the earliest caretaker. "He was a jack-of-all-trades as were most of the early workers like Roy Giles and Carroll Lane" who also helped raise the structures at Menatoma. Norton and Nickerson were farmers on Nickerson Hill Road and Norton was also the Readfield Road Commissioner for several years. Lane was their neighbor on Lane Road and Giles lived on Giles Road in Readfield. Lane and Giles were both carpenters as well as "jacks of all trades".

Those local men moved fast. Twelve cabins were put up at Menatoma the first year along with the lodge, mess hall and the shower house. The cabins were originally numbered but were later given animal names by Jim. Camp Menatoma opened for business the summer of 1926 with seventy-five campers in attendance.

Wally Penrod of Johnstown, PA and a summer resident of North Wayne worked at Menatoma as a counselor and archery instructor from 1960 until 1976. Since then he has worked at several such camps in this area, including Caribou and Androscoggin. In Penrod's words, Menatoma had a physical layout superior to any he's ever seen. He recalled that bunkhouses were not built close to each other in a row like with most kids' camps but on a hillside, dispersed through the woods with space in between. Each cabin had its own running water and toilet and the shower house was conveniently located nearby. Six tennis courts and an athletic field were set above the boys' cabins. A large infirmary was situated off to the side for privacy and that building also included sleeping quarters for married (staff) couples. The office and arts & crafts buildings sat near the waterfront and each had two levels. The bathhouse was in the lower level of the office and

"Tom Two Arrows" was an Iroquois Indian and artist who lived at Menatoma for several summers.
Photo Courtesy of Dirk Peterson

boating equipment was stored below the arts & crafts room. There were two large docks – one for swimming and the other for canoes and sailboats. The riflery and archery ranges also sat at good locations. The mess hall was near the office and just beyond that was a cabin for the kitchen crew. Penrod also described the exterior of the buildings saying they were all well made, each with slab siding. On a recent visit he was surprised to see that the siding, bark and all, was still intact.[504]

Arnold Kidder worked maintenance for Friedenwald recalled Jim Lawrence. Kidder had lost one hand to dynamite but he used to push a big wheelbarrow that collected the trash from each cabin's trap door every day. He also took blocks of ice from the ice house to the ice boxes and put them in the barrels below the bubblers at the lodge and in the mess hall.

Originally there was a large bell mounted in a tower to keep them on schedule. Later they relayed bugle calls over a P.A. system. The camp colors were always blue and gray but the uniforms eventually changed from jerseys to Menatoma T shirts.

In 1941 Friedenwald and Marjorie Kirk of Camp Merrywold next door bought the North Wayne dam.[505] Her camp later became Camp Kirkwold. (see pg 286) "Apparently no one wanted to maintain the dam so they bought it for $10 or something like that." Jim recalled. That, of course, gave them water rights so they could raise or lower the level of the lake to suit their needs.

Jim Lawrence

Jim told of knowing Joe and Elliot Levy who later started Camp Belgrade with Mort Eisman. As a camper Joe was Jim's first counselor, but Jim was never a counselor himself. He worked as camp secretary for his father in 1948 and 1949 until they both agreed that working at camp was not for Jim so he went off to the Allagash as a bush pilot in 1949 and 1950. When Friedenwald died the following year Jim immediately returned to take over the leadership at Menatoma.

After his first season as the director Jim knew he had to hire some new staff which he did by the following spring. To find top administrators he visited some local colleges including Bates in Lewiston where he found and hired Lloyd Lux, the Bates College athletic director. "He was a God-send" Jim exclaimed. "What a jewel he was!" Lux had a lot of camp experience from working at several camps and was able to put in place professional systems in scheduling, inventory and general camp procedure. He was more than willing to do anything that the situation demanded --- including spring clean-up. Lux stayed at Menatoma for almost 20 years.

Former camper and counselor Dirk Peterson related this. "Once Jim told me that for every ten applicants he got for entry level counselor positions - he accepted only one. He told me the risk of a bad apple was just too high." Peterson added that "Many of Jim's former counselors will tell stories about his management style - which left the buck at his desk."

The strongest year at Menatoma was 1973 when the camp reached maximum enrollment by Christmas. Many new campers were added. Jim made a mistake after that, he admitted to Peterson. During that last two to three years, when the economy was tough and kids had other opportunities for summer break, Jim relied on parents and alumni to help with recruitment. He had stopped traveling to cities such as New York, Boston and Philadelphia, to bring in new campers himself - the old fashioned way. By 1976 it was over.

In hearing stories from men who were campers or counselors at Menatoma it seems most are in agreement with Wally Penrod who concluded our interview by saying "Two, three maybe four generations of campers came back to Menatoma. It was a wonderful camp. It really was!"

**Gilbert Friedenwald and two unidentified
ladies sometime in the 1930s**
Photo courtesy of John Lawrence

"In the 1970's I went to a girls' camp in northern Indiana for nine years. As an adult I worked in a summer camp in northern Wisconsin for six years. Camping is in my blood. In 1998 I took my oldest daughter on a college trip 'out east'. Our last stop was Colby College. We stopped at the Readfield Family Market for a sandwich where I noticed a real estate listing. From what I could tell it was in an old boys or girls camp. We had some time to kill so I thought let's just go look at it. I nearly died when I saw the property. There was the cutest little cabin for sale for the most reasonable price and it was in an old boys' camp that had gone out of business. The cabin was 'Bobcat' in the old Camp Menatoma property on Lovejoy Pond. We bought the cabin right then and there and have been spending our summers there ever since. It is my sanctuary and my most favorite place on Earth." ~ Adele Wolkoff, Indianapolis, Indiana

CAMP DON BOSCO ~ 1952

The Sisters of Charity, also known as the "Grey Nuns", came to Lewiston from Montreal, Canada before 1900 to provide health care and social support to the emergent French-Canadian immigrant population. One of several institutions founded by the Sisters of Charity was the Healey Asylum on Ash Street, a boarding school and orphanage which housed up to one-hundred boys at a time.[506] Providing so many youngsters with outdoor activities in a stifling city environment was challenging to say the least and organizing a summer camp on a lake seemed like the ideal solution.

Camp Don Bosco is the only camp, of all those included in this book, that was run by a religious community. It was situated on 150 acres of land partly in Fayette and partly in Wayne.[507] The Roman Catholic Sisters of Charity from Lewiston acquired this property[508] in 1952 and developed a camp for orphaned boys. They opened in June of that same year, exactly one week after the Girls Scouts had launched Camp Kirkwold across the lake.[509]

Tom Mathews has been the owner of this entire property since 1981. His great-grandfather and name-sake[510] bought a camp lot from the original farm in 1933. Since then four generations of Tom's family have summered there. Throughout his life Tom has collected stories from his parents, grandparents and some of the Camp Don Bosco alumni.[511] Tom related that Dennis Fournier owned this land previous to the Sisters of Charity. He was a Franco American logger from the Lewiston area who bought the farm in 1947 and built four bunkhouses for his woodscrew who harvested all the standing timber. Five years later the Sisters of Charity convinced Fournier to donate the clear-cut property where they would start Camp Don Bosco.[512] The existing structures – a farmhouse, two barns and the lumberjack camps would be their primary buildings. Several lakeside lots had been sold by then but there was still about 700 feet of water frontage and ample acreage that made for an ideal location.

The Sisters of Charity solicited for donations and enough materials to convert the big red four story barn into a dormitory. It would take construction workers, from Lewiston, at least eight weeks to complete the project but that did not stop the Sisters from moving the boys there a good six weeks before renovations were completed. They were all anxious to get out of the hot city no doubt. Four teenage girls were hired to help prepare meals. They and Rev. Bernard Remillard, who was the priest in charge, occupied the former lumberjack camps by the lake.[513] In later years they became quarters for teenage boys who were hired as counselors.[514] Four nuns bedded down in the dormitory while another sixteen slept in the farmhouse.[515] "An industrial bathroom was added to the back side of the barn" said Mathews "but there were no showers. They must have bathed in the lake." In the beginning a dining room on the first floor doubled as the chapel and confessional. Father Remillard held Sunday services there for the campers. The older boys slept on the second and third floors and the youngest ones slept on the fourth floor. "There was no fire escape and only one set of stairs and it got really hot up there" Mathews said. "It's a wonder they never had a fire or tragedy there, really." They eventually built a dining room onto the back of the farmhouse and turned the ground floor of the barn exclusively into a chapel.

An arts & crafts and recreational hall was added to the grounds along with a play area which was comprised of rockers, swings and a merry-go-round. A cleared field behind the barn served as a sports field. Mud was scooped out of the lake with a power shovel to create a beach and swimming area and a bathhouse was built in that area.[516] "There wasn't much for watercraft, just one rowboat and no canoes" related Mathews. Activities included swimming, fishing, boating and hiking[517] which were done on the grounds or locally. Apparently extended off-campus field trips like the ones offered at other kids' camps were not offered at Don Bosco.

The lake and a second barn were located on the opposite side of the road from the farmhouse. The barn blocked the view of the lake and, although the nuns lived conservatively, they did take a leap and had the barn moved aside. This barn was used for storage and some livestock was kept there as well.[518] They raised pigs for meat,[519] maintained a large vegetable garden and an orchard that helped fill the pantry. The boys had hearty appetites. They consumed thirty loaves of bread and one-hundred quarts of milk every day - three times more than they ate in the city. One boy exclaimed that he could eat "eleven slices of bread for lunch" after a busy morning of fresh air, some work and lots of play. They also generated a lot of laundry which was hauled to and from Lewiston every week on "wash day".[520]

"Camp Don Bosco was self-sufficient so there was little interaction with the community" said Mathews. Neighbors did share their catches of fish and made other donations to the camp though. According to Mathews two discontinued transit busses were given by the City of Lewiston and transported to the camp where the wheels and axles were removed. One was set near the farmhouse and used as a concession stand. The other was moved to the lakeside and served as housing for the camp custodian, Gregoire Baillargeon of Lewiston. The Sisters of Charity gave the makeshift bungalow and the lot it sat on to Baillargeon when the camp ceased operation.[521]

Brian Donohue was 7 years old when he started summering with some family members at Tall Timbers (see pg. 279) in 1946. He recalls going to Camp Don Bosco on Sundays. "I used to ride with my aunt and uncle in a rowboat across the lake and we would go to church there on Sunday mornings. The Priest spoke French so we did not understand what he was saying but we still went."

Sadly, Camp Don Bosco was discontinued and put up for sale in 1968 and the Healy Asylum closed two years later. The realtor's advertisement for the camp read "…An excellent opportunity to enter a worthwhile service to youth…The property consists of 150 acres, the dormitory will accommodate over 100 campers, the administrative building has sleeping quarters for 36 administrative and employed personnel, and it includes several other buildings and camps…completely furnished and ready for business." In spite of this appeal the property never functioned as a summer camp again. In 1969 it was purchased by a New Jersey couple and then reverted back to private ownership.

Some of the campers had been orphans since birth and others were older when, for various reasons, their parents surrendered custody. Mathews related "For a good fifteen years after I bought this place I quite often found (former campers) sitting in their cars in my driveway and revisiting the place. Sometimes I would find someone crying because he had been abandoned as a child and being here brought back painful memories. Then there were others who told me those summers at Camp Don Bosco were the happiest times of their lives."

The house and barn at Camp Don Bosco as it appears today

Some of the nuns and orphans at Camp Don Bosco, 1952
Courtesy University of Southern Maine, Franco-American Collection

INLAND TOURIST HOMES

During the 1940s and 50s several private homes in this area opened their doors to summer guests. Today they would be called Bed & Breakfasts but in that era they were known as "Tourist Homes". Most of them were not located on the lakes but "inland". In this final section of the book are personal accounts of two tourist homes, the "Torsey View House" and the "Dr. Wright Place".

TORSEY VIEW HOUSE ~ 1930

Nearly twenty years ago George S. Cates, Jr. shared his memories of growing up on Kents Hill for inclusion in the 1999 Readfield Heritage Days booklet. In July 2015 he wrote and shared additional memoires with this author. Below are excerpts from both of those writings, as they pertain to the Torsey View House, with additional comments from this author. George's parents were Agatha and George Cates, Sr.

"I (George Cates) was born (1927) in Togus, Maine where my father was head baker at what was known at that time as the Soldiers' Home. After my father retired from Togus we moved to Kents Hill in 1930. There were eight of us children in all, four boys and four girls (Nellie, Rachel, George, Kenneth, Gilbert, Geneva, Elzina (Tillie) and Gleason). The youngest, Gleason, was the only one born at Kents Hill. My folks bought a huge house with many, many bedrooms and a large front porch. As us kids grew up and moved away (my parents) turned the place into a tourist home. Today I guess they are known as Bed and Breakfasts. The sign that hung for years above the front porch read 'Torsey View House' named that because of the nice view of Torsey Lake."

"Our guest rooms were booked by parents who came to visit their children at the various camps such at Camp Menatoma, Camp Merrywold, Camp Vega and Winnebago. Too, we would have vacationers and fisherman stay there - mostly people from New York and New Jersey. I remember two lawyers from Baltimore who came by seaplane and landed on Torsey Pond just down the road. They would circle around the house a couple of times, a signal that they would be landing on the pond. Then Dad would go pick them up in his car. I loved fishing and so did those men, so they used me as a guide and we'd fly and land on some remote lake miles away. Back (in 1940), most lakes had no roads to them nor anyone living around them."

The Cates raised and stored most of their own food supply in order to feed such a large family in addition to the guests. "Our basement was quite large, where we had storage bins for vegetables we grew in our gardens. There was a field (where Gleason Cates built his house) where we had a huge garden for raising vegetables and there was also an apple orchard on the south end. We also had a cow pasture east of that (later this was Ed Wills pasture). I remember as a kid, going hunting every winter with a .22 through a rough woods road looking for any game I could shoot. Then I would dress what I killed and take it home for Mother to cook. I also remember going across the

Agatha Cates

main road, down what we called the Indian Trail to Torsey Lake and I would shoot a dozen or more grey squirrels and Mother always made great meals of the squirrels."

The porch became a lunch room for Kents Hill School students. George's mother, Agatha, also took phone orders from the boarding students and teachers as well as residents on Kents Hill. During the school year she provided a home away from home for the Kents Hill School dormitory students. She cooked hamburgers, hot dogs, sandwiches and pasties including homemade doughnuts which were especially popular. Following Sunday church services at the Methodist Church students would walk to Torsey View House for lunch although reservations were required because space was limited. Agatha was a hard disciplinarian and was not afraid to redirect students towards following the rules but that never seemed to deter them from filling the house.

George, Sr. died in 1940 but Agatha continued to operate Torsey View House. She catered to people from all over the country, especially during the summer months. Parents of Kents Hill School boarding students and those visiting their children at local summer camps rented rooms from Agatha throughout the year. Camp directors and staff members who came to town off season also took rooms at Torsey View House. One in particular, who Evelyn Potter, Readfield Historian recalls, was Mr. Friedenwald, the Camp Menatoma director. Seeing his unmistakably large car parked in front of Torsey View House was one indication every year that camp kids would be coming in soon.

Agatha Cates sold her home in 1965 after which Torsey View House was no more. She lived with her daughter Rachel Gordon and husband Lee on P Ridge Road until her death in 1981.

Torsey View House on Kents Hill as it looked in 1960
(Yannelli 2016)

The view of Torsey Pond from
"Torsey View House" on Kents Hill

"THE DR. WRIGHT PLACE" ~ 1946

> ### This is an abstract of an ad Berry placed in a Maine Bureau of Tourism publication
>
> **Inland – Readfield**
> Lovely old Dr. Wright Place with apartments for summer guests. You can enjoy the advantages of exclusive living close to the shores of beautiful Maranacook Lake, with hot and cold water and electric cooking for your convenience. Just a short drive to Augusta, the State Capital, with golf, movies, etc. There are stores within a short walk of this charming village place.
> **Prices:** See custodian for rates which are low for a month or part of a month. *G.M. Berry, owner, Moweaqua, Illinois.*

In 1946 George Berry, a temperance worker from Illinois, bought what was known by locals as the "Dr. Wright place" on Church Road in Readfield. Berry owned the house until 1955 during which time he let out rooms to summer tourists.

In the summer of 1952 Berry enlisted the help of five teenage boys from Illinois who were children of some people he knew through his temperance work. They would spend the summer painting the exterior of the Wright house and barn. On the morning they were about to embark on their 1,500 mile five-day road trip to Maine one of the boys backed out. Calvin Boyer, who was 13 and significantly younger than the others, was invited to fill the vacancy. More than sixty years later Boyer wrote of the experience from his home in Pasadena, California. He has kindly given permission for us to include excerpts from his entertaining account of that summer.

"For a young farm boy who had never been further from home than the neighboring states of Indiana and Missouri, it "turned out to be one glorious, unbroken adventure..." Boyer wrote. Their mode of travel was a "Kaiser Virginian with a tear-drop trailer hitched behind. At that time there was no high-speed interstate highway system, yet to Boyer 50 mph seemed lightening fast – "...unimpeded driving contrasted against driving on the roadways of (Boyer's) community often strewn with farm machinery…"

Boyer's story varies from those in previous chapters in that his observations come from several personal perspectives – through the magical eyes of a young boy; as a highway traveler from simpler times; as a fledgling tourist; and as a summer employee with some interesting insights into the proprietor and his style of operation.

Excerpts from "Heaven on Earth" by Calvin Boyer

With no advance warning or planning, here I was in a car with four other young people who I had never met, all in tow of a man named Berry. We ranged in age from 13 to 17, I was the youngest. We were all farm youths. Ahead of us lay nearly 3,000 miles of road travel on pre-interstate highways and seven weeks away from home. The three oldest boys bonded the first day and declared the back seat theirs leaving us younger two to sit in the front with Berry. I found that enormously advantageous (because) Berry as our seat mate was our personal guide pointing out a myriad of sights that I would have missed on my own. The tear-drop trailer had a small ice box and a two-burner gas stove which was never used. We stopped daily at a grocery store (to get food for that day) and we ate two picnic-like meals a day for the entire trip (except) for one hugely memorable stop at a Howard Johnson's on the Pennsylvania Turnpike for ice cream sundaes.

Boyer's musings tell of Berry's tight budget and frugality such as bad brakes replaced by some he found in a junk yard; and how they slept on the ground near the car on the shoulder of the road. One such night they slept uncomfortably close to a fast moving highway in Boston. Another night they all bedded down in a huge mining bucket in the strip mining region of western Pennsylvania. More thrilling than all that were the sights Berry showed the boys along the way. They toured old Philadelphia, West Point and historic Boston. They gleefully splashed in the waves one "late afternoon at the seashore" - the first time any of them had ever seen an ocean. From there it was on to Portland, Maine where Berry arranged for an interview with a newspaper reporter and by the time the group reached Readfield many of the residents had already read the resulting article about the "Coast-to-Coast Campers". They knew all about the boys before they had even pulled into town.

Northeastern Headquarters of Coast to Coast Campers
READFIELD, MAINE

This postal size advertising card of the Wright house was produced by Berry for another entrepreneurial scheme. "Coast to Coast Campers" had its origin in the trip to Readfield. Berry bought a can of red paint and added "Coast to Coast Campers" on each side of the tear drop trailer. The acronym 'CTCC' appeared in the Portland newspaper story.
~ Photo Courtesy of Calvin Boyer

When we arrived the house was clean and the interior was in fine order. The furniture, although modest, was sufficient in quantity and quality that, as a guest house, would have been quite attractive to families of the middle class. The kitchen had not only basic appliances but table service and glasses sufficient for

8-10 people. There were linens in the bedrooms and bathrooms. It was easy for us to keep the house clean as the floors were largely barren of throw rugs. There was even a Hoover.

The extensive lawn around the house and barn was evidently cared for by someone in the village as it was well maintained when we arrived. The exterior of the house was in rather good shape. That is, very little scraping of old paint was needed before the new paint was applied. Indeed, wooden siding allowed to deteriorate can require sometimes almost as much preparatory work as the actual painting. Clearly that was not the case with the Wright House.

Upon arrival we toured the house and each of us selected our room for the stay. Not one of us had come from such a large spacious house. Before the first weekend was over we had settled comfortably into the Wright house, attended church, had a swim in the lake and had (eaten) our first hot meal since we had left home.

Day one was divided between purchasing paint and supplies in the morning and grocery shopping in the afternoon. The more fascinating of the two was Berry's strategy for feeding the crew well but inexpensively. To do this, we drove to a supermarket in a larger town…Berry sought out the fruit and vegetable manager to ask if he might have that which was being discarded…He would go three times each week to pick up what was available… Once he secured a no-cost supply of fruits and vegetables for our stay, he proceeded to stock our fridge and pantry. I still recall (food preparation) foreign to my own household such as adding a large amount of crackers and eggs to ground beef to make hamburgers. But the bottom line was that our three meals a day were simply delicious, healthy and plentiful.

On day two and the following week days we began painting the house after breakfast… we took a brief break for lunch and then painted again until mid afternoon... when the thermometer reached the high 80s or even the 90s we would end our work for the day. Without fail we young people would then change into our bathing suits and head for the lake. Oh, what joy that lake provided... That summer much of the time we were there it was especially hot and dry...at most we lost only part of one day to rain..."

As the lightest of the five painters I was assigned the high ladder work. In order to reach the highest points...two long ladders were cobbled together. While they were sufficiently attached they were still wobbly...Later I think my parents were horrified to hear (of my) climbing and working from those ladders.

From a local library Berry obtained permission for us to borrow books. Each one of us was an avid reader and the library shelves were a rich storehouse...Many evenings after supper I would climb up the barn roof to the cupola and view the surrounding world. Then I would settle in with my book...I think I was the only one who made regular use of the cupola. Among the house furnishings was a phonograph (and) Berry had a collection of classical music recordings. Each evening he would play a few discs (and say) some words about the music or composer. This was my first introduction to classical music...

In essence, Berry had the house painted for little more cost than that of the paint and brushes. To underscore this fact, you may recall his strategy for feeding us youngsters largely on over-the-hill produce that the grocery stores were discarding... Later after my return to Illinois, my parents were puzzled over why Berry owned the house which he did not intend to ever personally occupy. The puzzlement was heightened by his modest income as a temperance worker with a large family that surely lived frugally of necessity, with little money for the upkeep of a second home.

Among my public school classmates, no one then or later had any summer adventure which rivaled my summer in Readfield! Later I read Wouk's "City Boy, the Adventures of Herbie Bookbinder". The portion of the book devoted to his summer camp adventures was no more exciting than what I lived that summer. And it cost my parents not one dime! That I have made my way back to Readfield twice as an adult to see that house firsthand surely does suggest how indelible the impressions made on me. Nearing the end of year 75, that summer in Readfield is still one of the highlights of my life.

Time and again throughout my life I have curiously glanced down camp roads in passing. I have heard reveille and taps play from nearby kids' camps; seen the "summer kids" paddling canoes on our lakes; or riding in open-backed trucks past my childhood home. I tried to imagine what it would feel like to leave my own family for an entire summer. I wondered what the campers did to pass the time and what those kids' camps were really like.

I have marveled at how many out-of-state cars appeared in town come July and day dreamed about where their passengers might be going. I have seen strangers in our country stores and eateries and heard them speak with unfamiliar accents. I wondered where they came from and where they "hid" during their visits here. Now, I won't wonder so much and for the first time in my sixty-eight years I feel "connected".

Dale Potter-Clark, 2016

ENDNOTES

---

1 State of Maine Development Commission; Augusta, ME; 1928; pg.41
http://digicom.bpl.lib.me.us/; accessed 1/11/2016

2 Daniel Craig was a grandson of James Craig, Sr. who was a Readfield pioneer in 1765. He built the first sawmill and grist mill in Readfield. By doing so he created an industrial center called "Craig's Mills" (Factory Square) that endured for well over a century. Land lots were sold from that 200 acres by his heirs and developed into a significant section of Readfield Corner.

3 Craig's farm was located on the east corner of "Whittier (North) Road" and the "Road to Hallowell" (route 17). In our time known as "Sonny's Seafood" (Payson)

4 David W. Craig developed Tallwood Peninsula when he built the Sir Charles Hotel and cottages. The land was called "Craig's Point" for several years after. See the chapter on Tallwood pg.62

5 KCRD book301 page94 3/14/1848 James and Alton Sedgeley to A&KRR

6 Given, Charles S.; Railroad History, Issues 1-10; pub. 1921; pg.45; hereafter Given

7 Kennebec Journal (KJ), "Opening of the Railroad to Waterville"; 12/6/1849; Vol. XXV No.51; pg. 1; hereinafter KJ and date

8 ibid

9 ibid

10 Anson P. Morrill became the first Republican Governor of Maine in 1861. He also served as president and vice-president of the Maine Central Railroad between 1864 and 1887.

11 Annual Reports of the Maine Central Railroad Company 1879-1893; hereinafter referred to as MCRR

12 Schultz, Mary; Reflections of Readfield; Readfield Bicentennial Comm. 1976; pgs.27-28

13 www.american-rails.com/yankee.html; accessed 1/1/2016

14 Rondi Nelson who runs Camp Skoglund in West Mt. Vernon, is a direct descendant of George S. Page. She is in possession of a mounted, record setting trout that he caught in the Rangeley Lakes.

15 New exhibits at the Outdoor Sporting Heritage Museum draw visitors; Daily Bulldog;

16 A brief Biography of George Shepard Page; unpublished; in the collection of his g-granddaughter Rondi Nelson, Camp Skogland, 2015. Also in her possession is the 11.5 pound mounted brook trout affectionately called "Stanley" by the family

17 Hallock & Bruette; Forest and Stream ; New York City; 1873; pg.293

18 Hallock & Bruette; Forest and Stream Vol. 46; New York City; 1896

19 Bean and Bane Family Genealogy of Saco Valley Maine: Capt. Joseph Bane (Bean) was born in 1676. He was taken captive by the Indians, in 1692, at the age of sixteen, and remained with the tribe eight years, learning their language and afterwards acted as interpreter. There is a document in the Massachusetts archives written by him, April 25, 1755, which shows him to have been about 80 years of age. Col. Phillips, in his journal, now in the Massachusetts archives, date Jan. 24, 1698, mentions "Joseph Bean, of York, a young man," as then a captive with Indians. He was living in Falmouth as early as 1710 and had five children born there, the first three having been born in York. He was probably connected with the fort at New Casco; served in

Indian war of 1722; was captain in 1724, in which year he and a file of soldiers had an engagement with about thirty Indians, killing their leader, whose scalp was carried to Boston, and Lieut. Bean received £100 bounty. He commanded a company in the Norridgewock expedition. He and Joanna had five children.

[20] Kennebec County Registry of Deeds (KCRD) book301 page94 3/14/1848

[21] KCRD; book327 page374 7/7/1880 and book327 page377 8/2/1880

[22] MCRR Railroad Commissioners Annual Report; 1880; pgs. 18-19

[23] Maine Central Railroad Commissioners Annual Report; 1881; page pg.82; hereinafter MCRR

[24] KJ; 8/3/1880

[25] KJ; 8/5/1880

[26] KJ; 8/6/1880

[27] The Defender, Volumes 8-13; monthly periodical by The New England Sabbath Protection League; pg. 72

[28] Haynes, Charles H.; Charming Retreats of Maine via the Maine Central Railroad; 1890

[29] http://www.fishermensvoice.com/201401TheKate.html accessed 1/19/2016

[30] http://www.fishermensvoice.com/archives/0409mainesteamers.html accessed 1/19/2016

[31] Security on Steam Vessels on inland waters; 53rd Maine State Legislature, 2/18/1874; Chapter 172, Sections 1-13; hereinafter MSL 1874

[32] ibid

[33] An Act to authorize the Maine Central Railroad Co. to form steamboat connections; 62nd Maine State Legislature; 1/10/1885; Chapter 367, Section 1

[34] Kingsbury & Demo; History of Kennebec County; pub. 1892; pg.838; hereinafter HKC

[35] Biographical Sketches of Representative Citizens of the State of Maine; New England Historical Publishing Company; pub. 1903; Pages 124-125

[36] KCRD; book459 page 21 7/23/1902

[37] Portland Press Herald; June 4,1901

[38] Wilson, Donald A; Maine's Steamboating Past; Acadia Publishing, 2007; pg.41; hereinafter Wilson

[39] Portland City Directory, 1895; pg.

[40] Chamber of Commerce Journal of Maine, Volume 19; 1905; pg.225

[41] ibid; pg.601

[42] Genealogical and deed research by Dale Potter-Clark; unpublished collection, 2016; hereinafter Potter-Clark collection

[43] ibid

[44] Per 1910-1930 U.S. Census

[45] Dale Potter-Clark interview with C.W. Knight's grandson, Andrew Knight, Jr., of Wayne, ME 1/21/2016; hereinafter Knight

[46] 1900 U.S. Census

[47] State of Maine Auditors Annual Report, 1909

[48] Day & Beattie, pg.13

[49] Wilson, pgs. 13, 88, 92

[50] Bangor Daily News; Ed Knight, Dean of Maine Guides; 1/23/1952

51 KCRD book337 page419 9/1/1882

52 Adams, William; extensive research of land and house lots at Readfield Corner; 2014-2015

53 John O. Craig's grandfather was James Craig, the founder of Factory Square, whose homestead lot encompassed two-hundred acres from Church Road west to Handy Stream on Factory Square and 1 mile north to south. When James' son Thomas died at age 49, his son J.O. was next in line to own the Craig estate.

54 See pages 1 and 58

55 Potter-Clark collection

56 During the mid-twentieth century this Cape Cod house was owned by Benjamin and Mary (Williams) Smith, co-owner of Newton's Camps. (see pg. 175)

57 Adams, William, Readfield Corner research in collaboration with Dale Potter-Clark; 2014-2016; hereinafter Adams

58 ibid

59 Hoyt & Fogg; Maine State Yearbook and Legislative Manuel; 1882; pg.394

60 Burleigh, Charles; History of Guile Family; 1887; pg.286; hereinafter Burleigh

61 The 5th district school house eventually became Readfield's town office and is known today as Asa Gile Hall.

62 Kennebec News; *Lewiston Evening Journal*; Aug. 29, 1876

63 Kingsbury & Deyo;, History of Kennebec County; pub. 1892; chapter on Readfield; and Potter-Clark collection

64 Burleigh, pg.286

65 Potter-Clark collection

66 The Anson P. Morrill mansion on Sturtevant Hill Road was destroyed by fire. It was located in the vicinity of Morrill & Sturtevant Hill Roads.

67 KCRD book196 page414 11/8/1854 ; 1856 map of Readfield

68 Potter, Evelyn; Hints of a Glorious Past; *The Summer Times*; 8/3/1989; pg.20. Note: Most of these features remain intact as of this writing.

69 Readfield news; *Lewiston Evening Journal*; March 4,1874

70 Annual Report of the Bureau of Industrial and Labor Stats; pub. 1893; pg. 13

71 Recent Sales at Readfield with other facts of interest in regard to a prosperous town; *Lewiston Evening Journal*; June 27, 1887

72 1879 map of Readfield Corner

73 KCRD book337page 419 9/1/1882

74 Potter-Clark collection; determined through extensive deed research on Lake Maranacook properties 2013-2016

75 Recent Sales at Readfield with other facts of interest in regard to a prosperous town; *Lewiston Evening Journal*; June 27, 1887

76 Among Harvey's business ventures was North Wayne Scythe Manufacturing Co. and Dirigo Salt Co. William Harvey's ancestral home was a very large farm, with lakefront property on Lake Maranacook which included Harvey Island. That homestead went to William's son James E. Harvey, who founded a boys' camp on Harvey Island around 1915. (Dale Potter-Clark interview with Marjorie Black, Harvey's granddaughter; 1/2016)

77 Inflation estimate $41,250 (2015)

78 Inflation estimate $43,000 (2015)

[79] Maine, Wills and Probate Records for Asa Gile; www.ancestry.com; accessed 2/13/2016; Gile Hall was sold to the Inhabitants of Readfield after Asa Gile's death.

[80] Emery O. Beane was married to a daughter of John O. Craig.

[81] Inflation estimate $58,000 (2015)

[82] Panic of 1893; https://en.wikipedia.org/wiki/Panic_of_1893; accessed 2/13/2016

[83] Orville H. Johnson was president and treasurer of Blake & Johnson; *Iron Age*, Volume 54; Chilton Company, 1894; pg.906

[84] Marriage record of Charles and Sadie (Adell) Stevens; 11/28/1895

[85] Potter-Clark collection

[86] George K. Adell was the first manager of the Sir Charles Hotel and later managed the Granite Hill House in Hallowell. He was married to Mary Gordon, Sadie's Stevens' sister. Prominent Readfield Depot businessman, Nelson D. Gordon, was another sibling. George and Mary Adell were parents of Lottie and Myrtle Adell who worked at the Elmwood and Maranacook Hotel at the turn of the century. Myrtle Adell married Linwood Townsend and they ran Townsend Farm. Linwood Townsend's first cousins Nellie and Lottie Townsend were married to the Maranacook Hotel proprietors Mark and Charles Collins. Family helped family. (per Potter-Clark collection)

[87] Charles E. Stevens obituary; South Portland, ME; March, 1932; hereinafter Stevens

[88] Dale Potter-Clark interview with Readfield native, the late Ruth Mullen in 1986

[89] ibid

[90] Adams

[91] KCRD book1109 page14 3/19/1958

[92] Kingsbury & Deyo; History of Kennebec County; pub.1892; Readfield

[93] Readfield news; Lewiston Evening Journal; 10/8/1881

[94] The Hutchinson's loss was estimated at $4,500 = $112,000 in 2015 http://www.westegg.com/inflation; accessed 2/21/2016

[95] KCRD book326 page291 4/1/1880; and KCRD book395 page339 4/11/1893; also Annual Report of the Bureau of Industrial and Labor Statistics; 1893

[96] See Daniel O. Craig house pg. 2

[97] See page 29, Maranacook House

[98] Hoyt & Fogg; Maine State Yearbook, and Legislative Manual, for the Year 1882; pg.392

[99] This paragraph compiled from information in Potter-Clark collection

[100] Death certificate, signed by Dr. Warren W. Wright of Readfield

[101] Potter-Clark collection; this branch of the Stanley family was cousins of the Stanley twins who were creators of many inventions including the Stanley Steamer. One of the twins also started the Stanley Hotel in Estes Park, CO. All of those Stanleys were also cousins of George S. Page and Henry O. Stanley who are discussed in our chapter titled "Cometh the Sports" pg.11

[102] KCRD book413 page247 3/21/1896; KCRD book413 page248 3/21/1896

[103] Hutchinson family oral tradition says that Edwin had the house built but research by Dale Potter-Clark indicates that he enlarged or converted it, or both. The building was in place when he purchased this property.

[104] See the chapter on Coleman Grove, pg.44

[105] Tyner

[106] Tyner

[107] Tyner and Potter-Clark collection

[108] Edwin and Ida's daughter Alice married Roy Giles of Readfield. Alice was given a lakeside lot by her father before she died in 1928. Her husband, Roy Giles, afterwards owned the lake lot and built a cottage on it. The property was passed on to his daughters Natalie and Jean who sold it to Laurence and Nancy Perkins in 2001. The Giles camp burned in the interim.

[109] Convalescents Escape; *Portland Sunday Telegram*; 2/15/1948; After the Hutchinson family sold "the summer home" it was converted yet again – this time into a home for the elderly called "Sunset Home". In 1948 Sunset Home was destroyed by fire. Later the same year the land was purchased by Ruth Townsend and her sister Mary Hock. Ruth built a house there which is owned and occupied by her grand-nephew Eben Dumaine as of this writing.

[110] KCRD book39 page222 5/17/1821

[111] See the chapter on Hutchinson House, pg38

[112] Ibid

[113] This house was razed decades ago. It sat on the south corner of South Road & Pine Rest Cottage Road.

[114] KCRD book620 page199; 8/15/1924

[115] Dale Potter-Clark interview with Catherine Bliss, September 2014; hereinafter Bliss

[116] Bliss

[117] Pinerest Housekeeping Cottages brochure, Fred and Catherine Bliss, proprietors

[118] KCRD, various as researched by Dale Potter-Clark

[119] KCRD Book 119 Page 105; 10/28/1839

[120] http://readfield1791.blogspot.com; Robert Waugh; accessed 8/19/2015

[121] KCRD; 1) Samuel Waugh, Robert's grandson, to Benjamin Cushman of Harrington, ME for $1,000 7/7/1834 KCRD book84 page275; 2) Benjamin Cushman of Readfield to Samuel Chandler of Winthrop for $4,000 10/28/1839 KCRD book 119 page 105 excluding the 8-12 acre Pine Island which Chandler reserved for self; 3) Samuel Chandler to Joel Howard of Canton, ME for $3,000 11/27/1839 KCRD book119 page 106; 4) Joel Howard, Sr. of Readfield to Joel Howard, Jr. for $1,000 3/26/1947 "...90 acres and all of Waugh farm..." KCRD book154 page491; 5) Joel Howard to George Hunt for $1,600 11/4/1848 90 acres and Waugh farm KCRD book163 page545; 6) Hunt to Inhabitants of Readfield book258 page173 3/21/1861 KCRD book258 page173.

[122] Baker, Charles; Veterans, Tramps, and the Economic Crisis of 1873; http://voiceseducation.org/node/208; accessed 1/16/2016

[123] Potter-Clark, Dale; Readfield, Maine Town Farm and the evolution of how we supported and cared for our poor 1771-1991; 2012; unpublished

[124] After Craig bought the "town farm" the farmhouse and barn were rented to various families over the years. Merrill and Faith Rourke, and their two older sons Dick and Bill, lived there for about six years in the 1950s. They rented from Mr. Bloomfield, who owned Tallwood at that time. During the years the Rourkes lived there the barn burned, and the Rourkes lost several farm animals. The house was torn down about 1960, about five years after the Rourkes moved out. Bill Rourke recalls the house was three stories and one upstairs room was full of books – shelves and

boxes of them. He never knew what happened to those books and always wondered who they belonged to. (by Dale Potter-Clark interview with Bill Rourke, 2/6/2016)

[125] Day, Charles L. and Beattie, Donald; *Maranacook's Southern Lakeside Resorts*; pub. 2013 by Day and Beattie; pg. 12; hereinafter Day and Beattie

[126] Henry Whittier's workshop is owned by craftsman / carpenter Tom McPhedran in 2015.

[127] George K. Adell is 2nd great grandfather of author Dale Potter-Clark

[128] Later known as Butler Island

[129] Previously known as Stevens Island. In 1920 Charles A Collins (Hotel Maranacook) placed the highest bid for Center Island, which had been seized by the town of Readfield for unpaid taxes from David W. Craig's heirs. Charles son Parkman sold it to William Morgan in 1940 (Camp Maranacook).

[130] Forest and Stream Magazine; July-Dec, 1894 issue; 8/11/1894 pg.120

[131] Day and Beattie pg. 10 NOTE: The Anita was built by C.W. Howard of Peak's Island. Howard was a Readfield native whose grandfather Joel Howard was the last to own the 200 acre Tallwood Peninsula in its entirety. He split is into two 100 acres farms, between his three sons Joel, Jr, Charles and Anderson (C.W.'s father) in the 1840s. This discovered through a genealogical study and research at KCRD by Dale Potter-Clark, 2015. See chapter on steamboats pg.20

[132] "A.G. Wing is reported to be plans for a hotel to be erected at Craig's Point, Winthrop, Maine for Mrs. Wm S Butler of Boston Mass." (The Engineering Record, Building Record and the Sanitary Engineer, Volume 51; 1905; pg.336

[133] Day and Beattie, pg. 13

[134] This murder was solved three years after the murder when a Hallowell innkeeper confessed and then committed suicide but the event still made great fodder for a ghost story. (Early Readfield, Maine 1791-1991; Readfield Sesquicentennial Committee; copies available at Readfield Historical Society)

[135] KCRD book480 page495 9/5/1907

[136] Letter from Charles A. Collins to his son Parkman, 12/27/1919; personal collection of Judith Collins, Montpelier, VT 1/2016

[137] Day and Beattie; pg 10

[138] KCRD book741 page547 9/12/1938

[139] Day and Beattie page 10

[140] KCRD various

[141] http://www.tallwoodcottages.com/History.html; accessed 8/20/2015

[142] Panic of 1893; https://en.wikipedia.org/wiki/Panic_of_1893; accessed 1/11/2016

[143] A Brief History of the Sandy River & Rangeley Lakes Railroad; http://www.srrl-rr.org/hist.htm; accessed 1/12/2016

[144] New England Historical Society; Cornelia Fly Rod Crosby, The First Maine Guide; www.newenglandhistoricalsociety.com; accessed 1/11/2016; hereinafter NEHS

[145] ibid

[146] Hallock & Bruette; Forest and Stream Vol. 46; New York City; 1896; pg 254

[147] ibid; page 475

[148] NEHS

[149] Wilson, Donald A; Glimpses of Maine's Angling Past; Arcadia Press; 2000; pg.22; Dale Potter-Clark email exchange with the author 1/2016 inconclusive.

150 Stack, Jennie Borodko; Wielding a fly rod in northwestern Maine won Crosby a nickname; Bangor Daily News; 3/30/1991 (hereinafter Fly Rod)

151 Some sources relate that Maranacook Hotel was built in 1880, the same year the Maine Central Railroad (MCRR) built "Maranacook Grove." In 1905, when Maranacook Hotel burned, the Kennebec Journal reported it was twenty-seven years old, and that it was owned by the MCRR. In fact several writings about the Hotel say that MCRR owned it and the land it sat on – one claiming the MCRR owned 60 acres at that location. An extensive search of land deeds revealed that the MCRR never owned land at this location, other than where the tracks and right of way ran through. They did enter into a 25 year lease for about 10 acres where they built Maranacook Grove in 1880. (KCRD book 301page 94; document 3/14, 1848; recorded 4/21/1875). An 1883 publication about vacationing Downeast describes a "...charming point on Maranacook, 'owned' by the railroad... (with) pavilions, seats, dance halls, wharves and other conveniences..." There is no mention of a hotel. (Sweetser, Moses Foster; Lakes and Streams Illustrated; Passenger Department, Boston and Maine Railroad; 1896; pgs.53-54). In 1895 Mark Collins bought 100 acres from George Sedgley, which included those ten acres, he agreed to a 30 years lease on the same land and included rights for the MCRR to run water pipes from Collins spring to "the grove". That document expressly mentions the excursion center but no hotel. (KCRD book407 page108 5/15/1895) In 1896 the Boston & Maine Railroad published a booklet that included information about Maranacook Grove but there is no mention of a hotel at that location. (Sweetser, Moses Foster; Lakes and Streams Illustrated; Passenger Department, Boston and Maine Railroad; 1896; pgs.47-48) Additionally, the Maine State Railroad Commissioners' annual reports of that era tell in detail what buildings were erected at Maranacook Grove and Maranacook Hotel is not included in those reports. There is mention of the 30x100 ft. dining hall built Maranacook Grove in 1880. It is important to note those reports reference hotels that were owned or built at other Maine locations by railroad companies.

152 KCRD book330 page134 ; book309 page480 (properties bought by Charles A. Collins in Clinton, ME 1877 and 1880)

153 Genealogical and deed research by Dale Potter-Clark; unpublished collection, 2016 (hereinafter Potter-Clark collection)

154 Dale Potter-Clark's telephone interview with Mark and Nellie Collins' grandson Mark Collins III and his wife Katherine of Ventura, CA; January 2016; hereinafter Collins

155 Potter-Clark collection

156 KCRD book379 page349 11/2/1889

157 KCRD book381 page 499 7/1/1890

158 This purchase also included the cattle pound lot adjacent to the store lot. (KCRD book387 page446 12/23/1891) NOTE: Daniel Craig inherited this store from his step-father William Luce. After Daniel it was owned and run by his son David W. Craig. David moved to MA then later bought and bought Tallwood Peninsula and built the Sir Charles Hotel and cottages. Collins sold the store to Nelson D. Gordon in 1897 who converted it to a tenement house. Still later his son Nelson T. Gordon built a Pontiac garage and dealership at that location, using part of the old railroad freight

shed for his garage. This building has recently been torn down (2016) but part of the old freight shed was retained.

[159] Potter-Clark collection

[160] KCRD book406 page445 and KCRD book 406 page 404 4/17/1895

[161] KCRD book327 page374 7/7/1880 and KCRD book407 page108 5/5/1895

[162] KCRD book415 page545 2/25/1897

[163] Potter-Clark collection and KCRD book426 page513 6/30/1899; Charles and Lottie were living in Yarmouth at this time.

[164] This cove has historically been called Waugh's Cove and Townsend Cove.

[165] KCRD book423 page10711/4/1897 NOTE: This farm eventually found its way back to members of the Townsend family who ran it as the summer hotel, "Townsend Farm".

[166] KCRD book417 page462 1/11/1897

[167] Rusticators was a term used for city dwellers who came to Maine in the 19th and early 20th centuries to spend summers at resorts and inns; Today's Tourists–Yesterday's "Rusticators; https://mainehistory.wordpress.com; accessed 2/3/2016

[168] KCRD 432 page 520 6/22/1899

[169] ibid book432 page13 8/8/1899

[170] 1900 U.S. Census, Winthrop, ME. This is the earliest documentation we found of the Hotel

[171] The engineer was C.W. Knight. See more about him in the chapter about steamboats pg.20

[172] One of the lady servants was Myrtle Adell, who married Nellie and Lottie Townsend's cousin, Linwood Townsend. Myrtle and Linwood later ran Townsend Farm as a summer hotel. See pg.99

[173] 1900 U.S. Census, Winthrop, ME

[174] Maine Railroad Commissioners Annual Report; 1881; page 6; hereinafter MRRC

[175] Four Lives Lost at Maranacook; Kennebec Journal; 8/28/1905; pgs.1-2

[176] Potter-Clark collection

[177] Maranacook, Maine local news; Kennebec Journal; August, 1906

[178] KCRD book474 page4010/4/1906

[179] 1910 U.S. Census, Winthrop, ME

[180] Printed on the backs of postcards from this era.

[181] Potter-Clark collection

[182] ibid

[183] Per his occupation on the 1910 U.S. Census, Readfield, ME

[184] Collins

[185] Potter-Clark collection; his last recorded land transaction in Kennebec County was dated 1934

[186] KCRD book550 page290 12/1/1915

[187] KCRD Plan book7 page84 11/1/1915

[188] The original station was further north, near the trestle. The hotel was out of sight from the old train station which was actually located in Readfield. The land where the hotel, cottages and camps were located fell within both Winthrop and Readfield.

[189] KCRD book566page 490 4/15/1918

[190] Day and Beattie; pgs.47-48

191 Charlie Day interview with Stephen Dacorta; email to Dale Potter-Clark 2/1/2016
192 KCRD Plan book7 page84; 11/1/1915
193 Dale Potter-Clark's telephone interview with Charles Collins' g-grandaughter, Judy Collins, of Montpelier, VT; January 2016. The steamer *Maranacook* was entered into service about 1900, by Mark Collins, after his first steamboat, *Lorna*.
194 Scott Davis, owner of said building in 2016, who relates this to the best of his knowledge; email to Dale Potter-Clark 2/1/2016
195 KCRD Plan book20 page98 9/30/1958
196 ibid
197 Day and Beattie; pg 43
198 1) Dale Potter-Clark's interview and emails with Charles Collins g-grandaughter, Judy Collins, of Montpelier, VT 1/2016; hereinafter Judy Collins; 2) Potter-Clark collection
199 As told by Joe Maloney to Dale Potter-Clark, 8/5/2016
200 Dale Potter-Clark interviews and emails with Katherine and Mark Collins III of Ventura. CA 12/2015—1/ 2016; hereinafter Mark Collins 2) Potter-Clark collection
201 Streetcar, Cable Car: What's the difference? http://www.streetcar.org; accessed 1/16/2016
202 The Electrical Age, Volume 33; 1904; pgs.451-452 (hereinafter electric age)
203 The Commissioners made this decision noting that access by rail from Augusta to Winthrop and Monmouth only existed by a circuitous MCRR route via Waterville or the Lewiston & Brunswick railroad
204 Annual Report of the State of Maine Board of Railroad Commissioners; 1900; pgs.83-86; hereinafter SMRC
205 ibid
206 Electric age, pgs.451-452
207 KCRD book459 pg21, lease from Fred H. Beane; 7/23/1902
208 Townsend Cove was known as Waugh's Cove in earliest days of settlement. Robert Waugh settled 200 acres on Tallwood Peninsula in 1768. Also see Sir Charles Hotel and Townsend Farm.
209 Day and Beattie; page 12
210 The Trolley Parks of Maine by Carney, Leclair, and Rogan; Maine Memory Network; www.mainememory.net; accessed 1/17/2016
211 Memories of Island Park by Vivian Dennett; Summertime in the Belgrades; 8/18/2006
212 https://en.wikipedia.org/wiki/Moonlight_Bay; accessed 1/18/2016
213 Oral histories conducted by Dale Potter-Clark and Evelyn Adell Potter 1987-1989, transcriptions available at Readfield Historical Society, Main St. Readfield Depot
214 Special Collections, Colby College http://web.colby.edu/specialcollections/2011/03/15; accessed 1/15/2016; hereinafter Special Collections, Colby College
215 Electric Railway Journal, Volume 38, 1911; McGraw Hill Publishing Company; pg.210
216 Ibid; 1910; pg.176
217 Special Collections, Colby College
218 KCRD; book 10 page6; 5/20/1929

[219] Day & Beattie; pg.1. NOTE: When it became Memorial Drive is not known at this time, but in 1942 a plan registered with Kennebec County Registry of Deeds book14 page19 still named it Memorial Road.
[220] Winthrop Comprehensive Planning Process Historical Resources; June 8, 2009
[221] http://kennebecriverrailtrail.org; accessed 1/18/2016
[222] KCRD book442 page460, 3/27/1903; Linwood rented this farm for 3 years until he bought it.
[223] Potter-Clark collection; House Lineage: Josiah Whittier pre 1824; Henry White 1824-1846; Samuel Gove 1846-1855; Moses Whittier 1855-1865; Alson Whittier 1865-1870; George Wadleigh 1870-1878; Miles E. Williams 1878-1898; Jerome Messinger 1898-1900; W.H. Jackson 1900-1902; Minnie Atherton 1902-1903; Elmer Gibbs 1903; Linwood Townsend 1903-1947.
[224] Dale Potter-Clark interview with Holly Hock Dumaine, grandaughter of Linwood and Myrtle Townsend: 2/10/2016; hereinafter Holly Hock
[225] KCRD book786 page69, 1/22/1942
[226] Myrtle's father George K. Adell, who was the first manager at the Sir Charles Hotel, was living in Hallowell and managing the Granite Hill House at this time. (per 1900 Census)
[227] See the chapter on Maranacook Cottages, Camps and Hotel, page 74
[228] Potter-Clark collection
[229] Dale Potter-Clark interview with Linwood Townsend, son of Lee and Helen Townsend, 2/8/2016 (hereinafter Townsend)
[230] Townsend
[231] KCRD various 1908-1912
[232] Holly Hock
[233] Dale Potter-Clark interview with Irene Adell Potter who worked at Townsend Farm as a chambermaid and waitress in the 1950s; 2/9/2016; hereinafter Irene Adell Potter
[234] 1) Compiled from interviews with Holly Hock, Townsend and Adell; 2) Dale Potter-Clark interviews with Robert Ifill (he since decreased) who bought Townsend Farm from Helen Townsend; 2/9/2016; hereinafter Ifill; 3) Dr. Alex McPhedran, current owner; 2/9/2016; hereinafter McPhedran
[235] Holly Hock
[236] Bliss, Catherine; Maranacook Yesterday and Today; address to Lake Maranacook Assoc; Aug., 1996; pg.4; hereinafter Bliss
[237] Potter
[238] Holly Hock
[239] Holly Hock
[240] Townsend
[241] The trolley stop called Tallwood Landing was also known as Bearce Landing.
[242] Townsend; and Ruth and Marion Townsend oral history; by Dale Potter-Clark and Evelyn Adell Potter, Readfield Historian; 1980s
[243] Bliss, pg.3
[244] Townsend and Holly Hock
[245] Dale Potter-Clark interview with Evelyn Adell Potter, Readfield Historian and Readfield Depot native; 2/6/2016

[246] KCRD book558 page300 and book564 page323

[247] Dale Potter-Clark interview with William Rourke, grandson of William and Iva Rourke; 2/6/2016

[248] When Lee and Helen Townsend took over the business in 1947 their brochure more bluntly stated "transportation to the Catholic and Protestant churches in Winthrop is available." (Townsend) The hotels and camps of the times were, for the most part, segregated and accepted people of either Christian or Jewish faiths, but not both. Notation in brochures of transportation to a Christian church was a "secret code" of sorts, that let potential guests know which religious persuasion that particular resort or camp would accept and that it was set up with a kosher kitchen. (Per Dale Potter-Clark interview with Stephanie Wilson Hatch, July 2014. Hatches' grandparents founded Cebennek Boys' and Chase Lodge and Cottage Colony on Torsey Pond in 1898. Chases Camps was one of the few in this area that would take both the Jewish and Christians, although they did not have a kosher kitchen and made that known to potential clientele first.)

[249] Day and Beattie, pg.18

[250] Irene Adell Potter

[251] Holly Hock and Potter-Clark collection

[252] Irene Adell (Potter) was working there at the time and was the one to find him in distress on August 6th. She sought help from Helen and found out the following day that Mr. Hinds had died soon after she left work.

[253] For a few years in the early 1950s employees were Irene Adell (Potter) of Readfield Depot and Avis Dunn (Butman) of Dunn's Corner, Mt. Vernon

[254] Adell, Townsend, Holly Hock

[255] Townsend

[256] Potter-Clark collection

[257] McPhedran

[258] Joel and Philura (Bean) Howard moved here after they sold Tallwood Farm in 1847. She was a daughter of Oliver Bean and sister of Judge Emery O. Bean, who were both neighbors. Joel and Philura eventually moved to northern Maine.

[259] Research by Dale Potter-Clark, unpublished collection, 2016; hereinafter Potter-Clark collection

[260] Occupation listed on US Census and death certificate.

[261] 1910 U.S. Census, Readfield

[262] Edwin and Tamson Nelson are buried in Readfield Corner Cemetery

[263] Tamson Austin Nelson obituary, Mill Valley, CA; Sept. 1916

[264] Potter-Clark collection

[265] Frost also purchased other properties in town and became a landlord.

[266] Dale Potter-Clark interview with Velma McDougald Bellville; 2/2014

[267] Kennebec County Registry of Deeds 3/29/2000 Book 6174 Page 191.

[268] Oral histories conducted by Dale Potter-Clark and Evelyn Potter 1987-1989 of C. Willis Brown and Ruth and Marion Townsend.

[269] Potter-Clark collection

[270] ibid

[271] The couple's legal sir name was Mathieu but they went by Martinetti. Ignacio, called "Nash" by people close to him, went by the stage name Ignacio Martinetti and

Caroline's stage name was Carrie Radcliffe. Both appeared in Broadway plays in the 1920s. He died in Long Island, NY 1931 and she died in 1933. Her son John Ferris, from a previous marriage, inherited "The Pines" and sold to Golsners in 1934. The Martinettis were the second owners of the cottage, having bought it in 1913 from the original owners, the Vincent family. (Letter from John Ferris in Readfield Historical Society vertical files; and KCRD book703 page403 6/22/1934)

272 The owners at that time were Albert and Mae Golsner who also owned Coleman's Camps (Pinerest) further north on the lake from 1944-1949. They bought the Martinelli cottage from Carrie Martinelli's son John Ferris in 1934. The Golsners actually called "Tall Pines" cottage Pinerest.

273 Potter-Clark collection

274 Maine Chamber Catalogue, 1911

275 Private collection of Judith Collins, great-granddaughter of Charles Collins 1/2016

276 Stewart Edward White was a well known American author and conservationist during the early 20th century. Among his works were history, travel and adventure books. White and Theodore Roosevelt became great friends and they went on many outdoor adventures together. Roosevelt said of White, he's "the kind of young American who is making our new literature." In 1903 White wrote "Silent Places" in which the hero was an Indian named Haukeemah – perhaps this story was Mabel Harvey's inspiration? The Literature Network, Stewart Edward White; www.online-literature.com/stewart-white/; accessed 2/22/2016

277 Lake at Readfield Keep Names Founded in Romance of English Girls with Indians; *Portland Sunday Telegram and Evening Express*; after 1929, between 1907-1929 - exact date unknown. The last paragraph in this news article was this: William H. Morgan, proprietor of Camp Maranacook now owns Mount Hunger and a few years ago had the old apple trees cut down and had the cellar filled in.

278 Vergne Harvey, grand-nephew (born 1939) of James and Mabel Harvey to Dale Potter-Clark 2/22/2016: "My father James Willard Harvey found the spring mentioned in the story. We used it thereafter for our drinking water. It was about 1/4 of a mile from our camp so my father fashioned a wooden cradle to carry a 5 gallon jug back to the camp. He had remembered it as a boy so he and my sister Judith set out to find it. By then the whole area was deeply wooded and it took them about 4 days to find it. I think this was about 1948."

279 This was called "Adams Island" when it was bought from Hallowell Savings Bank (2* to a bank foreclosure on one Norton) by the Harvey family in 1882 (KCRD book356 page491). The island was 22 acres at that time but since then the lake level has increased and some of the island may have also washed away, which reduced the acreage significantly.

280 A newsy letter from Tamson Nelson to her daughter Bertha Johnson dated 1910 and included a photo of this island with buildings. Letter courtesy of Stephen Johnson, Nelson's g-grandson. Tamson Nelson ran Tamsonhurst, see pg. 110

281 KCRD book255 page170; 12/28/1864

282 The Harvey farm was eventually sold with some of the land to the mayor of New York City. With subsequent owners it fell into disrepair and had to be torn down Dale Potter-Clark interview with Marjorie Black, granddaughter of James and Mabel Harvey; 1/25/2016; hereinafter Marjorie Black

283 When the Asa Gile estate was auctioned off William Harvey bought the Asa Gile house. See pg 37

284 Marjorie Black; Interesting notes about this house is it was built by a shipwright so the floors were not level, as it would be on a ship, so water would flow towards the outside edge. There was also a secret compartment in the basement that Marjorie's grandfather told her was used to hide runaway slaves as part of the Underground Railroad.

285 Dale Potter-Clark interview with Vergne Harvey, grand-nephew of James E. and Mabel Harvey; 2/14/2016; hereinafter Vergne Harvey

286 ibid

287 1) Vergne Harvey 2) *A Handbook of Private Schools and for American Boys and Girls*; 1922; Boys Camps, pg.529

288 Marjorie Black

289 A 1914 post card of Dead Stream Bridge shows the red roof of this building and a large boat entrance facing the lake. This property had buildings on it when sold to Gordon and Annie Smith in 1953 although there had been alterations made or they may have been replaced. Their daughter Lynn Stufflebeam and husband Herbert ran "the Tackle Box" in those buildings – an ice cream and fishing bait shop. In 1960 it was sold by members of the Smith family to the "Readfield Fish and Game Club" and in 1966 the Readfield Fish and Game Club president, Harry Mullen, gifted it to the State of Maine Parks and Recreation Dept. at which time they created the Dead Stream Boat Landing that has been there since.

290 Vergne Harvey

291 At the same time James and Mabel Harvey conveyed a lot on the northeast corner of the island to Asaphine's brother Jim who eventually passed it on to his sister and took over the building on the mainland; per Vergne Harvey

292 Vergne Harvey

293 Libby, Jason C.; Poland Spring Preservation Society; Images of America, Poland Spring; Arcadia Publishing; 2009; 128 pgs.

294 Vergne Harvey

295 ibid

296 U.S. Patent; Marine propulsion; Publication No. US 1786997 A; Dec 30, 1930; www.google.com/patents/US1786997; accessed 3/5/2016

297 Charles Day, Jr. email to Dale Potter-Clark; 2/22/2016

298 1) Broadside; Maine State Museum newsletter; The Harvey Inboard Motor Case; 2) Natalie Liberace, Collections Manager, Maine State Museum

299 Information for this chapter gleaned from a 1910 newspaper article in Readfield Historical Society vertical files; and research by Dale Potter-Clark

300 After James Craig sold this property to Armstrong he moved on to build the first sawmill and grist mill in Readfield at what became known as Craig's Mills or Factory Square. His mill house remains to this day and is currently being rescued.

301 Potter-Clark collection

302Dale Potter-Clark interview with Lawrence Rolfe; 1986; Larry worked on building Martha Washington Inn also. His family moved to Readfield in 1921. Larry, his father and brothers were in the logging and lumber business at that time.

---

[303] Farkas, Tom; *Pieces of empty Readfield Inn will find a home*; Capital Weekly, 1992; hereinafter Farkas

[304] Day & Beattie, pg. 57

[305] Ibid, page 56-59

[306] The woodie station wagon originated in the mid-1930s. The passenger compartment portion of the vehicle was manufactured in hardwood. They were popular in the U.S. and were produced as sedans, convertibles and as station wagons.

[307] Dale Potter-Clark interview with Jean Poulin Pratt, whose parents Gerard & Noella Poulin bought Martha Washington Inn in 1967.

[308] Extracted from Martha Washington Inn brochures in Readfield Historical Society collection.

[309] Mangle irons are large rollers used to press or flatten sheets, tablecloths, kitchen towels, or clothing.

[310] Dale Potter-Clark interview with Phyllis Rolfe Rourke who worked there as did her sister Jean.

[311] Potter-Clark collection

[312] Potter-Clark collection

[313] Farkas

[314] Kingsbury & Deyo; History of Kennebec County; pub.1892; Chapter on West Gardiner

[315] Banquet given by the Maine State Bar Association to the retiring Chief Justice, Wm. Penn Whitehouse; Maine Bar Association; Kennebec Journal Co.;1913; pg.115; Included in this publication is a letter written to the Chief Justice by Peacock which says in part: "… *I was admitted to the bar in 1907 at Bath at a term of court held by you there. From time to time I have had various matters before you and I appreciate more than words can tell your kind help and counsel which have made easy the many shortcomings which have been mine as a new attorney*

[316] The property where Kiwanacook sat was drawn partly from the Greeley-Brown (Colon 2016) farm and the Will Bourne farm (St. Andre 2016).

[317] Kiwanacook brochure; How Kamp Kiwanacook Originated; 1927; hereinafter Kiwanacook brochure

[318] Kiwanacook brochure, The Buildings

[319] A ring-tossing game

[320] The Rangeley Lake rowboat was developed during the late 19th century in the Rangeley Lakes region of western Maine. The Rangeley boat was used by local guides to carry vacationing city "sports" on fishing trips. It was sturdy, stable enough to carry a load and seaworthy enough to take on sudden chops. They were not limited to the Rangeleys but came into common use by fishermen on the Winthrop and Belgrade Lakes as well as other lakes in Maine. The name and sight of Rangeley Lake rowboats cast a romantic air that became almost synonymous with fishing adventures in Maine.

[321] Dale Potter-Clark interviews with some of Fred E. William's former players and friends have included Thomas Adell, Gaylord Bouthlier, Joe Maloney, and Fred's wife Evelyn Peacock Williams.

[322] KJ, August 27, 1931

[323]There are no specifics in the ad as to what those conveniences were. Gene and Carrie Dixon were the ones who added indoor plumbing in all the cabins, and

converted them to housekeeping cottages, in 1950. (per interview with Ron Dixon 2/24/2016)

[324] Ruth was first married to Wesley Adell, divorced in 1947 and married in 1957 to Harry Mullen. Her daughter Evelyn Adell married Henry Potter in 1947 and is a Readfield author and Town Historian. She is also the mother of this book's author Dale Potter-Clark.

[325] Ruth was born in 1912 and was a modern woman before her time. She worked outside the home all of her adult life. As a very young woman she worked at Nelson Gordon's sawmill at Readfield Depot. She and her second husband Harry Mullen ran the Coffee Cup at Readfield Corner from the late 1950s into the 1960s. She also became Readfield's first licensed beautician in 1948 and ran "Ruth's Beauty Shop" for many years along with her other jobs. Also in 1948 she received her GED diploma which was considered an accomplishment for a woman of her age at the time. Those feats were especially notable because she also became a grandmother for the first time that year (Dale Potter Clark born 7/28/1948) and the Kennebec Journal featured a story about all that at the time. Ruth also earned certification as a mental health worker around 1960 and became evening supervisor of the Marquardt Building at the Augusta Mental Health Institute where she worked until her retirement.

[326] Dale Potter-Clark interview with Evelyn Adell Potter; 2/25/2016; hereinafter Adell-Potter

[327] See photo of tenement house, pg 55

[328] A mangle is a mechanical laundry aid consisting of two rollers in a sturdy frame, connected by cogs and are used to press or flatten sheets, tablecloths, kitchen towels and other laundry. www.wikipedia.com; accessed 2/25/2016

[329] Adell-Potter

[330] His daughters were Evelyn Williams, Eleanor Bickford and Hazel Adams. He lived with Hazel on the Winthrop Road in his final years.

[331] Dale Potter-Clark interview with Ronald Dixon, son of Eugene and Carrie Dixon; 2/24/2016; hereinafter Dixon

[332] Dixon

[333] See Craig's Point, pg 62

[334] See Coleman Grove, pg 44

[335] This chapter compiled from genealogical and deeds research by Dale Potter-Clark.

[336] May (Williams) Smith was a paternal aunt of Fred E. Williams who is discussed in the chapter on Kamp Kiwanacook, pg. 160.

[337] J.O. Newton Kents Hill Trustee honored on 85th birthday; Kennebec Journal; April 6, 1949

[338] Fred E. Williams is the same man who partnered with E.E. Peacock at Kamp Kiwanacook. He predeceased both Benj. And Mary (Williams) Smith sold they sold their house on Church Road to Bill & Wilhelmina Harris in 1957 and moved to Winthrop. Both were nearly 80 at that time.

[339] Dale Potter-Clark interview with Evelyn Adell Potter, Readfield Town Historian; Kents Hill School alumnus class '47; and former secretary to three headmasters at Kents Hill School 1962-1975.

[340] Dale Potter-Clark interview with Roger Lane of North Fayette, first cousin of Ralph Lane; 3/10/2016; hereinafter Lane

[341] Elmer Elvin farm as of this writing

[342] Dale Potter-Clark interview with Beverly Norton Newton, Lane family historian; 1/7/2016; hereinafter Newton

[343] Dale Potter-Clark interview with Robert Bryant of Readfield; 3/9/2016. Bryant related the land where Lane Cottages sat was at one time part of J.O. Butman's farm (Vorpagel 2016). The right of way to them and some of the shoreline was part of Albion Bryant's property (per Dale Potter-Clark research). The Lanes bought from Bryant first in 1932 and then another 35 acres in 1936.

[344] Dale Potter-Clark interview with Emery Nason of Winthrop; 3/9/2016; hereinafter Nason

[345] William Rourke, W J Rourke Construction Inc, Readfield; John Cushing, Cushing Construction, LLC, Readfield

[346] KCRD Plan book 1980 page 116; 2/3/1980

[347] David Giroux was the Readfield Code Enforcement Officer and also a land surveyor at the time so he knew town properties well. Evelyn Potter was already the Town Historian then, and at that time she was working in the Readfield Tax Assessors office, so she knew town properties as well as the Readfield history. For those reasons Giroux and Potter were asked by Steve Musica, the Readfield town manager, to work on their own time to name the roads per the new E911 system.

[348] See Hutchinson Tavern, pg 38

[349] The Capt. John Smith mansion house was donated by Asa and Ursula Gile to the Union Meeting House in 1868 and moved to its present location on Church St. adjacent to the Union Meeting House. Asa and Ursula built a new home at that time. See the Elmwood House pg. 29

[350] ibid

[351] Mariah bought another house nearby where she lived until her death in 1888 (Barton 2016; known as Frank and Mae Ramsey's house by many). Mariah lived with her daughter Mary O. and husband Thaddeus Hammond and their son Frederic Hammond. The Hammonds continued to live here after Mariah died. Interesting that after the Hammonds it was owned by Augustus and Mary E. (Townsend) Brainard (see Brainard pg.185)

[352] 1883 Augusta City Directory

[353] Ibid, various years 1886-1892

[354] Potter-Clark collection

[355] 1900 US Census, Augusta

[356] Dale Potter-Clark correspondence with Dr. David Wood of Texas, son of Edna (Galouch) Wood and grandson of Freeman Galouch.

[357] The Mace family owned this building when the Readfield Fire Dept. was given permission to take it down in a controlled burn as a training session.

[358] Owned by Vorpagel in 2016. Nancy Brainard was a daughter of Joseph Johnson who settled the land where these two farms sit. In 1870 one Nancy Johnson, age 82yrs, is living in the Benjamin Brainard house. She is the head of household and boarding twenty brick masons, carpenters and laborers – most of them Irish and Canadian immigrants. Research has not yet determined who this Nancy Johnson was. She was 16 years older than Mrs. Asahel (Nancy Johnson) Brainard so not the same person.

[359] Readfield Bicentennial Commission; *Reflections of Readfield*; 1976; page 18.

[360] Dale Potter-Clark research reveals that Mrs. Augustus (Mary Esther) Brainard held a $1,150 mortgage on this house (Collins 2016), property of Jonas Packard Dudley, during those years from 1883 to 1908 but no documentation has been found saying the Brainards actually lived there. When Mary Esther Brainard released the mortgage in 1908 the document stated "where Jonas Packard Dudley was living at the time of his death." He died in July 1908. Augustus Brainard owned (his father's) house next door (Vorpagel 2016) from 1861 until 1904. OF NOTE: Mary Esther Brainard was Augustus' third wife. She was Mary E. Townsend when she married him and she was the one who held the purse strings no doubt. She bought, mortgaged and sold several properties in East Readfield and Readfield Depot. She was an aunt of Ernest Linwood Townsend who ran Townsend Farm and held a mortgage on his property for one. After selling his ancestral home in East Readfield Augustus and Mary E. Brainard moved to Readfield Depot to what many remember as the Ramsey house (Barton 2016). Mary Esther (Townsend) Brainard was a sister of Thomas Townsend and after his death his widow Mary J. Townsend lived with Augustus and Mary Brainard. Mary J. Townsend was the mother-in-law of Mark S. and Charles Collins who were early proprietors of Hotel Maranacook. Confused yet? Suffice it to say the Brainard, Collins and Townsend families were interconnected and very much had their hands on the tourist industry of the times.

[361] This Nancy Johnson was sixteen years older than Mrs. Asahel (Nancy Johnson) Brainard so not the same person. They were surely related though. The Brainard properties were originally settled and lived upon by the East Readfield pioneer Joseph Johnson.

[362] Dale Potter Clark interview with Lenny and Sue Reay; 2/28/2016; hereinafter Reay

[363] Potter-Clark collection

[364] Reay

[365] See Daniel O. Craig, pg. 1

[366] Andrew served as a Private and Corporal in the New Hampshire and Massachusetts Regiments. He lost both hands in a militia muster, from a premature cannon explosion; and in 1832 he was granted a lifetime Revolutionary War pension. Andrew moved to Readfield from Hampton Falls, New Hampshire between 1790 and 1795. He was married twice, having been widowed the first time, and his wives gave him seventeen children. A variation of Andrew's name is Andron. His 6th great grandsons, Peter and Larry Mace carry on the family name and both currently reside in Readfield. (Potter-Clark collection)

[367] See Coleman Grove pg. 44

[368] See Kamp Peacock, pg.160

[369] Reay

[370] Dale Potter-Clark interview with Peter Mace, great-grandson of Roy and Alice Mace; 2/26/2016 (hereinafter Peter Mace)

[371] Reay (The family was asked to suggest a name for the road when the E911 system was set up. Sue Reay, Larry and Peter Mace talked it over, Sue suggested "Alice's Way" and the brothers agreed)

[372] Maces Cottages brochure

[373] Reay

[374] See Tamsonhurst, pg. 110

[375] KCRD Book 880 Page 323 11/19/1948

[376] KCRD Book 80 Page 559 1/22/1949

[377] Dale Potter-Clark interviews with Margaret Mast of Brunswick, ME; Valerie Sulya of Bucksport, ME; and Jack Turcotte of Arundel, ME; March 1 & 2, 2016; hereinafter Turcotte

[378] KCRD Book 1800 Page 201 3/19/1975

[379] Potter-Clark collection, Readfield History Walk #17

[380] Kennebec Valley YMCA website; http://www.kvymca.org/content/camp-programs; accessed 3/1/2016

[381] Julia Inspires; http://clukeyluge.com/camp/; accessed 3/1/2016

[382] Julia Inspires; http://clukeyluge.com/camp/; accessed 3/1/2016

[383] Dates Announced for Julia Clukey's Camp; Maine Beer & Wine Distributors Association; www.mainebeerandwine.com/; accessed 3/1/2016. Clukey has been their spokesperson since 2010, encouraging people to make wise choices regarding alcohol consumption.

[384] Julia Clukey's Camp for Girls opens in Readfield, New director's cabin unveiled as camp opens June 17 for fourth season; Central Maine Newspapers; 6/26/2015

[385] Dale Potter-Clark interview with Schuyler Ludwig; 3/15/2016; hereinafter Ludwig

[386] Folsom Brothers Day Camp for Boys on Lake Maranacook, Winthrop, Maine; camp brochure 1970; hereinafter Folsom brochure

[387] The land included parts of two early homesteads, one settled in 1815 by a Daniel Johnson whose farmhouse is owned today by Wendel and Joyce Adell. The land had been subdivided long before the Folsoms and Adells came into the picture. The remainder of Folsom's land was originally that of James Sedgley, on which Maranacook Hotel and Cottages were built. After that property was subdivided in 1949 a piece was ultimately sold to Bob and Elaine Folsom.

[388] *Day Camp is Part of a New Trend*; Kennebec Journal; 1968; hereinafter Day Camp

[389] Robert Folsom obituary; Central Maine Newspapers; 5/10/2008

[390] Day Camp

[391] Dale Potter-Clark interview with Joyce Adell; 3/1/2016. (her husband Skip Adell died 17 days after this interview)

[392] Folsom brochure

[393] Bob Folsom's journal; summer of 1967; hereinafter Bob's journal

[394] ibid

[395] Dale Potter-Clark interview with Deb (Folsom) Harvey, daughter of Bob & Elaine; 7/17/2016; hereinafter Folsom-Harvey

[396] Folsom brochure

[397] *Campers to Take 4-Day Canoe Tour*; Kennebec Journal, 8/9/1965; hereafter Canoe trip

[398] Day Camp

[399] *Canoe Trip to Maine slated for local boys*; Branford, MA; news article shared by Deb Folsom Harvey; date or pub. unknown

[400] Folsom brochure

[401] Bob's Journal

[402] ibid

[403] Folsom-Harvey

[404] Newton, John O. and Young, Oscar E; *Kents Hill and its Makers*; pub.1947; pgs.49-55

[405] Evelyn Adell Potter, Readfield Historian is the mother of this book's author, Dale Potter-Clark.

[406] This section on Chase / Allen family compiled from 7 sources: 1) Dale Potter-Clark interviews in 2014 with Stephanie Wilson Hatch, grandaughter of John & Irene Chase. Hereinafter Hatch; 2) *Face Value* by Joseph Cumming Chase, his autobiography, pub. 1963. Hereinafter Chase; 3) *Kents Hill and its Makers* by J.O. Newton, pub. 1947. Hereinafter Newton; 4) *The History of Methodism in Maine* by Rev. Stephen Allen, pub.1886. Hereinafter Allen; 5) *The Life of Rev. John Allen – Better known as Camp Meeting John* by Rev. Stephen Allen, pub.1888; hereinafter Allen; 6) Potter-Clark collection; Dale Potter-Clark interview with Dorothy Wilson Crockett, grandaughter of John and Irene Chase; hereinafter Crockett

[407] Translation of "Jollity Manse" is the cheerful home of a minister. This house was built for Rev. William Larrabee in 1838, an early headmaster at Maine Wesleyan Seminary. After Larrabee it was owned by Readfield Methodist minister Rev. George Webber for 30 years. He sold it to A.F. Chase in 1875 and the Chase family immediately started calling it Jollity Manse (ascertained through deeds research by Dale Potter-Clark)

[408] Joseph Cummings Chase was the only child of A.F. & Louise Chase who did not return to live in Kents Hill in 1897. He was living in New York City by then and attending the Pratt Institute of Art. He went on to become a world famous portrait artist. Joseph was also a semi-professional baseball player as well as an artist. He also became a professional singer and once said he could read the musical notes before he could read the words. A.F. and Louise's daughter Crystal never married. She was an English teacher at Kents Hill School for several years until she moved to Middleborough, MA and taught in public school there. She founded "the Crystal Club" in Kents Hill village which remained an active benevolent women's society until after 1956. Her sister Louise moved to Fort Fairfield to fill a teaching position where she married a man who worked in the lumber industry. They eventually moved west to Portland, Oregon.

[409] In 1918 the house became Kents Hill School's property and was named "Chase Hall".

[410] His grandaughter Stephanie Wilson Hatch related that John Chase taught at Haverford for 10-20 years but does not know exactly how many.

[411] Kennebec County Registry of Deeds; 8/1916; book 546 page572

[412] Kennebec Lakes Association; Kennebec Lakes Region the Playground of Central Maine, 1939; Maine State Library collection

[413] Per Stephanie Hatch, the buildings were Brookside, Birches, Happiness, Pine Point, Rose Point, Old Lodge, Kids' Cabin, Eagle's Nest, Tree Top, Warratah, Crow's Nest (burned), The Funny House and the Lodge (came down in a 1960s snow storm).

[414] *Mother Earth* (magazine); https://en.wikipedia.org/wiki/Mother_Earth_(magazine); accessed 7/11/2016

[415] Goldman, Emma; Living My Life; published 1931, reprint by Cosimo, Inc., 2011, 1028 pages; pgs.335-336; hereinafter Goldman

[416] Read more about Emma Goldman and associated anarchist activities at https://en.wikipedia.org/wiki/Emma_Goldman

[417] Goldman; pg.392

[418] The Brooklyn Daily Eagle; Brooklyn, New York June 6, 1926, page 148; and April 14, 1929, page 88

[419] G.R. Armstrong Manufacturers Supplies Inc. was founded by G.R. Armstrong in 1916 in Boston, MA. In 1972 the company was purchased from the original George R. Armstrong family by one of their salesmen. Today the company is known as Lehigh-Armstrong and is celebrating its 100th anniversary. This company is one of the nation's oldest full-line fastener distributors. www.lehigh-armstrong.com; accessed 6/21/2016

[420] When Ethel Bishop sold Castle Hill Farm to John & Mary Tyler in 1956 she reserved "… the wooden shop across the street (and) right to move within a year…" (book 1041 page 141). It was moved next door where it remains to this day (Kathleen Choate property, 117 Thundercastle in 2016).

[421] Dale Potter-Clark interview with Evelyn A. Potter, June 2016

[422] The Bishops bought Castle Hill Farm in 1930 and sold it to John and Mary Tyler in 1956. It is currently owned by their son John and his wife Marjorie Tyler.

[423] The Methodist chapel was located on Church Road, next to the Grange Hall. It is a privately owned building in 2016 that houses business offices.

[424] This campground was located at the Bishop farm on Thundercastle Road.

[425] Sturgis and Elizabeth Coffin owned a camp and lot on the east shore of Torsey Pond, adjacent to Chase's Boys Camp. Later became the site for camp Thunderbird. They also owned the Albert Bean farm.

[426] A special thank you to Stephanie (Wilson) Hatch who provided most of the information for Camp Thunderbird. Without her input we would not have known about this camp's existence.

[427] Sturgis and Elizabeth Coffin of Fitzwilliam, NH owned this property from 1917 until 1941. During the years they owned it local guests were welcomed as were those from afar. This is the cottage that Girls Scouts hiked to in 1936, as mentioned in the chapter re Castle Hill Farm. pg.222

[428] Dale Potter-Clark phone interview with Ralph Ives III of Washington D.C.; 6/30/2016

[429] Potter-Clark collection

[430] 30 Mile River Watershed Association; www.30mileriver.org/; accessed 6/23/2016

[431] Wight-Smith, Beverly; Turning Back; pub Vienna Historical Society 1985; page 85

[432] Underwood, Joseph; History of Fayette; pub.1950, reprinted by Fayette Historical Society 1990; pgs. 29-47; hereinafter Underwood

[433] Kennebec County Registry of Deeds; 1795; book 3 page 32

[434] www.maine.gov/ifw/fishing/lakesurvey_maps/kennebec/echo_lake.pdf; published 1940; accessed 6/23/2016

[435] www.state.me.us/ifw/fishing/lakesurvey_maps/kennebec/lovejoy_pond.pdf; published 1940; accessed 6/23/2016

[436] 1) Underwood page 15; 2) KCRD various, Potter-Clark collection

[437] Formed in 2008 as a nonprofit coalition of lake associations, municipalities and local conservation organizations with a shared mission: To preserve, protect and improve the land and water quality in the 30 Mile River Watershed; 2015 Annual

Report; pg.2; www.30mileriver.org/wp-content/uploads/2016/06/30MRWA-2015-Annual-Report.pdf; accessed 6/23/2016

[438] The Foord family owned a 470 acre tract and Seth Foord sold 148 acres of their tract to one Moulton Bodge in the 1820s. The Bodge family owned it for more than a century. Henry Bodge sold to Frank Bodge in 189 and the first mention of buildings was under Frank Bodge's ownership. Thus the estimate that be built the first cabins at this site circa 1900. Frank Bodge sold to Leon and Mavill Sanborn of Fayette in 1932.

[439] These mills were called "Foords' Mills" and later became known as "Fayette Mills".

[440] This mill stone was moved to its present location, from a nearby location on the lake, decades ago by people staying at Twin Springs; Judy Whitten, Oct. 2014.

[441] www.twinspringscamps.com; accessed 6/24/2016

[442] William ("Wild Bill") Donovan was a United States soldier, lawyer, intelligence officer and diplomat. Donovan is best remembered as the wartime head of the Office of Strategic Services (OSS), a precursor to the Central Intelligence Agency, during World War II. He is also known as the "Father of American Intelligence" and the "Father of Central Intelligence" A decorated veteran of World War I, General Donovan is the only person to have received all four of the United States' highest awards: https://en.wikipedia.org/wiki/William_J._Donovan; accessed 6/24/2016

[443] Kennebec County Registry of Deeds; book832 page 532; 3/13/1946

[444] Melzar Fish was the father of Ruth Fish Hight, who inherited this farm. She and her husband Stanley lived there all their married lives and ran their own tourist home there in the 1940s and 50s.

[445] College and Private School Directory of the United States and Canada, Volume 13; Educational Bureau Publishing Company, 1922; pages 78. Camp Mowana is advertised in the same publication on page 86.

[446] Alexander Ross "A.R." MacMahon was born in Basswood Ridge, New Brunswick, Canada only 11 miles from Calais, Maine. He immigrated to the US in 1905 at age 21. His place of origin may explain why he later took campers on adventures to that part of Maine and Canada.

[447] The booklet in its entirety is on file at Readfield Historical Society.

[448] A sponson extends a watercraft hull dimension at or below the waterline to increase flotation or add lift when underway; www.wikipedia.com; accessed 6/26/2016

[449] In 1919 Fred Guggenheimer, an attorney from New York City, bought the 60 acre Smiley farm on Echo Lake in Fayette. How Guggenheimer found his way to this property is not known, but we do know that for fourteen years prior to that it was owned by James and Emelie Dunn of Boston. A mill was erected on part of this property and leased to "the Gordon brothers of Livermore Falls" when Smiley and Dunn owned it. The Smiley farm was established by one Matthew Keating of Boston, a stonecutter, in 1830 and remained his until 1859 when Keating signed it over to one Jacques Littermough (Letourneau) of Fayette. Conditions of the conveyance were that Litternough would care for Keating and his wife Sarah for the rest of their natural lives. Letourneau sold to Josiah Taylor in 1870 who sold to John Couture in 1877 and his estate sold to Cynthia Smiley in 1879

[450] Further research revealed that in 2013 the Peace Corps awarded Phil Lilienthal the prestigious Sargent Shriver Award for Distinguished Humanitarian Service.

[451] Steiner, Helen Cohen; "So You Want to Run a Camp?": How I got into and out of trouble in no easy stages; March 1, 1976; private collection at Camp Vega, Fayette, Maine. Contact Kyle Courtiss, Director, Camp Vega.

[452] Dale Potter-Clark interview with Joan Pfaffle, daughter of Bill and Hope Pfaffle; 7/15/2016; hereinafter Pfaffle

[453] Maine Department of Economic Development, "Maine Developments, May 1962" (1962). *Economic and Community Development Documents.* Paper 94; http://statedocs.maine.gov/decd_docs/94; accessed 7/15/2016; hereinafter ME-DOD

[454] 1) Pfaffle 2) Central Maine Newspapers; William H. Pfaffle obituary; 12/2007; Bill Pfaffle died at age 90. Hope predeceased him in 1970 and he remarried in 1972 to Ruth Innes Allen who survives him; hereinafter Pfaffle obit

[455] 1) Dale Potter-Clark interview 7/13/2016 with Phyllis Nason Hewitt of Fayette who worked for the Pfaffles as their cook from 1970 until 1983; hereinafter Hewitt 2) Fire destroys lodge on Maine lake by Keith Edwards; Portland Press Herald; 9/3/2016; hereinafter Edwards

[456] ME-DOD

[457] Ernie's full / last name was recalled by Ronnie Hewett of Fayette

[458] Dale Potter-Clark interview with James Feagin; 7/20/2016

[459] As told by Ronda Luce to Dale Potter-Clark, 8/5/2016

[460] *Camp Skoglund: The Home of the World's Most Awesome Camp*; a 29 minute video produced by John and Peter Fitzpatrick in honor of Wilbur Nelson's 91st birthday; June, 2016

[461] Coincidence or fate? Rondi Nelson who owns Camp Skoglund on a part of this very farm is a cousin of Belle Stanley. When Rondi's parents came from New Jersey and bought land for Camp Skoglund from the Fish / Hight family in 1957 they were not aware that Rondi's Page & Stanley (maternal) ancestors hailed from Readfield, say nothing of Interlaken Farm where they ended up establishing their business! Rondi is also a direct descendant of George S. Page whose grandfather Simon ran Page's Tavern in East Readfield.

[462] Catering in the Farm Home by Ruth Hight; American Agriculturist; January 21,1956; pg. 32; hereinafter Ruth Hight

[463] This statement indicates that boarders were being taken in as early as 1870. Benjamin Davis, Jr. was living there at that time.

[464] Ruth's mother was Edna Stevens Hight 1864-1938. After her husband Melzar's death Edna continued to live with Stanley and Ruth at Interlaken Farm until her death.

[465] Robert died in Erie, PA in 2012 but Rolfe is still living at age 98. Robert had two daughters, Karen and Katherine, and Rolfe's sons are Mark and Alan.

[466] Jessie Welch later went to work as the cook for Wilbur Nelson at Camp Skoglund.

[467] Ruth Hight, excerpts from the American Agriculturist article that Ruth Hight wrote in 1956.

[468] Dale Potter-Clark interview with Gary Hight, grandson of Stanley and Ruth Hight and son of Rolfe Hight; 7/21/2016

[469] John Sprague's Journal of Maine History; Vol. 3; page 112; May 1915

[470] Dale Potter-Clark interview with Brenda Joseph of Fayette, gg-niece of Ellsworth Crosby and keeper of family artifacts; hereinafter Joseph

471 Dale Potter Clark interview with Andrew Knight, Jr. of North Wayne; 7/16/2016; hereinafter Knight
472 Kennebec County Registry of Deeds; book456 page344; 4/29/1904. In 1936 book714 page116 he sold a parcel from the NE corner to Miss Marjorie Kirk of Syracuse, NY – she being the founder of Camp Merrywold. This land made up only a part of Merrywold, however. See the chapter of Camp Merrywold FMI
473 John Canwell was a drover, originally from England, and he also raised sheep. He settled east of Lovejoy Pond before 1790 and was a business partner of another English settler, Robert Cornforth of Readfield, who owned the woolen mill on Factory Square in that town. In March, 1810 as Canwell returned home on horseback from Portland, he was murdered, presumably by a robber who knew he was carrying cash from the sale of cattle. A man brought Canwell's horse, overcoat, and spurs to his wife with the assurance that her husband would return in a few days. He never did. The identity of this man and why he had possession of Canwell's horse and knowledge of his situation is a mystery. The murderer was never identified, and Canwell's fate remained unknown until many years later, when during the renovation of the Baptist church in Wayne, remains presumed to be those of Canwell were found. A tale passed down by Canwell descendants says that his widow identified the remains by recognizing the clothing she had sown for him. No documentation for this story has been found. Unfortunately, editions of the Kennebec Gazette for the time period have been lost. In the late 1800s, a grassy knoll in the Canwell pasture, one could still see the graves of Canwell's two wives and the cellar hole where his house once stood. Source: Alan Spaulding, family historian, 7/2013; alanwspaulding@verizon.net; 7/2013
474 Kennebescoggin Camps brochure by Ellsworth Crosby, proprietor; year unknown; in possession of his g-g-niece, Brenda Joseph of Fayette, ME; hereinafter Crosby brochure
475 The *Bar Harbor Express* began in 1902 with its southern terminus in New York. Trains ran north to Springfield, Massachusetts, over the New Haven, where they were handed off to the Boston and Albany Railroad (B&A), which carried them, to Worcester. From Worcester the B&M hauled them to Union Station in Portland, Maine. From Portland the Maine Central hauled the cars to their final destinations in the northeast. Wikipedia; accessed 7/24/2016
476 ibid
477 Lewiston Saturday Journal; Maine Town News; 11/21/1906, pg.10; https://news.google.com/newspapers; accessed 7/16/2016
478 Augusta area city directory, 1907; and 1910 U.S. Census
479 Green Dragon Gift Shop, 24 East 28th Street, New York City; business card in possession of g-niece Brenda Joseph
480 Dale Potter-Clark interview with Brenda (Wells) Joseph, gg niece of Ellsworth Crosby, g-niece of Lula Wells; 7/23/2016; hereinafter Joseph
481 When Ellsworth's father Charles W. Crosby died the family home in North Wayne was conveyed to Ellsworth by his siblings; Kennebec County Registry of Deeds book534 page474; 7/30/1913
482 McKee and Joseph

[483] Central Maine Newspapers; Wayne Williams House hosts rare bookplate exhibit; by Craig Crosby; 10/22/2012

[484] The Crosby-Wells curtain hung in the school until 1961 at which time it was given to their g-niece Brenda Joseph of Fayette who returned it to the school years later.

[485] The Crosby-Wells painting was, perhaps, inspired by an 1899-1900 New York City production of Ben-Hur, a stage adaptation of a popular novel by Lew Wallace.

[486] Linda Rogers McKee, co-president of Wayne Historical Society and Steward of the "Old North Wayne School House"; email 7/22/2016; hereinafter McKee

[487] The name of the company who bought it was Voos, Smith & Nelson", a business that had been established in Winthrop. Kennebec County Registry of Deeds; book836 page235; 4/10/1946. Crosby had owned this property since 1904 having bought it from W.G. Hunton of Readfield.

[488] Ibid; book3482 page21; 12/27/1988

[489] Knight

[490] Central Maine Newspapers, Robert A. Nelson obituary; March 1, 2004. Bob died at age 95 in Winthrop, ME.

[491] Kennebec County Registry of Deeds; Plan book2004 page 203

[492] Information for Camps Abenaki and Merrywold gleaned from 1) Genealogical and deeds research by Dale Potter-Clark; 2) Various news articles from the Syracuse, NY Herald; 3) "Brief History of Camp Kirkwold"; circa 1964; copy provided by Mary Ellen Deschenes, Chief of Outdoor Operations, Girl Scouts of Maine, Sept. 2014

[493] This land was part of the original Dudley and Peleg Hains homestead. The Hains family owned large parcels of land on Nickerson Hill Road and North Wayne Road. This parcel passed from the Hains family to Thomas Weston in 1880 and after him eventually to Albert Wells of New Vineyard in 1912 who sold it to Dr. Emma Greene Wood in 1919.

[494] Drs. O. J. Snyder and Mason W. Pressly founded Philadelphia College of Osteopathic Medicine in 1899 as the third osteopathic medical school in the world and the first osteopathic medical school in the northeastern USA; www.pcom.edu accessed 7/11/2016

[495] Dale Potter-Clark phone interview 7/11/2016 with Jen Kennedy, Institutional Advancement Coordinator, Alumni Department, Philadelphia College of Osteopathic Medicine.

[496] "The Osteopathic Physician"; The Bunting Publications, Chicago, IL; 9/1920, Volume 38 No.3, page 31; www.atsu.edu/museum/subscription/pdfs/osteopathicphysician/; accessed 7/9/2016

[497] "The Osteopathic Truth"; Vol. 5 No.6, 1/1921, page 73; www.atsu.edu/museum/subscription/pdfs/osteopathictruth/; accessed 7/9/2016

[498] Laura Mattoon founded the country's first girls' camp in New Hampshire in 1902. Her ideas were often misunderstood and met with some social resistance because they were in advance of her time. Two camps for girls opened in Maine 1902 as well including Camp Arey Pinelands in Center Harbor and Wyonegonic Camps in Bridgton. Then Aloha Camp opened in 1905 and Alford Lake Camp in 1907, Gulick Wo-he-lo Camp in 1910 and the first Girl Scouts camp in 1912. By 1925 there were 125 girls' camps in the U.S. *His Story, Her Story, Our Story: 100 Years of the American Camp Association* by Rita Yerkes, Ed. D.; www.acacamps.org/; accessed 7/10/2016

[499] Death notice from Philadelphia College of Osteopathic Medicine archives: Dr. Emma Greene Wood, of Maplewood, N. J., died April 24th, 1930, after a short illness. Dr. Wood was born in Surry, Maine, July 4th, 1868. She was married to Otis Elms Wood in Portland, Maine, in 1888, where she lived until her husband's death in 1908. Dr. Wood graduated from the Philadelphia College of Osteopathy in 1911 and was the first osteopath in Maplewood, N. J., where she located in 1912 and practiced her profession until less than a month before her death. Dr. Wood leaves two daughters, Mrs. Hollis G. Mollson, of Portland, Maine and Mrs. Philip L. Carter, of Philadelphia, PA.

[500] Picture map of Camp Merrywold; drawn by Edith (Pete) Laurie circa late 1920s – early 1930s; copy provided by Mary Ellen Deschenes, Chief of Outdoor Operations, Girl Scouts of Maine, Sept. 2014

[501] 1952 Newspaper article posted on Girl Scouts of Maine web site re history of Camp Kirkwold; accessed 12/2013

[502] For additional information about Kirkwold's operations today visit the Girl Scouts of Maine web site www.girlscoutsofmaine.org

[503] Jim's last name was changed from Friedenwald to Lawrence - that of his step-father.

[504] Dale Potter-Clark interview with Wally Penrod, counselor at Menatoma 1960-1976; 7/24/2016; hereinafter Penrod

[505] Friedenwald and Kirk purchased the North Wayne dam from the North Wayne Tool Co. Included water rights to the dam. Kennebec County Registry of Deeds; book784 page15; 8/15/1941

[506] Remembering Healey Asylum School in Lewiston by Juliana L'Heureux; Portland Press Herald; 8/23/2012

[507] This farm was known as the circa 1855 Josiah Taylor homestead which had been separated from the circa 1805 Ebenezer O. Lovejoy homestead. Coincidentally, Brenda (Wells) Joseph, the gg-niece of Ellsworth Crosby (see Kennebescoggin) lives today (2016) in the Lovejoy homestead which is located adjacent / north of the Taylor (Don Bosco) farm.

[508] Another Franco American camp existed in this area as well. Camp Tekakwitha on Androscoggin Lake in Leeds was founded in 1938 by the Dominican fathers of SS Peter and Paul Catholic Parish in Lewiston. It was intended originally to cater to local French-speaking boys. However, by 1949, the majority of its campers were from Quebec. The camp was run for 40 years by Rev. Remi Clark. After his retirement in 1978, the camp was turned over to a private board of directors. It was, and remains, the only French-speaking camp in the United States. www.mainememory.net/artifact/67728; accessed 7/13/2016

[509] *New Camp Bosco Scores Big Hit with Healy Lads* by Francis Giusti; Lewiston Daily Sun, Lewiston, ME; July 2, 1952; pgs 1,11; hereinafter Giusti

[510] Tom Mathews was an Augusta native who built his camp in order to get his children out of downtown Augusta in the summertime. He was a chauffeur for the Gannett family and managed the garage at the Kennebec Journal. His wife and children spent summers on Lovejoy Lake.

[511] Dale Potter-Clark interview with Tom Mathews of Fayette, Maine; 7/12/2016; hereinafter Mathews

[512] Saint John (Don) Bosco was born in Italy in 1815, became an ordained Catholic Priest in 1841 and died in Italy in 1888. There are several boys' camps and schools named in his honor throughout the world. Father Bosco believed that education was a matter of the heart and said that "the boys must not only be loved, but know that they are loved". His three components of teaching included reason, religion and kindness combined with music and games. In spite of opposition from various quarters and several attempts on his life, Bosco gained a reputation of being a holy man and miracle worker through his work with orphaned boys and the elderly in Europe. Bosco was canonized by the Roman Catholic Church on Easter Sunday of 1934 and given the title of "Father and Teacher of Youth".

[513] Giusti

[514] Mathews

[515] Giusti

[516] ibid

[517] ibid

[518] Mathews

[519] ibid

[520] Giusti

[521] Mathews

"Summer camps for boys and girls are no longer an experiment. They have proven their worth and each year notes an increasing attendance. The question is not "Shall we send our boys or girls to a summer camp?" but "which is the best camp for them to go?"
~ E.E. Peacock, Kamp Kiwanacook, Lake Maranacook, 1927

"The best part of Tallwood cannot be told in type – the friendly atmosphere – the meeting with people who came as strangers last year but now are friends – the dropping of Mr. and Mrs. to "John" and "Mary", a nap or a party – when desired – or absolute quiet and rest to lessen the weary."
~ Sam W. Patterson, Tallwood Inn, Lake Maranacook, 1930

"Few are insensible to the lure of the woods, the charm of days out-of-doors. Solitudes and watercourses appeal to the romantic and idealistic, and in his own peculiar way a boy absorbs and cherishes the thoughts which they arouse. Every detail of a canoeing trip – the scenes of natural beauty the experiences exciting and humorous, even his own throughout when plying the paddle or making camp – all recur to a boy in the after days with new delight; and the boy who having camped hard and well prefers the hotel or summer resort is very rare indeed."
~ A. R. MacMahon, Camp Mowana, Echo Lake, 1934

"Here one has a wonderful panoramic view of hill-encircled Torsey, mountains to the north, wooded shores, historic old Kents Hill to the south, and over all a gorgeous sunset sky with flaming hues of rose and gold reflected in the peaceful water. It is an unforgettable picture, equaled only by the silvery moonlight which later turns the lake into a fairy pool of beauty and romantic glamor."
~ Irene Chase, Chases' Cottage Colony, Torsey Pond, 1942

"For those who wish to fish there is a beautiful sheet of water at the very door and with nine lakes within a radius of ten miles, a variety of fish including trout, pickerel, perch and bass…Boats for the free use of guests to row, gather water-lilies, fish or make trips to the two nearby villages."
~ Ellsworth Crosby, Camp Kennescoggin, Lovejoy Pond, 1915